D1188497

Wildwood Library
St. Louis Community College
2645 Generations Drive
Wildwood, MO 63040-1168
636-422-2000

WITHDRAWN

## America and the Return of Nazi Contraband

*The Recovery of Europe's Cultural Treasures*

The Nazi war on European culture produced the greatest dislocation of art, archives, and libraries in the history of the world. In the ruins of the Reich, Allied occupiers found millions of paintings, sculptures, books, and manuscripts, from the mediocre to the priceless, hidden in thousands of secret hideaways. This book tells the story of how the American military government in Germany, spearheaded by a few dozen dedicated Monuments, Fine Arts, and Archives officers and enlisted men, coped with restoring Europe's cultural heritage. Caught up in often bitter diplomatic wrangling during and after the war, the American restitution effort struggled to uncover what the Nazis had hidden and to equitably return all that was found. Based on the pioneering study of cultural restitution first published in 1985, *America and the Return of Nazi Contraband* presents new insights into how the American government and Jewish organizations managed the painfully difficult problem of heirless Jewish cultural property.

Michael J. Kurtz currently serves as the assistant archivist for Records Services in Washington, D.C., with responsibility for all records management, archival, and museum program functions performed by the National Archives and Records Administration in the nation's capital. He is also an adjunct professor at the University of Maryland's College of Information Studies, teaching a course on the management of cultural institutions. Dr. Kurtz has published extensively in the areas of archival management and American history, including *Managing Archival and Manuscript Repositories* (2004) and *Nazi Contraband: American Policy on the Return of European Cultural Treasures, 1945–1955* (1985). He served as chair of the Archives Management Roundtable of the Society of American Archivists from 1987 to 2001.

*To the gallant men and women
who served in the U.S. Army as
Monuments, Fine Arts, and Archives
officers*

# America and the Return of Nazi Contraband

## The Recovery of Europe's Cultural Treasures

MICHAEL J. KURTZ

CAMBRIDGE UNIVERSITY PRESS

CAMBRIDGE UNIVERSITY PRESS
Cambridge, New York, Melbourne, Madrid, Cape Town, Singapore, São Paulo

Cambridge University Press
40 West 20th Street, New York, NY 10011-4211, USA

www.cambridge.org
Information on this title: www.cambridge.org/9780521849821

© Michael J. Kurtz 2006

This publication is in copyright. Subject to statutory exception
and to the provisions of relevant collective licensing agreements,
no reproduction of any part may take place without
the written permission of Cambridge University Press.

First published 2006

Printed in the United States of America

*A catalog record for this publication is available from the British Library.*

*Library of Congress Cataloging in Publication Data*

Kurtz, Michael J., 1949–
America and the return of Nazi contraband : the recovery of Europe's cultural treasures /
Michael J. Kurtz.
    p.   cm.
Includes bibliographical references and index.
ISBN 0-521-84982-9 (hardback)
1. World War, 1939–1945 – Reparations.   2. Cultural property – Repatriation.
3. World War, 1939–1945 – Destruction and pillage – Europe.   4. Art thefts – Europe.
5. Military government – Germany – History – 20th century.   I. Title.
D818.K85   2006
940.54'05 – dc22                                                    2005009622

ISBN-13   978-0-521-84982-1 hardback
ISBN-10   0-521-84982-9 hardback

Cambridge University Press has no responsibility for
the persistence or accuracy of URLs for external or
third-party Internet Web sites referred to in this publication
and does not guarantee that any content on such
Web sites is, or will remain, accurate or appropriate.

# Contents

# List of Illustrations

# Introduction

When *Nazi Contraband: American Policy on the Return of European Cultural Treasures, 1945–1955,* was published by Garland Press in 1985, I honestly believed that the story of cultural restitution after World War II and America's role in it was pretty much a settled story, a part of the past. Obviously, I am no seer, because unexpected events reopened painful and complex issues of historical and individual justice.

The collapse of the Soviet Union and communism in Eastern Europe, the opening of long-suppressed archives, and the reunification of Germany fueled a resurgence of demands not seen since the first decade after World War II for the settlement of restitution and compensation claims. Lost art and other cultural treasures were in the forefront of national, communal, and individual claims. Holocaust survivors, their heirs, and other supporters demanded a day of reckoning from governments – enemy, Allied, and neutral – and the corporate sector in seeking a measure of justice more than fifty years after the end of World War II.

Another set of events, not totally unexpected, involved the surfacing of looted art on the market, as looters died and artworks were bought by often legitimate purchasers. More and more court cases that posed difficult legal and moral issues came up in the United States and other countries. The demand for accountability touched the art and museum worlds in America and Europe.

National commissions in Europe, the United States, and Latin America often completely revised earlier understandings of what governments and peoples did during the war and the Holocaust. New information, new perspectives, and unfolding courtroom dramas provide the necessity for revisiting America's role in the saga of cultural restitution. Though the accomplishments of the U.S. Army Monuments, Fine Arts, and Archives (MFA&A) officers stand the test of time, the overall American diplomatic and legal performance is both more nuanced and ambiguous. This is often seen to an even greater degree with the records of various European governments.

In the first years of the new century, diplomatic and legal issues involving cultural restitution have reached a level of activity not seen since the 1940s. Indeed, a persuasive case can be made that, with the nations of Eastern Europe and the former Soviet Union beginning to engage actively on questions of restitution, the era ahead may rival that of the earlier period. So, a critical revisiting of cultural restitution and America's role in it, as well as bringing together the myriad actions and initiatives underway internationally in the legal and diplomatic arenas, will hopefully provide a framework in which to understand and evaluate actions that may, or may not, occur.

Cultural restitution is an ongoing phenomenon. Whether the ultimate judgment on the long saga that is the continuing response to Nazi barbarism is positive, negative, or mixed depends on what has been done and what others have yet to do. The enormity of the crimes committed during World War II and the Holocaust demands a final, historical accounting. Through the prism of plunder and restitution, we enter the darkest period of the most violent and bloody century in human history. What we find are the depths of human evil, acts of restoration and compensation, and all manner of behavior between the extremes. Let the story begin.

PART ONE

# CRISIS AND RESPONSE

I

# Plunder and Restitution

## An Historical Overview

> Restitution: (1) an act of restoring or a condition of being restored: as (a) a restoration of something to its rightful owner; (b) a making good of or giving an equivalent for some injury; (2) a legal action serving to cause restoration of a previous state.[1]

### Ancient and Medieval Eras

Throughout recorded history, armies have attacked the territories of other tribes, cities, or nations with the defeated enduring the pillage or loss of their property. Objects representing the most important values of the defeated peoples, such as religious articles, military banners or symbols, works of art, and archives were those most usually coveted by the victors. The Assyrian King Sargon II and the Babylonian ruler Nebuchadnezzar, for example, carried both captive peoples and their cultural treasures into exile.[2]

In the Old Testament book of the prophet Jeremiah, the biblical writer describes the looting in 586 B.C.E. of the most holy Jewish site in Jerusalem, the temple of Solomon:

The Chaldeans [i.e., the Babylonians] broke up the bronze pillars in the bronze sea, and carried off all the metal to Babylon. They removed also the pots, shrouds, snuffers, tossing-bowls, saucers, and all the bronze vessels used in the service of the temple.[3]

---

[1] *Webster's Seventh New Collegiate Dictionary*, revised ed. (Springfield, Mass.: G&C Merriam Co., 1965).

[2] Jeanette Greenfield, "The Spoils of War," in *The Spoils of War: World War II and Its Aftermath: The Loss, Reappearance, and Recovery of Cultural Property*, edited by Elizabeth Simpson (New York: Harry N. Abrams, 1997), p. 34.

[3] Jeremiah 52:17–18, *The Oxford Study Bible: Revised English Bible with Apocrypha* (New York: Oxford University Press, 1992), p. 846.

When the Romans sacked Jerusalem in 70 C.E., they not only destroyed the city but first looted valuable items for use in their military victory parade, the triumph, back in the capital. The Arch of Titus, erected in honor of the Roman victory, contained representations of the treasures seized from the defeated Jewish city.[4] Yet by 554 C.E., a different perspective emerged: Emperor Justinian promulgated his great revision of Roman law, the *Sanctio Pragmatica*, which contained perhaps the earliest legal restitution provisions. Despite the law, the only certain method of restoration was the eventual triumph of the defeated, an event of rare occurrence.[5]

Europeans, beginning with the decline of the *Pax Romana*, repeatedly experienced the loss of cultural treasures through the vicissitudes of warfare. Invaders, such as the Germanic tribesmen, the Norsemen, the Mongols, and the Turks, swept over the lands of the Roman Empire with devastating results. But cultural loss was not always at the hands of the "barbarian" outsiders. During the Fourth Crusade in the early thirteenth century, Latin Christians stole four bronze horses from the Hippodrome in Constantinople and brought them to adorn the piazza of San Marco in Venice.[6]

## Renaissance and Early Modern Times

The Italian wars of the French kings Charles VIII and Louis XII during the Renaissance accelerated the trend of European state-sponsored looting during wartime. During the Italian wars, the value Renaissance princes placed on artistic and literary treasures is clearly witnessed in the clauses of numerous treaties stipulating the transfer of tapestries, manuscripts, statues, and paintings to the victors.[7] The use of treaties to provide a legal framework for the transfer of looted property was a step beyond – though not necessarily an improvement on – a total reliance on brute force and conquest.

This trend of cultural looting again accelerated with the religious wars of the sixteenth century and the ensuing Thirty Years War. Examples of looting abound. Among the most notorious was the seizure of the Elector Palatine's library at Heidelberg by Maximilian of Bavaria and the subsequent gift of the library to Pope Gregory XV.[8] Some effort at restitution was made in the Treaty of Westphalia in 1648, which provided for a limited return of property to the Estates of the Holy Roman Empire.[9] In particular, article CXIV

---

[4] Greenfield, "The Spoils of War," p. 35.
[5] Louis E. Pease, "After the Holocaust: West Germany and Material Reparations to the Jews – From the Allied Occupation to the Luxembourg Agreements" (Ph.D. dissertation, Florida State University, 1976), p. 11.
[6] Greenfield, "The Spoils of War," p. 35.
[7] U.S. Department of State, *International Protection of Works of Art and Historic Monuments*, International and Cultural Series 8, Publication 3590 (1949), p. 823.
[8] Ibid.
[9] Pease, "After the Holocaust," p. 11.

provided "that the Records, Writings and Documents and other Moveables be also restored."[10] This was an important milestone in the evolution of international law and restitution.

The Treaty of the Pyrenees in 1659, ending an extended period of French-Spanish conflict, marked another significant milestone. The treaty not only called for specific restitution measures, but also established a joint commission to supervise the process and settle any disputes that might arise.[11] The concept of an internationally sanctioned body of arbitrators was one that would reappear, particularly in the twentieth century.

## The French Revolution and Its Aftermath

The wars of the French Revolution brought cultural looting and restitution fully into the modern era. Artistic and literary treasures were taken not only for their value or religious significance but also as part of an overall ideological attitude. Revolutionary France saw itself as the center of enlightened thought and practice, Europe's liberator from its feudal past, and thus the "natural repository" for Europe's artistic heritage.[12] Revolutionary and Napoleonic armies put this idea into practice and brought back to France many precious treasures from public and state collections in northern Italy and the rest of Europe.[13] In a practice carried over from the Renaissance, the French cloaked much of their pillaging through the legal cover of armistices and peace treaties concluded with their defeated foes. In 1796, for example, agreements with the princes of Parma, Modena, and the Holy See all provided for the transfer of specific items. For example, in the 23 July 1796 Armistice with the Papal States (article VIII), the French required that

The Pope will give over to the French Republic 100 paintings, busts or statues according to the choice made by the commissioners who will come to Rome, among these objects one should find in particular the bronze bust of Junius Brutus and the marble bust of Marcus Brutus which are now located in the Capitol, additionally 500 manuscripts chosen by these commissioners.[14]

The commissioners called for in the armistice with the Holy See obviously functioned differently from the body established by the Treaty of the

---

[10] Wojciech Kowalski, "Introduction to International Law of Restitution of Works of Art During Armed Conflicts, Part II," *Spoils of War International Newsletter* No. 3 (December 1996): p. 10.

[11] Ibid., p. 11.

[12] Sharon A. Williams, *The International and National Protection of Movable Cultural Property: A Comparative Study* (Dobbs Ferry, N.Y.: Oceana Publications, 1978), pp. 7–8.

[13] Janet Flanner, *Men and Monuments* (New York: Harper and Brothers, 1947), p. xiv.

[14] Wojciech Kowalski, "Introduction to International Law of Restitution of Works of Art During Armed Conflicts, Part III," *Spoils of War International Newsletter* No. 4 (August 1997): p. 40.

Pyrenees. Whether a military campaign ended in victory, defeat, or stalemate determined how any joint bodies would function. The aftermaths of
World War I and World War II would make this abundantly clear. Another
Napoleonic feature that set an example for future developments was the
conqueror's display of looted art in the Musée de la République for his own
and France's glory.[15] Revolutionary fervor, nationalist pride, and greed were
a formidable combination. Not all French actions were so negative. A law
of December 1790 provided for restitution to Huguenots for property seized
after the revocation of the Edict of Nantes in 1666.[16]

At the Congress of Vienna, the reaction of the Allies to Napoleon's looting
marked the first substantial efforts in the modern era to develop a legal and
ethical framework for the old Latin concept *restitus*. The question facing
the Congress was whether items transferred to France by treaties concluded
during the French Revolutionary wars were, in reality, looted or valid transfers now legally belonging to France. The English representatives, Lords
Liverpool and Castlereagh, at first saw a distinction between items that were
clearly spoils and those covered by treaties. Insistent claims to the contrary
by the King of the Netherlands, German and Italian princes, and the Pope
forced a reconsideration of the issue.[17]

After protracted debate, the Allies finally decided to return items taken
either by force or through treaty provisions to the country of origin. Promulgated in the 1815 Convention of Paris, this was the first international
condemnation of looting and the establishment of the principle that all loot
should be returned to the country of origin.[18] This decision was based on
the concept of the artistic integrity of a nation, an idea first propounded
by French scholars and artists such as Jacques-Louis David, Jean Louis
Darmond, and Antoine Quatremère de Quincy, who had forcefully objected
to Napoleonic looting.[19] Thus, the four bronze horses taken from the Byzantines by the Venetians, and then in 1797 from the Venetians by the French,
were returned to Venice,[20] but not to their original home. This highlighted
a political reality in cultural restitution. It was actually difficult in many situations to return an object to its point of origin. In this case, the Byzantine
Empire had long since disappeared, and in the eyes of Europe, the successors
to the Byzantines, the Turks, had no right to make a claim. No one, however,

---

[15] Flanner, *Men and Monuments*, p. xiv.
[16] Pease, "After the Holocaust," p. 11.
[17] *International Protection of Works of Art and Historic Monuments*, p. 826.
[18] Lawrence M. Kaye, "Laws in Force at the Dawn of World War II: International Conventions
and National Laws," in *The Spoils of War: World War II and Its Aftermath: The Loss,
Reappearance and Recovery of Cultural Property*, edited by Elizabeth Simpson (New York:
Harry N. Abrams, 1997), p. 101.
[19] Charles Estreicher, ed., *Cultural Losses of Poland: Index of Polish Cultural Losses During
the German Occupation, 1939–44* (London, 1944), p. xi.
[20] Flanner, *Men and Monuments*, p. xiv.

asked the Sultan for his views. The Turks were not accepted as part of the political or diplomatic concert of Europe.

Politics also affected cultural restitution in other ways. The peacemakers in Vienna, though accepting restitution in principle, did not want to turn French opinion against the restored Bourbons. Hence, an overly rigorous approach was avoided. French sensitivities had an even more direct effect on restitution efforts. Two hundred Prussian troops were needed to get Prussian art stored in the Louvre past sullen French National Guardsmen and irate citizens.[21] Diplomacy, politics, and popular feeling would always affect cultural restitution.

## Developments Prior to World War I

By the mid-nineteenth century, the romantic notion of the integrity and unity of a national cultural heritage dominated. This belief, along with developments in the technology of war, created a great deal of anxiety about the fate of art and other cultural property during war.[22] The American Civil War stimulated the first attempt to codify principles of international law for the protection of cultural property. At the request of Abraham Lincoln, Dr. Francis Lieber of Columbia College in New York developed a code of conduct, subsequently issued for use by the Union Army, designed to protect cultural, educational, and charitable property from looting and destruction.[23] The Lieber Code served as the basis for the 1874 Brussels Conference. The Declaration of the Conference, which contained principles of international law never ratified but significant for later developments, clearly stated that cultural and educational property, even where state-owned, should be treated as private property and thus be exempt from seizure.[24] Another building block in the search for international consensus on the conduct of war came in 1880 when the Institute of International Law issued the Oxford Manual. Based on the Lieber Code and the deliberations of the Brussels Conference, the Oxford Manual sought to codify the rules for land warfare.[25]

Two conferences at The Hague, in 1899 and 1907, attempted to regularize the rules of warfare and to limit its destructiveness. The second conference, building on earlier efforts, approved Convention No. 4: "Laws and Customs of War on Land." The convention contained articles that became the essential statements in international law on the protection of property. Article 47 forbade pillaging, while Article 56 specifically prohibited the "seizure or destruction or willful damage to institutions dedicated to religion, charity,

[21] Kowalski, "Introduction to International Law...Part III," p. 40.
[22] Williams, *The International and National Protection of Movable Cultural Property*, p. 12.
[23] Kaye, "Laws in Force at the Dawn of World War II," pp. 101–2.
[24] Ibid.
[25] Ibid.

education, [or] the arts and sciences," as well as "historic monuments, [and] works of art and science."[26] The taking of private property was expressly prohibited.[27] Equally significant were provisions that permitted legal proceedings for violations of the convention and for payment in compensation by those deemed as violators.[28] This agreement was signed by the major European and non-European powers, including the United States, Germany, Russia, France, and Great Britain.

In the tense years prior to the outbreak of war, several nations took related steps to protect their cultural heritage. Italy in 1902 and 1909 passed laws controlling the sale or transfer of cultural objects in public and private institutions as well as items in private hands.[29] The French in 1913 placed similar restrictions on cultural objects that the government classified as protected property.[30] The Italian laws, in particular, would affect cultural restitution disputes with Germany in the post–World War II period.

## World War I and Restitution

The events of 1914 through 1918 showed how fragile were the results of the Hague Conventions. Among other Convention articles, those on pillaging and property were flouted. Because of sensitivity in neutral nations after the burning of part of the University of Louvain and the bombardment of Rheims Cathedral, the Germans in late 1914 created an organization in their conquered territories in Belgium and northern France that was supposed to protect historic monuments and cultural objects.[31] Many items, though, were sent to Germany for "protection," setting a precedent zealously imitated in World War II. One particularly notorious item sent to Germany was sections of the Van Eyck altarpiece from the church of St. Bavo in Ghent. The Allies viewed all this as looting, and German actions created an intense amount of ill will.

In the harsh peace treaties that concluded the Great War, the provisions in the Hague Convention pertaining to restitution and compensation were used as the basis for strong Allied measures. In the Versailles Treaty, Article 245 required Germany to return all "trophies, archives, historical souvenirs, or works of art carried away from France by the German authorities in the course of the war of 1870–1871 and during [the World War]." The restituted items would be drawn from a list prepared by the French government. The Germans were ordered in Article 247 to provide for restitution-in-kind to

[26] Ibid.
[27] Ibid.
[28] Ibid.
[29] Ibid.
[30] Ibid.
[31] Ernst Posner, "Public Records Under Military Occupation," *American Historical Review* 49 (January 1944): 215.

Belgium for the destruction in Louvain. Specifically, the Germans were forced "to furnish the University of Louvain, within two months after a request is made by it...manuscripts, incunabula, printed books, maps, and objects of collection corresponding in value to those destroyed in the burning by Germany of the Library of Louvain."[32]

In response to a strong Belgian demand, the second clause of Article 247 directed the Germans to return not only the looted Van Eyck altarpiece panels but also panels sold to Prussian King Frederick William III in 1821 by an English collector and kept in the Kaiser Friedrich Museum in Berlin. Along the same lines, the Germans had to return to the church of St. Peter in Louvain panels from the triptych of the *Last Supper* by Dirk Bouts, which had been legitimately purchased by German museums before 1914.[33] The return of these altarpieces was an innovative step in international law. Here for the first time was articulated a requirement to reintegrate works of art into a nation's historical and artistic heritage. Though Article 247 was only a small part of the Versailles Treaty, it would have long-term consequences. The return of the altarpieces stirred bitter German resentment, and both works, destined to be looted again, would fit well into the Nazi racist view of art history.

Through those actions, the Allies clearly established the principle of using works of art as reparations (i.e., compensation for other, destroyed works of art). In requiring reparations for cultural losses, the Allies determined that legitimate purchases could be voided and that public collections of the defeated were fair game. These measures and the one that mandated restitution for an earlier conflict provoked a fierce German reaction, which manifested itself in the next war and would also complicate restitution efforts after that conflict.

Treaties with Austria and Hungary and the settlement of the Polish-Soviet-Ukranian conflict all featured prominently the restitution principles of returning items to the countries of origin, compensating these countries for objects destroyed during war and replacing lost objects with objects of comparable nature and value.[34] The Poles, for example, regained cultural treasures taken at the time of the first Polish partition in 1772. Many valuable artworks, tapestries, and other cultural items were returned to Poland.[35] An interesting point to note is that, in going back to 1772 and 1870–1871

---

[32] Kaye, "Laws in Force at the Dawn of World War II," p. 103; Leslie Poste, "The Development of U.S. Protection of Libraries and Archives in Europe During World War II," 2 vols. (Ph.D. dissertation, University of Chicago, 1958), vol. 1: 9.

[33] Kaye, "Laws in Force at the Dawn of World War II," p. 103; Gladys E. Hamlin, "European Art Collections and the War," *College Art Journal* 5 (March 1946), p. 233; Andrea Gattini, "Restitution by Russia of Works of Art Removed from German Territory at the End of the Second World War," *European Journal of International Law* 7 (1996): 1–6.

[34] Kaye, "Laws in Force at the Dawn of World War II," p. 103.

[35] Ibid.

in settling restitution issues, the Allies ignored the concept of the statute of limitations, a legal concept that required much time and attention in the decades after the Second World War.

Much bitterness ensued from the application of the cultural restitution provisions in the various treaties. For example, during the course of the war the Germans had stolen many cultural items from private owners. The issue of restoring private property was new. The Allied and German responses were inadequate. The 1919 peace agreements did not specifically address the practical aspects of returning various categories of property. Owners of looted items often spent years in futile efforts to recover their property from their own governments. The Germans, for their part, responded to Allied restitution efforts with bitter passive resistance.[36]

## Interwar Years

International tensions during the period between the wars, particularly in the 1930s, made it clear that another general conflict was in the offing. The efforts of the International Museums Office of the League of Nations reflected intense concern about the protection of fine arts. A series of conferences, beginning in 1931, focused on the protection of fine art during wartime. The issues of distinguishing between public and private cultural property and the alienation of cultural property through illegal export and sales also figured prominently in the international discussions. A draft convention prepared in 1933 by the International Museums Office required repatriation for all objects illegally exported and the cancellation of all transactions in which objects were illegally alienated, no matter what the means. The draft convention failed to address questions related to statutes of limitations and did not clearly distinguish between public and private cultural property.[37] The League, distracted by crises in the Far East, Africa, and Europe, failed to act.

The worsening international climate prompted another effort, this time clearly focused on war-related threats to cultural property. The International Committee on International Cooperation for the Year 1937–8 urged the International Museums Office to draft yet another new convention.[38] As a

---

[36] Memorandum, "Restitution after the War of 1914–18, 1 September 1944," File "Restitution – Study on Restitution of Works of Art after World War I," Reports from Advisors Overseas, 1944–1945, Records Relating to Restitution of Cultural Materials, 1943–1946, RG 239, Records of the American Commission for the Salvage of Artistic and Historic Monuments in War Areas (the Roberts Commission), National Archives at College Park, Maryland.

[37] Kaye, "Laws in Force at the Dawn of World War II," pp. 103–4.

[38] Report, "The Director's Committee of the International Museums Office to the International Committee on International Cooperation for the Year 1937/38, Together with a Preliminary Draft International Convention on the Protection of Historic Buildings and Works of Art in Time of War," File "League of Nations – Draft of International Agreement to Protect Arts and Monuments in Time of War," Correspondence, 1943–1946, RG 239.

result, the International Museums Office appointed a committee of experts to prepare a new draft convention. The committee, interestingly enough, consisted of legal and military experts, with no one from the fine arts.[39] In April 1938, shortly after the German annexation of Austria, the group submitted a draft "International Agreement to Protect Arts and Monuments in Time of War." This agreement provided for inspections of cultural objects and sites in time of war and specifically stated that works of art stored abroad in wartime were exempt from confiscation or any other form of disposition.[40] But the withdrawal of Japan, Germany, and Italy had fatally weakened the League. This, along with the bitterness of the Germans about the Versailles Treaty and its cultural restitution obligations, made it certain that Germany would pay no attention to this League initiative.

The outbreak of war in September 1939 blocked any further diplomatic efforts to gain assent on the draft international agreement. The secretary general of the League unilaterally issued a declaration containing the basic principles of the draft convention, but only Belgium, Greece, the Netherlands, Spain, and the United States (a nonmember) announced adherence.[41] Thus, the Fourth Convention of the Second Hague Convention remained the fundamental statement in international law regarding the protection of property in wartime. All the issues raised in the First World War – protecting cultural heritage from plundering, appropriately distinguishing between public and private cultural property, instituting restitution measures involving reparations and compensation-in-kind – remained to be resolved.

But the events of the Holocaust era and World War II would result in destruction and loss beyond anything experienced in the dreadful conflict of 1914–18. The cataclysm that convulsed Europe between 1933 and 1945 affected every aspect of existence, including cultural heritage. The issues involving cultural protection and restitution were beyond anything heretofore experienced or imagined. To understand the disaster that befell Europe's cultural heritage, we must turn to the author of the calamity: Nazi Germany.

[39] Ibid.
[40] Ibid.
[41] Ibid.

## 2

# Nazi Looting

## *The War Against European Culture, 1933–1945*

Nazi looting of cultural property was radically different in nature and scope from previous historical experience. Events that began in Germany spread throughout Europe and then the world, culminating in the horrific losses of World War II and the Holocaust. Sixty million died in the global conflagration, and twenty-five million perished in the Soviet Union alone. Approximately six million Jews died, 15 to 20 percent of the Polish population perished, and millions of displaced persons roamed devastated Europe at the conclusion of the war. Economically, Europe was ravaged. A quarter of Britain's wealth was gone, 30 to 40 percent of the Soviet Union's industrial infrastructure was destroyed, and Germany lay in ruins.[1]

Amidst the carnage and devastation, damage to Europe's cultural heritage was likewise immense. Libraries, archives, works of art, and precious artifacts had all been swept up in the Nazi vortex of plunder and destruction. In the aftermath of the war and the looting, the survivors' heirs, those who sought to redress the wrongs committed, and even perpetrators had to ask not only "how" this had all happened, but "why." The answer to "why" lay in the very nature of the Nazi regime.

## The Regime

The Nazi regime was rooted in a racist ideology with potentially vast geopolitical implications. Based on a crude Social Darwinism, the Nazis viewed the world from the perspective of racial groups fighting for existence in a ceaseless effort to expand, dominate, and destroy other, "inferior" races.[2] The Aryan race, of which the Germans were the highest expression, had to remain "pure" in order to attain dominance and expand. Adolf Hitler in

---

[1] Gerhard L. Weinberg, *A World at Arms: A Global History of World War II* (New York: Cambridge University Press, 1994), p. 894.
[2] Ibid., pp. 20–21.

*Mein Kampf* clearly stated that the German race had to expand eastward for living space (*Lebensraum*). This meant moving into Poland and then into the territory of the Soviet Union, and this would require war, the preferred policy instrument of the National Socialist regime.[3] Those who were in the way, the Slavs and particularly the Jews, had to be eliminated so that the Germans could migrate to much needed agricultural territory. The communists and the Nazis shared a deterministic view of history, with the Nazis substituting race for social class as the key factor.[4] Hitler's ideological fanaticism and geopolitical aspirations made war inevitable. All efforts to dissuade, appease, or compromise were futile.

In addition to the ideological and geopolitical tenets, the Nazis were animated by a bitter rejection of the results of World War I and the subsequent Treaty of Versailles. To the Nazis and many other nationalist Germans as well, Germany had not lost the war. With German troops deep in French and Belgian territories, it was difficult to comprehend or accept how swiftly the war ended and the home front collapsed in October and November 1918. Thus, the stab-in-the-back legend came to be. The belief that traitors – communists, socialists, the Jews – had betrayed the Reich and caused defeat.[5] Once Hitler was in power, many of his plans and policies were built on lessons learned from the first conflict. A dictatorship at home would stifle any traitorous actions while fighting abroad. One enemy at a time would prevent an alliance of enemies that could blockade and attack the homeland on multiple fronts.[6] But more profound than these tactical considerations were the imperatives of race and ideology, and art and culture played vital ideological roles.

The ideology of the Nazi regime profoundly affected how it dealt with art and culture. The belief that German culture was superior to other cultures or racial groups was buttressed by the underlying tenet that the Aryan race, from which Germanic culture developed, provided the vitality and vigor that protected and promoted Germanic cultural expression. The foundational notion that undergirded this whole structure was the notion that the Aryan, Germanic race was purer and biologically superior to all other races.[7] From this perspective, artistic expression is not just a phenomenon of civilized society. Rather, it represents the expression of the superior race, with the art of other cultures viewed as inferior, if not degraded.[8] From the Nazi perspective, art which expressed the purity of Aryan and Germanic culture,

---

[3] Ibid.

[4] Ibid.

[5] Ibid., p. 8.

[6] Gerhard L. Weinberg, *World in the Balance: Behind the Scenes of World War II* (Hanover, N.H. and London: The University Press of New England, 1981), p. 4.

[7] Jonathan Petropoulos, *Art as Politics in the Third Reich* (Chapel Hill: University of North Carolina Press, 1996), p. 7.

[8] Ibid.

at least as they understood it, was the heritage of the German nation. If such art was currently in other hands, it did not matter. It belonged to the German nation, and the Germans had a right to it.

The troubled years of the Weimar Republic were filled, from the Nazis' point of view, with defeatism, pacifism, socialism, and economic collapse, which was expressed culturally in a decadent modernism. Berlin, the heart of the Old Reich, was, for the Nazis, a hotbed of cultural decadence. Adolf Hitler in *Mein Kampf* and Alfred Rosenberg in *The Myth of the Twentieth Century* focused on Jews, communists, sexual deviates, and inferior races, particularly the Slavs, as the "spiritual" enemy. These races and groups sapped the vitality of the Aryan race and had to be eliminated. The art and culture of these enemies presented a threat to the purity and integrity of Aryanism and so had to be eliminated as well.

Besides ideology, the regime also sought social recognition as the legitimate heir of its pre-Weimar predecessor. Less than twenty years separated the Third Reich from the monarchical era. Association with works of art and masterpieces linked them with the still extant aristocratic class, which continued to dominate the nation's aesthetic sensibility.[9] As a right-wing party that never won a majority at the polls, the Nazis desperately needed the support of the former ruling classes, as well as that of the military officer corps and the industrial barons. Social recognition and acceptability were critically important. Hitler and most of his cohorts came from the lower middle class. Although some, such as Joachim von Ribbentrop, affected aristocratic pretensions, in fact, most of the Nazi leaders had little in common with their erstwhile upper-class allies. Art collecting and artistic patronage became vehicles to meet the upper class on a level field and, eventually, to supplant it. As the years of the regime went on, particularly during the period of all-out war, the Nazis ground into the dust the elite they had once needed.[10]

Another factor that came to the fore as the regime matured was the spirit of intense competition that animated the senior leadership. Continually, ministers maneuvered, made and broke alliances, and sought the patronage of the Führer. With art and culture a key component in Nazi ideology, there was a particularly intense competition for dominance and control. As the regime became more entrenched and corrupt, the elements of personal gain and avarice exacerbated the leadership rivalries for the control of art and culture.[11] In many ways, the Nazi handling of cultural property, particularly the appropriation of property belonging to the enemies of the state and the party, provides a lens through which we can understand the very essence of the regime. Historian Jonathan Petropoulos has identified four key elements

[9] Ibid.
[10] Ibid., pp. 299–307.
[11] Ibid., pp. 8–9.

of Nazi rule, which found expression in the appropriation of cultural property and ultimately in the Holocaust.

1. The programs against the enemies of the regime began with relatively nonviolent, modest steps and evolved into ever-increasing levels of terror, confiscation, and destruction.
2. Cultural policies, including the appropriation of cultural property, stemmed from a combination of Hitler's orders and decisions and the initiatives of various leaders in the state and party.
3. The seizure of Austria in 1938 provided the critical testing ground for plundering operations. Vienna would serve as the model for what would happen in Germany and the rest of Europe.
4. The laws and directives against the Jews and other enemies of the regime became inextricably linked with the Holocaust. Seizure of cultural property preceded the mass murders. Works of art drew particular attention from the Nazis.[12]

Totalitarian fervor, with the theft of cultural property as its hallmark, reigned unchecked in the Germany of the Nazis.

## The Jewish Plight

Amongst all their foes, the Nazis hated and feared the Jews the most. The Jews were regarded as "culture-destroying non-humans," a continued threat to Germany's racial purity because of the dangers of intimate relations between Jews and non-Jews and intermarriage. The Jews, according to the Nazis, sought to subvert German culture and vitality and to destroy the "Master Race." To fanatical Nazis, the removal of Jews from German life was absolutely critical. Further, the Jews were seen as being the motivating force behind international criticism of the Nazis as well as being responsible for the "encirclement" that the Nazis always feared.[13] Shortly after Hitler took office as Reich chancellor on 30 January 1933, violent attacks on the Jews by Nazi storm troopers, the SA (*Sturmabteilung*), broke out in Berlin and other German cities. To control and channel the violence and, more importantly, to begin segregating Jews from German society prior to their removal, the Nazis passed the first in a long line of legislative decrees. The Law for the Protection of the Professional Civil Service, issued on

---

[12] Jonathan Petropoulos, "German Laws and Directives Bearing on the Appropriation of Cultural Property in the Third Reich," in *The Spoils of War: World War II and Its Aftermath: The Loss, Reappearance, and Recovery of Cultural Property*, edited by Elizabeth Simpson (New York: Harry N. Abrams, 1997), p. 106.

[13] Weinberg, *A World at Arms*, pp. 20–4; Raul Hilberg, *The Destruction of the European Jews* (Chicago: Quadrangle Books, 1967), pp. 11–14.

7 April 1933, defined the term *non-Aryan* and forced Jews from the civil service. Thus, the pattern of terror, propaganda, and legislation was set.[14]

What began with a definition of *non-Aryan* would grow into the framework for the Final Solution. For after definition would eventually come the concentration of the Jews in ghettos and, ultimately, annihilation. With each stage came expropriation measures. The seizure of assets, property, and, finally, even the personal belongings of victims was an integral part of the Holocaust.[15] Given Hitler's implacable determination to remove the Jews from German life, first through forced emigration and later by extermination, the 500,000 German Jews were doomed from the beginning. Raul Hilberg, historian of the destruction of the European Jews, put it this way: "When in the early days of 1933 the first civil servant wrote the first definition of 'non-Aryan' into a civil service ordinance, the fate of European Jewry was sealed."[16]

The business acumen of German Jews was needed to restart the depression-plagued German economy, and this, along with the effects of international boycotts of German goods, meant that Jews were at first not completely excluded from the economy. However, pressure on the Jews in the cultural life of the nation was uniform and relentless. Laws establishing the Cinema Office (14 July 1933), the Reich Office of Culture (22 September 1933), and the Newspaper Editors' Law (4 October 1933) drove Jews from public cultural life and forced them into their own schools, clubs, and cultural associations.[17] Despite these efforts at segregation, waves of anti-Jewish violence again broke out in 1935. Needing a calm international and domestic environment in order to rearm, Hitler decided to deal with the "Jewish problem" by further legal action.[18] The Nuremberg Laws of 8–14 September 1935 were designed to clarify the question of German citizenship and to separate the races completely. Hitler saw the Reich Citizenship Law and the Law for the Protection of German Blood and Honor as milestones in purging the Thousand Year Reich of the Jews.[19]

Despite the intensifying pressure, many Jews remained in Germany. After all, the Jews had existed as a persecuted minority for over 2,000 years and had always survived as a people.[20] The German Jews regarded themselves as Germans first and foremost and had little desire to leave their homeland. Their patriotic sentiments were the reason behind the prohibition against Jews flying the German colors. A fundamental issue, which would come to

[14] Leni Yahil, *The Holocaust: The Fate of European Jewry* (New York and Oxford: Oxford University Press, 1990), p. 60.
[15] Hilberg, *The Destruction of the European Jews*, pp. 640–1.
[16] Ibid., p. 669.
[17] Yahil, *The Holocaust*, p. 67.
[18] Ibid., pp. 67–70.
[19] Ibid., p. 71.
[20] Ibid., p. 91; Hilberg, *The Destruction of the European Jews*, p. 666.

haunt all European Jews, was where they could go. The British sought to restrict emigration to their mandate in Palestine, the Depression-era United States had very restrictive immigration laws, and most other nations were as unwelcoming.[21] Perhaps the strongest and most subliminal factor inhibiting flight was that no one, probably including the Nazis, could imagine the Final Solution. The year 1938, however, was to prove a turning point. Among other factors, widespread expropriation of property and looting came to the fore. Prior to this, Jews were pressured to forsake their professions, and those who wished to emigrate had to pay various taxes and sell their assets, but now things became immeasurably worse.

The Nazi annexation of Austria in March 1938 (*Anschluss*) provoked fierce anti-Jewish persecution in Vienna and throughout the country. Thousands of Jews were arrested and put in concentration camps, and Jewish businesses were "Aryanized" (i.e., Jews were forced to turn over their firms to "Aryans" and suffered catastrophic economic losses). The cultural property of prominent Jewish families, such as the Rothschilds, the Bondys, and the Lacoronskis, were seized, along with all other assets.[22] After this terror and the continued propaganda about the Jewish plot to control the world and destroy Germany came legislation to force Jews to register their property and to sell off their assets before emigration. Thus was born the "Vienna Model," the combination of "Aryanization," plunder, and repressive legislation that Germany and Europe would soon come to know well.[23] Adolf Eichmann, a senior officer in the SS (*Schutzstaffel*), was sent by his chief, Heinrich Himmler, to rid Vienna of the Jews. Within six months, Eichmann, using a full range of terror tactics, forced 50,000 Austrian Jews to emigrate destitute and without resources. All elements of the state and party competed for spoils. In Austria, as in the Alt Reich, Hitler's pattern of governing was to assign overlapping jurisdiction to government and party units so that he alone would remain in control.[24]

Out of this fierce free-for-all, Himmler could proudly report that the looting operation in Vienna had netted RM70 million of artworks, which the Nazis kept in depots at the Neue Burg palace and the Rothschild family's hunting lodge outside Vienna. In June 1938, Hitler, using a 31 May law as the basis, set forth the Führervorbehalt (prerogative of the Führer) as the governing concept of what was to happen with the seized art. The Führer alone, at least in theory, controlled each object seized.[25] This paved the way for his henchmen to begin trafficking in stolen art for their personal gain. What had

---

[21] Ibid., p. 93.

[22] Yahil, *The Holocaust*, pp. 105–9; Jonathan Petropoulos, "German Laws and Directives," p. 106.

[23] Yahil, *The Holocaust*, pp. 105–9.

[24] Petropoulos, *Art as Politics*, p. 8.

[25] Petropoulos, "German Laws and Directives," p. 107; Petropoulos, *Art as Politics*, p. 85.

FIGURE 1. Burning of Jewish books by a Nazi crowd in Berlin, ca. 1939. *Credit:* Courtesy of National Archives, photo no. 242-HB-1340.

begun with the seizure and sale of modernist "degenerate art" from German public collections in 1937 became endemic to the Nazi system. Great gains lay ahead for the plunderers and their collaborators.

Hard on the heels of the *Anschluss* came the *Kristallnacht* pogrom of 9–10, November which swept Germany and Austria. Orchestrated as the result of the murder of a minor German Embassy official in Paris by a Jew, the orgy of violence resulted in the murder of 91 Jews, the imprisonment of 30,000, the burning of 191 synagogues with seventy-six totally destroyed, and the destruction of 7,500 Jewish businesses.[26] This terror was again justified by the Jewish "threat" and Jewish "responsibility" for what had occurred. Again, repressive legislation followed swiftly after terror and propaganda. On the same day (12 November 1938) that the First Ordinances on the Exclusion of Jews from German Economic Life were passed, Joseph Goebbels banned Jews from entering museums and theaters or attending cultural events. Hermann Göring, chief of the Four Year Economic Plan, among other posts, levied a RM1 billion "atonement" tax on the Jewish

[26] Yahil, *The Holocaust*, p. 111.

community. Ordinances enacted on 20 November and 3 December permitted authorities to Aryanize Jewish businesses and seize Jewish property.[27] These decrees and others like them were issued as Implementation Orders to the Reich Citizenship Law issued in Nuremberg in September 1935. The last would come on 1 July 1943, ordering the final liquidation of German Jewry.[28] German and Austrian Jews now fully recognized their peril, and by the time war broke out less than a year later, almost 250,000 German Jews and 80,000 Austrian Jews had fled.[29] What was in store for the Jews of Europe had been made stunningly clear by Hitler in a January 1939 statement: "Today I want to be a prophet once more: If international-finance Jewry inside and outside of Europe should succeed once more in plunging nations into another world war, the consequences will not be Bolshevization of the earth and thereby the victory of Jewry, but the annihilation of the Jewish race in Europe."[30]

## Wartime Looting and the Holocaust

The outbreak of war in 1939 dramatically expanded the arena for Nazi plundering. After the one-month blitz of Poland, events in the west settled into a quiet lull until the April 1940 attacks on Denmark and Norway and the May assault on Belgium, the Netherlands, and France. The aftermath of these assaults, as well as events in the east, brought the Nazi looting machine into full swing. Immediately upon the conquest of Poland, the Polish military caste, the intelligentsia, the clergy, and most of all the Jews were subjected to the harshest treatment. Many were executed, and the Jews were concentrated into urban ghettos, where over time they would be joined by the Jews from Germany, Austria, and other parts of Europe.[31] Once more, terror was accompanied by propaganda (the Jews were responsible for the war) and repressive legislation that seized assets of the former Polish state, including cultural treasures, and assets of Nazi enemies, most particularly the Jews.

When the Nazis invaded the Soviet Union in June 1941, SS mobile killing squads (*Einsatzgruppen*) followed the invading forces with orders to kill communist commissars, partisans, and Jews. Almost 2.8 million Soviet prisoners of war were dead within a year of capture, and hundreds of thousands of Jews were slaughtered.[32] The war blocked the possibility of emigrations, forced or otherwise. Fanciful Nazi schemes for sending all Jews to the island

---

[27] Petropoulos, *Art as Politics*, pp. 84, 92.
[28] Yahil, *The Holocaust*, p. 71.
[29] Ibid., p. 121.
[30] Hilberg, *The Destruction of the European Jews*, p. 654.
[31] Yahil, *The Holocaust*, p. 48.
[32] Weinberg, *A World at Arms*, pp. 267, 300; Hilberg, *The Destruction of the European Jews*, pp. 219–24.

of Madagascar in the Indian Ocean were plainly not feasible.[33] But for Hitler the elimination of the Jews remained a political, military, and psychological urgency. Thus began the period of annihilation. Jews from the ghettos in the east and from the cities and towns of western Europe were sent to death camps, such as Auschwitz, Treblinka, and Sobibor.[34] At the infamous Wannsee Conference in January 1942, Nazi leaders settled on the details of the Final Solution, with Adolf Eichmann as the chief executioner.[35] All agencies of the state and party were engaged in this gigantic bureaucratic killing machine. The Ministries of Interior and Finance, the Post Office, the Railway Administration, the Army, and the SS all played a role, so that by the spring of 1945 over six million Jews were dead along with millions of others.

Because there were numerous organizations involved in the killing operations, there were many, often competing, entities struggling for control of European art and cultural property. But standing above all the others were four major players. The first, and most prominent, was the Sonderauftrag Linz (the Linz special project), operating under Hitler's aegis, with the goal of transforming the Führer's boyhood home into the cultural mecca of Europe. This idea was vaguely forming in Hitler's mind for a number of years, and it crystallized upon his visit to the fabulous art galleries of Rome and Florence in May 1938. Hitler wanted to reduce the influence and prestige of Vienna, the polyglot city that had rejected the artistic ambitions of the young artist. The fabulous Rothschild collections of Vienna, conveniently available since the *Anschluss*, formed the core of the collection Hitler intended to build in Linz.[36] This project was Hitler's great obsession, along with the elimination of the Jews, both of which were mentioned in his last will and testament. Hitler personally created the architectural scheme for a vast array of public buildings, the most prominent of which was to be the Führermuseum, modeled on the Haus für Deutsche Kunst in Munich. The building would have a 500-foot colonnade and house an art collection, library, theater, and collection of armor.[37] Hitler also planned to turn Linz into a modern, industrial metropolis, the new capital of the Nazi empire.[38]

---

[33] Weinberg, *World in the Balance*, p. 10; Hilberg, *The Destruction of the European Jews*, pp. 260–1.

[34] Hilberg, *The Destruction of the European Jews*, pp. 572–86; Weinberg, *A World at Arms*, p. 528.

[35] Hilberg, *The Destruction of the European Jews*, pp. 264–5.

[36] Lynn Nicholas, "World War II and the Displacement of Art and Cultural Property," in *The Spoils of War: World War II and Its Aftermath: The Loss, Reappearance, and Recovery of Cultural Property*, edited by Elizabeth Simpson (New York: Harry N. Abrams, 1997), p. 40.

[37] James S. Plaut, "Hitler's Capital: Loot for the Master Race," *Atlantic Monthly* 178 (October 1946): 73.

[38] Ibid.

Even as Soviet troops fought their way to the bunker in Berlin, Hitler was still working on new design schemes. The May 1938 law, which gave Hitler authority over all objects brought under the control of the state, provided the basis for Hitler's right of first choice of all looted art. Hitler's colleagues deferred, at least nominally, to the Führer's right of first choice. Over the five years of the war, the Linz project expended RM90 million to acquire eight thousand paintings and the rights to tens of thousands of other works.[39] A library of twenty thousand volumes, along with precious coins and medieval armor, were also brought together from collections across Europe. The Nazi methods included not only confiscation but also forced sales and even legitimate acquisitions. The various methods of dispossession, some involving complex currency transactions, would prove difficult to untangle after the war.

The second major player was Reichsmarshall Hermann Göring, chief of the Luftwaffe, head of the four-year economic plan, and Hitler's designated successor. Göring had a tremendous lust for art, both as a collector and a seller, to feather his own nest. Taking advantage of his power and authority, Göring manipulated the various occupation authorities and for a time controlled Alfred Rosenberg's looting operation.[40] Göring, despite obeisance to Hitler, often kept the best art for himself. The avaricious Reichsmarshall crammed his country estate with priceless items. Karinhall, named for Göring's first wife, was located in a vast game and hunting preserve on a small lake called the Wuckersee, about seventy miles northwest of Berlin. Among the many objects Göring collected and proudly displayed at Karinhall were Beauvais tapestries and a writing table that supposedly once belonged to Cardinal Mazarin.[41] By the end of the war, Göring had eight residences packed with art, practically none of it German. Göring's minions scoured occupied Europe confiscating seized art, manipulating hapless victims into forced sales, and dealing with collaborators in the art market, such as Theodor Fischer of the Fischer Gallery in Lucerne, Switzerland, to buy and trade for additional objects. At the peak of the Nazi empire, Göring made twenty visits to the Jeu de Paume museum in Paris, the Nazi depot for looted art in France, for private showings of the best holdings of French Jewish collectors and art dealers.[42]

A third major player was the SS under Heinrich Himmler. As the Reichsführer SS, head of the Gestapo and the Waffen-SS, and Minister of Interior from 1943 on, Himmler had great resources at his command. Along with his obsessions with the occult, mesmerism, and homeopathic remedies, Himmler was a fanatical racist and a true believer in the Aryan

[39] Nicholas, "World War II and the Displacement of Art and Cultural Property," pp. 40–1.
[40] Ibid.
[41] Janet Flanner, *Men and Monuments* (New York: Harper and Brothers, 1947), p. 243.
[42] Petropoulos, *Art as Politics*, p. 136.

myth.[43] He had his own ideas about art and culture, and his interests centered around "the sphere, spirit, deed and heritage of the Nordic Indo-Germanic race."[44] As head of the SS, he controlled the Ahnenerbe (legacy of ancestors), which purported to be a research and teaching community. Initially, the organization focused on archeological excavations and scholarly research to validate the Nazis' racial ideology. However, with the coming of the war, it also began to plunder and loot, particularly in Poland, the Baltic states, the south Tyrol, and parts of southeastern Europe.[45] Another important organization Himmler controlled was the Reich Main Security Office (*Reichssicherheitshauptamt* RSHA), formed in September 1939 out of the merger of the Security Police (*Sicherheitspolizei*) and the Security Service (*Sicherheitsdienst*). The RSHA was the single greatest looter of archives and libraries from Jews, Freemasons, and other enemies of the regime.[46] The RSHA seized between 300,000 and 2,000,000 books, including valuable Judaica and Hebraica archival materials from Masonic organizations and records of French security agencies seized after the collapse of France in 1940.[47]

The final and one of the most ambitious looting efforts revolved around *Reichsleiter* Alfred Rosenberg's organization, the Einsatzstab Reichsleiter Rosenberg (ERR), created in 1939. Rosenberg, the Nazi Party's official ideologue, had a long-term interest in studying the "Jewish Question." He obtained permission from Hitler in January 1940 for what he termed the Hohe Schule project, a planned network of ten institutions to serve as the focal points for studies of national socialist theory and ideology. The exigencies of war permitted only two of the research units to begin operations, the Institute for Jewish Research in Frankfurt am Main and the Institute for Biological and Racial Studies in Stuttgart.[48] When Hitler authorized Rosenberg on 15 July 1940 to collect libraries and archives of Jews, Freemasons, and communists, Rosenberg used his institute in Frankfurt as the site for all the collections he seized. The ERR initially confined itself to materials seized from Jews, socialists, communists, and other enemies of the regime.[49] Over 100,000 books were taken from France, along with 470 cases from the Netherlands seized from over ninety Masonic lodges, the Bibliotheca

---

[43] Robert A. Wistrich, *Who's Who in Nazi Germany* (London and New York: Routledge, 1995), p. 111.

[44] Hilberg, *The Destruction of the European Jews*, p. 608.

[45] Petropoulos, *Art as Politics*, p. 9.

[46] Patricia Kennedy Grimsted, "Twice Plundered or Twice Saved? Identifying Russia's 'Trophy' Archives and the Loot of the *Reichssicherheitshauptamt*," *Holocaust and Genocide Studies* 15 (Fall 2001): 197.

[47] Ibid., pp. 198–201, 206–7, 216.

[48] Donald E. Collins and Herbert P. Rothfeder, "The *Einsatzstab Reichsleiter Rosenberg* and Looting of Jewish and Masonic Libraries During World War II," *Journal of Library History* 18 (Winter 1983): 23–4.

[49] Ibid.; Petropoulos, "German Laws and Directives," p. 109.

FIGURE 2. Alfred Rosenberg, chief of the ERR. *Credit:* Courtesy National Archives, photo no. 242-HB-5107.

Klossiana, the Bibliotheca Rosenthaliana (100,000 volumes), and the Institute for Social History (160,000 volumes), among many others.[50] The ERR between 1940 and 1943 opened branch offices in Amsterdam, Brussels, Paris, Belgrade, Riga, Minsk, and Kiev.[51] In the east, Rosenberg's looters seized the holdings of 375 archives, 531 institutes, and 957 libraries. Altogether, the ERR seized 552,000 books, manuscripts, documents, and incunabula.[52]

Their most lucrative field remained France, where Rosenberg's empire dramatically expanded after he received authorization from the Führer on 17 September 1940 to seize and control all "ownerless" Jewish property in occupied France.[53] Rosenberg, aided by the other arch-looter and "Renaissance man" Göring, was able to ward off competitors, such as Foreign

[50] Collins and Rothfeder, p. 27.
[51] Leslie I. Poste, "Books Go Home from the Wars," *Library Journal* 73 (December 1948): 1699.
[52] Collins and Rothfeder, "The *Einsatzstab Reichsleiter Rosenberg*," p. 29; U.S. Chief of Counsel for Prosecution of Axis Criminality, *Nazi Conspiracy and Aggression,* vol. I (Washington, D.C.: U.S. Government Printing Office, 1946), p. 1101.
[53] Petropoulos, "German Laws and Directives," p. 109.

Minister Joachim von Ribbentrop and quash the objections of German military art protection authorities, headed by Franz Count von Wolff-Metternich. Literally tons of paintings, tapestries, and furniture flowed to Germany, particularly after the *M-Aktion* project seized the household goods "abandoned" by Jews and other Nazi enemies for redistribution to Germans suffering from Allied bombing.[54] By the time ERR operations ceased in France in July 1944, there had been 29 large shipments of art to the Reich containing 21,903 valuable objects.[55]

The Nazi looting apparatus, fully engaged from the Pyrenees to the Urals by 1942, brought about the greatest dislocation of cultural property in history. Millions of items were plundered, but three cases illustrate the why of Nazi looting. One element was revenge for the perceived injustices meted out to Germany after World War I in the Treaty of Versailles. In both conflicts, the Germans seized one of the artistic masterpieces of Belgium, the famous painting *The Adoration of the Mystic Lamb* by the brothers Hubert and Jan Van Eyck. Begun in 1420 by Hubert Van Eyck and completed in 1432 by his brother Jan, the painting is considered one of the great creations of the Flemish school. Though originally commissioned for the private chapel of a rich couple, the altarpiece was displayed in St. Bavo's Cathedral in Ghent. The artists portrayed the apocalyptic vision of St. John, with the Lamb of God as the figure surrounded by a number of biblical characters.[56] In 1816, several of the wings were purchased by an Englishman named Edward Solly, who lived in Germany. Later, they were sold to the king of Prussia and legitimately remained in Germany.[57] During World War I, other panels were taken from the church in Ghent and removed to Germany. After the war, all the panels, even those purchased in 1816, were returned to Belgium. This was to compensate for various German acts of destruction.

The Germans, oblivious to the havoc they wreaked on Belgium, bitterly resented the loss of the panels. In 1940, the Belgians decided to send the altarpiece to the Vatican for safekeeping. The masterpiece was caught in France with the Italian declaration of war. The altarpiece was stored in a museum at Pau, and French, Belgian, and German military authorities signed an agreement requiring the consent of all three parties before the altarpiece could be moved. In July 1942, Hitler ordered the masterpiece seized and brought to Germany. Dr. Ernst Buchner, director of the Bavarian State Painting Gallery,

54 Nicholas, "World War II and the Displacement of Art and Cultural Property," pp. 41–2.
55 U.S. Chief of Counsel for Prosecution of Axis Criminality, *Nazi Conspiracy and Aggression*, p. 1104.
56 "Ghent: *The Adoration of the Mystic Lamb* (1432)," Belgium Travel Network (www.trabel.com), September 2002; "The Ghent Altarpiece," excerpt from *The Story of Art* by E. H. Gombich, The Artchive (www.artchive.com), September 2002.
57 Gladys F. Hamlin, "European Art Collections and the War," *College Art Journal* 5 (March 1946): 223.

was ordered to conduct the removal. A special truck and passenger car with Buchner, a restorer, carpenter, and several movers arrived in Pau on 29 July.[58] Only with great reluctance did the Vichy French authorize removal, and the small convoy set off with a French Army escort on 4 August. The party arrived at Schloss Neuschwanstein, Bavaria, on 8 August, and the altarpiece was stored in a first-floor room.[59] In the fall of 1944, the castle was deemed unsafe because of enemy air raids, and the altarpiece was moved to the salt mine at Alt Aussee for safekeeping.[60] Reaction to the German seizure was very negative. Belgian and French officials protested vigorously and were met by soothing German replies emphasizing safety factors. Count von Wolff-Metternich, head of the German Army's Art Protection Unit, dissented. For his efforts, he was discharged.[61] In reality, this was Hitler's revenge for another provision of the hated Versailles Treaty.

Nazi racial ideology was another key element in the why of looting. The Nazis believed that any artwork created in Germany or by a German belonged in the Reich. Prior to the conflict, German scholars, led by Otto Kummel, director of the Reich's museums, had compiled a three-volume listing of artworks dating back to 1500, that fit the Nazi definition of what was "German" art.[62] Certainly such art did not belong in the midst of a "degenerate" culture such as that of the Slavs. The case of the Veit Stoss altarpiece in the church of Our Lady in Cracow illustrates the point. A few weeks before war broke out, the Poles dismantled the altar and sent crates for safekeeping to various sites around the country. Because Veit Stoss was a fifteenth-century Nuremberger, the Nazis considered the altar, newly restored in 1933, as "German." An SS unit, the Sonderkommando Paulsen, located the crates in early October, with the magnificent twelve-foot-high figures of the Apostles, and sent them to Berlin within a few weeks.[63] The rest of the altar followed shortly thereafter. Altogether, the twelve ornate side panels, the great central panel, and the statues of the Apostles were taken. The altarpiece was transferred to Nuremberg Castle where, in a triumph of faith over force, Polish slave laborers passed the word to the Polish resistance where their national treasure had been taken.[64]

---

[58] Statement by Dr. Ernst Buchner on the Removal of the Ghent Altarpiece, File "Restitution, Research and Reference Records, 1900–54," Prominent German Personalities, 1939–48, Records Concerning Central Collecting Points, Records of the Wiesbaden Central Collecting Point, RG 260, Records of the United States Occupation Headquarters, World War II, The National Archives at College Park, Maryland.

[59] Ibid.

[60] Ibid.

[61] Stacy V. Jones, "Art for Hitler's Sake," *Liberty* (April 1946): 48.

[62] Hector Feliciano, *The Lost Museum: The Nazi Conspiracy to Steal the World's Greatest Works of Art* (New York: HarperCollins, 1997), pp. 24–5.

[63] Petropoulos, *Art as Politics*, p. 103.

[64] Flanner, *Men and Monuments*, p. 237.

The third example brings in not only the Nazis' racist attitudes toward the Jews but also the relationships among the leading looters. When the Nazis occupied much of France in 1940, numerous Jewish families, some with significant private collections, were trapped. Among these was Mme. Edgar Stern, whose given name was Marguerite. Mme. Stern had ninety objects that were confiscated in Paris in 1941. Among the items was a still-life painting by the Flemish artist Frans Snyders. Entitled *Still Life with Fruit and Game,* the painting was done between 1615 and 1620. Mme. Stern's artworks were seized by the ERR and taken to the Jeu de Paume museum. On one of his twenty visits to the small museum in the Tuileries Gardens searching for art for his collection, Hermann Göring appeared on 3 May 1941 and selected the Snyders *Still Life.*[65] Subsequently, Göring exchanged the work for another item with art dealer Karl Haberstock. We will meet Haberstock again in this story because he is one of the key figures behind the Linz project. In the course of the war, Haberstock gave the painting to his friend, Luftwaffe officer Baron von Pöllnitz.[66] In fact, Haberstock was found by American troops at von Pöllnitz's castle in May 1945, where he had sought refuge from the Battle of Berlin.

These three cases not only illustrate various elements of the why of Nazi looting but also provide clear examples of the danger to art as the war progressed and the very real problems with restitution at the war's end. The return of the two internationally recognized treasures and the little-known Snyders work span the 1940s to the early twenty-first century and encompass the deep fissures of the Cold War and the decidedly difficult path heirs had to pursue to obtain justice.

## The Losses

The three examples of looted art just noted give but the merest glimpse into the incalculable cultural losses that resulted from the war. In the east, losses were vast. In addition to their hatred for Jews and communists, the Nazis had a particular disdain for Slavs, another "inferior" race. This disdain manifested itself clearly in Poland where, during the first six months of occupation, the Nazis plundered 43,000 churches, 74 palaces, 96 manors, 100 libraries, 15 museums, and many art galleries. What they didn't plunder, they often destroyed. For instance, an estimated 50 to 90 percent of the collections of the National Museum in Warsaw were plundered or destroyed, and 43 percent of the nation's architectural heritage

[65] Nancy H. Yeide, Konstantin Akinsha, and Amy L. Walsh, *AAM Guide to Provenance Research* (Washington, D.C.: American Association of Museums, 2001), pp. 68, 70.
[66] Ibid., p. 69.

was destroyed.[67] In the war against Slavic culture, the Nazis gathered manuscripts and rare books from all of Poland, took them to St. Michael's Church in Posen, and had them burned.[68] Hitler was determined that no trace of so-called Polish culture was to survive. However, some collections, such as those of the Cracow National Library and the library of the Parliament and Senate, survived only because the Nazis confiscated rather than burned them.[69]

After conflict broke out with the USSR in June 1941, looting units followed in the wake of the Wehrmacht. In October 1942, for example, the ERR looted wagon loads of material from Ukrainian museums in Tagonrog and Kharkov.[70] Losses overall for the Soviets were severe. Some 427 museums were plundered, and 1,670 Orthodox churches, 237 Roman Catholic churches, and 532 synagogues were destroyed or damaged.[71] Ancient churches in Vadus and the venerable Church of St. Sophia, built in 1050 C.E., were among those destroyed, many filled with irreplaceable frescos and icons.[72] The former imperial palaces around Leningrad were a particular target. Though half the state Hermitage collection was evacuated to Siberia, much remained vulnerable to the Nazi assault. The Nazis took 34,000 objects from the Peterhof Palace complex, including the panels from the Amber Room in the Catherine Palace, which were shipped to Königsberg.[73] The preservation of the panels illustrated the Nazi ideological touch. The panels were made in Prussia and thus considered "German" art and worthy of saving. Whereas the Tchaikovsky Museum in Klin, Slavic in its holdings, was culturally "inferior" and thus was ransacked and destroyed.[74] Ironically, Nazi ideological research interests ended up preserving many Slavic and Jewish materials that would have otherwise perished.

Despite undoubted Nazi depredations, the Soviets also bore responsibility for what happened to Russia's cultural and archival heritage. The Soviets time-bombed Kiev, which resulted in the destruction of the Uspens' Kyi Cathedral. Though half of the Kiev Archives of Early Acts was taken by the

[67] Jan P. Pruszynski, "Poland: The War Losses, Cultural Heritage, and Cultural Legitimacy," in *The Spoils of War: World War II and Its Aftermath: The Loss, Reappearance, and Recovery of Cultural Property*, edited by Elizabeth Simpson (New York: Harry N. Abrams, 1997), p. 51.
[68] Flanner, *Men and Monuments*, p. 239.
[69] Ibid.
[70] Petropoulos, *Art as Politics*, p. 146.
[71] Mikhail Shvidkoi, "Russian Cultural Losses in World War II," in *The Spoils of War: World War II and Its Aftermath: The Loss, Reappearance, and Recovery of Cultural Property*, p. 68.
[72] Flanner, *Men and Monuments*, p. 240.
[73] Shvidkoi, "Russian Cultural Losses in World War II," p. 69.
[74] Nicholas, "World War II and the Displacement of Art and Cultural Property," p. 41.

Nazis (and subsequently returned after the war), the remainder was blown up when the Red Army recaptured the city in early November 1943.[75] In fact, the Soviets ordered that archives that could not be evacuated were to be destroyed. This resulted in the extensive destruction of those Communist Party archives, local state archives, and the archives of government agencies that could not be evacuated in the face of the Nazi onslaught.[76] Soviet tactics and orders, revealed only by the post–Cold War opening of archives, were to complicate and poison later restitution efforts.

The situation in the west was different. The peoples and cultures in Western Europe were seen as being much more closely related to the Aryan Germans. Thus, state collections were for the most part left alone. However, Jewish collections and property were fair game. In France, for example, millions of books were stolen along with over 20,000 works of art, pieces of jewelry, and other precious objects. The more than 20,000 items looted came from 203 Jewish-owned collections, including the Rothschilds (5,009), Alphonse Kann (1,202), David-Weill (2,687), Levy de Benzion (989), and Seligmann Brothers, the art merchants (558). By the time the final object was sent to Germany, 138 freight cars of loot were removed from France.[77]

The liberal and tolerant Netherlands was another lucrative and tempting target because it had numerous archival and library collections of interest to the ERR and its research institutes. In 1940, the ERR confiscated all property belonging to the Freemasons, including the Bibliotheca Klossiana, a gift from Queen Wilhelmina's spouse Prince Hendrick to the Masons, which contained priceless incunabula and other books.[78] Jewish collections seized included the Bibliotheca Rosenthaliana taken from the University Library in Amsterdam and shipped in June 1944 to Germany in 153 crates. The archive and library (20,000 volumes) of the Portuguese-Jewish community in Amsterdam was likewise seized. In August 1942, 499 crates of Jewish antiquarian, theological, and philosophical books were sent to the Reich.[79] The repositories of other despised groups were also seized. The Library of the Institute for Social History, containing an extensive newspaper collection and 160,000 books, was sent to the Reich in the winter of 1944. The security police closed the International Archive of the Women's Movement in June 1940 and seized its holdings.[80]

---

[75] Patricia Kennedy Grimsted, "Displaced Archives on the Eastern Front: Restitution Problems from World War II and Its Aftermath," *Janus* 2 (1996): 44–5.

[76] Ibid.

[77] Flanner, *Men and Monuments*, pp. 223–4.

[78] Josefine Leistra, "A Short History of Art Loss and Art Recovery in the Netherlands," in *The Spoils of War: World War II and its Aftermath: The Loss, Reappearance, and Recovery of Cultural Property*, p. 55.

[79] Ibid., p. 56.

[80] Ibid.

Certainly unwittingly, the Nazis in fact helped rare Jewish books, artifacts, and manuscripts survive the war. Rosenberg's research institute at Frankfurt not only preserved the Jewish libraries and archives in Belgium and the Netherlands, but it also saved the holdings of the Yivo Institute in Vienna, the Warburg Library in Hamburg, the Rothschild archives from both Vienna and Paris, and the Berlin Theological Seminary, among many others.[81] This is one of the many ironies of the Holocaust era.

Perhaps the most unusual and significant Nazi activity in preserving Jewish cultural and religious objects was the Jewish Central Museum in Prague. Discussed from the spring of 1942 onward, the first organized steps to create the museum took place in July of that year. The needs of victims and perpetrators converged, at least to a certain point.[82] The Jewish ghettos of the Protectorate of Bohemia and Moravia were being emptied as victims were sent to extermination camps. Jewish leaders and scholars were desperate to preserve some memory of Jewish life as the community itself began to disappear. Thousands of items were being confiscated, and something had to be done with them. Local Nazi and SS officials were interested in creating a museum dedicated to the artifacts of what they planned to be an extinct race. This would serve the Nazi need for research and, in a sense, preserve the enemy on which their ideological edifice was built.[83]

So, under SS direction Jewish scholars began to catalogue, inventory, and preserve thousands of religious, cultural, and communal artifacts to document the vibrant Jewish culture that had existed in the area for hundreds of years. Though only one scholar would ultimately survive the Final Solution, the scholars preserved some 200,000 items in 8 buildings and 50 warehouses.[84] When the Nazis sought to organize exhibitions, which would deride and ridicule the Jews, the scholars were reluctant to cooperate, and during the Nazi era there were no public exhibitions.[85] Collection and annihilation were complementary phenomena during the period of the Final Solution.[86] By the end, in 1945, the largest collection of wartime Judaica created under Nazi management remained intact. As we shall see, the story of this museum will shed light on the bitter legacy of the Holocaust and the complexities of restitution in the postwar period.

---

[81] Sybil H. Milton, "Lost, Stolen, and Strayed: The Archival Heritage of Modern German–Jewish History," in *The Jewish Response to German Culture: From the Enlightenment to the Second World War*, edited by Jehuda Reinhauz and Walter Schatzberg (Hanover, N.H. and London: University Press of New England, 1985), pp. 320–31.

[82] Dirk Rupnow, "The Jewish Central Museum in Prague and Historical Memory in the Third Reich," *Holocaust and Genocide Studies* 16 (Spring 2002): 25–6.

[83] Ibid., p. 27.

[84] Ibid., p. 29.

[85] Ibid., pp. 33–5.

[86] Ibid., pp. 41–2.

Reichskommisar Artur Seyss-Inquart, transferred from Vienna to the Netherlands along with his crony Kajetan Mühlmann, zeroed in on Jewish art collections, as well as the libraries of Jewish art dealers. The collections of Jacques Goudstikker and Fritz Mannheimer were acquired through coerced sales, while the collection of the Jewish Historical Museum in Amsterdam was confiscated outright. In all, the Netherlands suffered over twenty thousand art losses with an estimated value of 150 million guilders.[87] As in the Netherlands, Belgium also witnessed the confiscation of cultural property belonging to Freemasons, Jews, and socialists. Jewish targets included the Belgian Federation of Zionists and the Alliance Israelite.[88] In the summer of 1942, as was the case in France and the Netherlands, Jewish property was confiscated, and transfers to concentration camps began.

In addition to the seizure of Jewish property and *The Adoration of the Mystic Lamb* altarpiece, the Belgians also lost two other masterpieces to German revanchist sentiment and greed. The Dirk Bouts altarpiece of the *Last Supper*, preserved in the church of St. Pierre in Louvain, was seized in the summer of 1942. Like the Van Eyck work, panels of the Bouts altarpiece had been legitimately sold to German museums. Again, as was the case with *The Adoration of the Mystic Lamb*, the panels were returned to Belgium as part of general reparations required by the Versailles Treaty after World War I.[89] In August 1942, wings representing the meeting of Abraham and Melchizedek, the feast of the Passover, the gathering of manna, and Elijah in the wilderness were brought to Germany.[90]

Another major blow to the Belgians came in September 1944, shortly before the arrival of the Allies. A prized possession of the city of Bruges since the sixteenth century was the sculpture of the *Madonna and Child* by Michelangelo. This work had continuously remained in Bruges, and there was no valid basis for German claims. So, the excuse for the seizure was to protect this masterpiece from the Americans.[91] Two German officers and a party of armed sailors used mattresses and a Red Cross lorry to complete their task.[92] Long before this last seizure, Belgian resentment of German high-handedness was practically universal.

Nazi ideological zeal and raw greed held sway over conquered Europe. All this had been well planned. Methods of despoliation had been worked out before the war ever began. Vienna, where Adolf Eichmann finely honed his techniques for expropriating Jewish property, provided a test bed, as

---

[87] Leistra, "A Short History," p. 56.
[88] Jacques Lust, "The Spoils of War Removed from Belgium During World War II," in *The Spoils of War: World War II and its Aftermath: The Loss, Reappearance, and Recovery of Cultural Property*, p. 58.
[89] Hamlin, "European Art Collections and the War," 223.
[90] Ibid.
[91] Ibid.
[92] Ibid., p. 224.

Guernica had for the German military. Persecution of the Jews in Germany had created a legal framework for persecution and the machinery necessary to handle all that was seized. Methods of transferring ownership, dividing up spoils, and arranging sales abroad – witness the notorious June 1939 sale of "degenerate" art in Switzerland – were well honed.

By the time the war came, the Nazis had clearly identified Jewish targets and works of art they claimed were Germanic in origin or once owned by Germans.[93] Heinrich Himmler was prepared for the resettlement of Germans from the Baltic back to the Reich and the clearing away from Germany's borders of "inferior" races. Himmler's relocation campaign, among other things, would involve the transfer of enormous amounts of cultural property. The Nazis, ever meticulous in planning, were ready.

## Operatives and Techniques

The top-tier Nazi leadership of Hitler, Göring, Himmler, and von Ribbentrop could never have implemented their racist cultural ideology, so inextricably tied to the Holocaust, without the invaluable assistance of second-tier operatives. In writing about several of the key operatives, historian Jonathan Petropoulos describes it this way: "The history of these operatives tells us much about how the Nazi regime functioned and how individuals responded to the unique circumstances of the time. Ultimately, National Socialist rule would have been very different, if not impossible, without their complicity."[94] The operatives – museum directors, art dealers, and art – historians are significant for what took place, for techniques employed that would raise difficult restitution issues after the war, and for a glimpse into denazification in the period after the war.

The highest-profile project, in many ways, was the Linz project. When Hitler returned from a 1938 visit to Italy, he was stirred by his tour of fabulous Italian galleries to convert his dream of a grand new museum in Linz into action. He discussed this with Berlin art dealer Karl Haberstock, a 60-year-old native of Augsburg in Bavaria, who was already selling art to the Führer and enmeshed in the disposal of "degenerate art." Though not particularly interested in art as such, Haberstock was ruthlessly competitive and known for sharp dealings. He suggested to Hitler that his project needed a professional museum director to ensure that only the highest-quality art was obtained. He had a suggestion as to a possible director: Dr. Hans Posse.[95]

93 Petropoulos, *Art as Politics*, pp. 123–4.
94 Jonathan Petropoulos, "The Importance of the Second Rank: The Case of Art Plunderer Kajetan Mühlmann," in *Austro-Corporatism: Past, Present and Future*, vol. 4, *Contemporary Austrian Studies*, edited by Gunter Bischof and Anton Pelinka (New Brunswick, N.J. and London: Transaction Publishers, 1996), p. 177.
95 Jonathan Petropoulos, *The Faustian Bargain: The Art World in Nazi Germany* (New York and Oxford: Oxford University Press, 2000), pp. 6–7, 74, 83–4.

Haberstock knew that his friend Posse, recently forced into semiretirement from his position as director of the Dresden Art Gallery, would be eternally grateful if Haberstock could rescue his career. Haberstock counted on major financial gains for himself if he proved successful in his scheme. After extolling Posse's virtues to Hitler and lamenting his ouster in Dresden because of a falling out with the local Nazi Gauleiter, Martin Mutschmann, Hitler descended in a fury on Mutschmann, excoriating him for his stupidity. The Führer then met with Posse and made him the astounding offer to head the Linz project.[96] Hans Posse, head of the Dresden Art Gallery since 1913, was a highly regarded museum professional with publications on the Dutch masters and Renaissance art. Though not a party member and an advocate of modernist art, Posse was an ardent German nationalist. He leapt at the opportunity to make what Petropoulos defines as the "Faustian bargain." He agreed to put his talent and loyalty in the service of the Führer in return for the chance to create the greatest museum in the world.[97] In fulfilling his part of the bargain, Posse, until his death from throat cancer in December 1942, would use art stolen from Jews, such as the Austrian Rothschilds; pressure owners to sell at ridiculously low prices; and insist that the Führer's prerogative of first choice of seized art be respected.[98] Though Posse and his successor, Hermann Voss, spent enormous sums of money to acquire over 8,000 pictures, the project ended in failure. Posse had sold his professional soul for a project he did not live to complete and that never became a reality. As for Voss, he was never tried or punished for his crimes.

Posse received his commission from Hitler in June 1939 to create the Sonderauftrag Linz, and he began to work feverishly to develop what became a multilayered project. Posse's principal assistants, who evaluated the merits of proposed acquisitions, were Dr. Fuerlrich Wolffhardt, a tall, blue-eyed, blond ardent Nazi, who specialized in rare books and manuscripts; Dr. Fritz Dworschak, an expert in coin collections; and Dr. Rudolf Oertel, Posse's aid in Dresden.[99] Posse, not only under pressure from Hitler but also in competition with other acquisitive Nazi warlords, relied on several agents to assist him with his searches. Posse naturally turned first to his friend and savior Karl Haberstock. This aggressive art dealer was already a member of the Commission for the Disposal of Products of Degenerate Art and working with Theodor Fischer of the Fischer Gallery in Lucerne to sell the art seized from German museums at, hopefully, a profit for all involved. Haberstock had built his business catering to wealthy right-wing anti-Semites in

[96] Ibid., p. 52.
[97] Ibid., p. 8.
[98] Ibid., pp. 53–4.
[99] David Roxan and Ken Wanstall, *The Rape of Art: The Story of Hitler's Plunder of the Great Masterpieces of Europe* (New York: Coward-McCann, 1965), p. 23.

FIGURE 3. Studio of Karl Haberstock, restorer, Buxheim. *Credit:* Charles Parkhurst Papers, National Gallery of Art.

Berlin before the First World War.[100] With the Nazi rise to power, Haberstock's opportunities grew. He had always sold what Hitler appreciated, nineteenth-century German genre paintings and Old Masters. To advance his career, Haberstock joined the Nazi Party in the spring of 1933. It helped, of course, that he was not Jewish in a field with many Jewish dealers. He eventually sold one hundred works to Hitler, laying the basis for his dramatic rise in income.[101] His appointment by Hitler to serve as Posse's chief advisor sealed his success. Like most plunderers (the most senior Nazi leaders were the exception), Haberstock avoided severe punishment after the war. After a brief imprisonment and interrogation, he was freed and resumed his art business.

Another operative who assisted Posse, as well as Göring and other top Nazis, was Kajetan Mühlmann. He was different from Haberstock. The latter, the most successful art dealer in Nazi Germany, was motivated primarily by greed. Mühlmann, a native of Salzburg, was an educated man with a doctorate in art history and an ardent devotion to bringing the Austrian Nazi Party to power.[102] He had a racist world view and wrote in a study on Cracow: "Securing German living space is the task. Achieving it through German spirit and culture is the result. Already centuries ago [this region] was

---

[100] Petropoulos, *The Faustian Bargain*, p. 74.
[101] Ibid., p. 77.
[102] Ibid., pp. 170–4.

settled and secured by our Germanic ancestors."[103] Mühlmann, "arguably the single most prodigious art plunderer in the history of human civilization," worked closely with his mentor Artur Seyss-Inquart in confiscating Jewish art and other cultural property in Vienna after the *Anschluss*.[104] He was intimately involved in developing the "Vienna Model" of expropriation followed by legal sanction.

Mühlmann entered Poland as soon as fighting ceased with a commission from Göring to serve as his "Special Delegate for the Securing of Artistic Treasures in the Former Polish Territories." Mühlmann could proudly report to the Führer on his work in Poland by stating that "within six months almost the entire artistic property of the land was seized."[105] Later Mühlmann would follow Seyss-Inquart to the occupied Netherlands and, as the only one of these operatives to achieve high rank in the SS, created his own organization, the Dienststelle Mühlmann.[106] As Dutch intelligence officer Jean Vlug put it after the war, "Rotterdam was still burning when Kajetan Mühlmann in his SS uniform arrived in Holland to take up the task of his Dienststelle."[107] Mühlmann dealt with expropriated art that he put up for sale at a substantial profit. He always made sure that Hitler and Göring had the right of first refusal, and he cultivated other leaders – such as Himmler; Hans Frank, head of the general government in Poland; and Baldur von Schirach, the leader of the Nazi youth movement, with special deals and offers. Mühlmann's activities in Austria and Poland were criminal, and those in the Netherlands had only a patina of legality about them. Posse, Haberstock, and Mühlmann were all involved in handling art and other cultural property stolen from Jews and other enemies of the regime. They were, in fact, intimately involved with the expropriatory process that complemented annihilation. Like Haberstock, Mühlmann avoided indictment and conviction for war crimes. He slipped away from a hospital while in Allied detention and lived quietly – and undisturbed – in the Salzburg-Munich region.

In addition to the three leading second-tier operatives just noted, there were others who aided, and profited from, the traffic in looted art. Among these individuals was a particularly successful woman, Frau Maria Almas-Dietrich. In 1933, she had a small art business in Munich, primarily selling paintings and turn-of-the-century scenes of Munich. In the feverish anti-Jewish atmosphere of the 1930s, Almas-Dietrich had two serious problems: Her daughter Mimi was illegitimate, and her husband was Jewish. In 1921, Almas-Dietrich had married a Turkish Jew, Ali Almas-Diamant, and

[103] Ibid., p. 190.
[104] Petropoulos, "The Importance of the Second Rank," p. 177.
[105] Petropoulos, *The Faustian Bargain*, p. 191.
[106] Petropoulos, "The Importance of the Second Rank," p. 195.
[107] Ibid., p. 197.

FIGURE 4. Governor General Hans Frank and Kajetan Mühlmann confer at Cracow Castle. *Credit*: Courtesy National Archives, photo no. 242-HB-4705-22.

converted to Judaism and become a Turkish citizen.[108] Eventually, her husband deserted her, though she kept the Almas name on her Munich gallery.
But Almas-Dietrich was not without resources. Her daughter Mimi was a
friend of Eva Braun and Heinrich Hoffman, Hitler's photographer and first
art advisor, who introduced her to Hitler. Hitler respected her business drive,
honesty, and generous nature and began to buy art, mostly of the nineteenth-
century German genre, from her. By 1937, Almas-Dietrich had divorced her
husband, and in 1940 she regained her German citizenship. Under Hitler's
patronage, her business flourished. She sold over 270 paintings to the Führer,
and her income soared from RM7,000 in 1937 to RM500,000 by war's
end.[109] Though fundamentally ignorant and easily deceived with artistic
fakes and forgeries, she retained the unique ability to sell to Hitler without
first going through Hans Posse or Hermann Voss. Despite some potentially
lethal liabilities, Maria Almas-Dietrich survived and succeeded in the Nazi
jungle because of her good contacts and strength of will.

Local Nazi officials often had agendas of their own, which influenced
plundering operations and the ultimate distribution of the spoils. The aftermath of the *Anschluss* provided the opportunity to settle some old scores.
One of these related to the crown jewels and coronation regalia of the defunct
Holy Roman Empire, which were stored in Vienna. Many of the items were
hundreds of years old. The imperial mantle, for example, dated from 1133,
when it was originally created for the Norman kings of Sicily. In 1424, the
regalia and the jewels, which were considered to confer legitimacy upon
the possessor, were deposited in Nuremberg for safekeeping. There they
remained until 1796 when, at the approach of French troops, Emperor Francis II removed them to Vienna.[110] German nationalists, particularly those
affiliated with Nuremberg, always sought to regain these treasures. After the
1933 Nazi ascent to power, Oberburgermeister Willy Liebl of Nuremberg
lobbied for repossession of the regalia and jewels. With the *Anschluss*, he
got his opportunity. Hitler issued a special decree on 16 March, 1938, returning the treasures to Nuremberg.[111] Liebl was ecstatic. At the opening of the
annual Party Congress in September, Hitler accepted the return of this portion of the German patrimony. Similar scenes and similar "repossessions"
would take place during the war.

[108] Roxan and Wanstall, *The Rape of Art*, p. 92.
[109] Ibid.; Lynn Nicholas, *The Rape of Europa: The Fate of Europe's Treasures in the Third Reich and the Second World War* (New York: Alfred A. Knopf, 1994), pp. 31–2; Edgar Breitenbach, "Historical Survey of the Intelligence Department, MFAA Section, in OMGB, 1946–1949," *College Art Journal* 2 (Winter 1949–50): 193.
[110] S/Sgt. Robert C. Armstrong, "The German Crown Jewels: A Modern Detective Story," File "General Reports, Special Reports, and Investigations Files, 1945–1951," General Records, 1945–1952, Records Concerning the Central Collecting Points, Records of the Wiesbaden Central Collecting Point, RG 260.
[111] Ibid.

Nazi oppression of Jews and other opponents before and during the war brought out of the woodwork thousands of opportunists. Many were attracted to the potential for gain involving looted property. These individuals were quick to bring to the attention of Nazi bigwigs and their art dealers, several of whom were described earlier in our story, valuable art and other cultural property. Wilhelm and Anni Ettle are vivid examples of this type of person. Herr Ettle's zeal for Hitler was clear as early as 1929, when he joined the storm-troopers and the Fighting League for German Culture. Ettle, an art restorer, joined the Nazi Party in 1932 and established his business in Frankfurt.[112] Ettle demonstrated his allegiance by being one of the first to raise the swastika in Frankfurt and by setting up loudspeakers in his studio for a Nazi Party demonstration in November 1933.[113] In case anyone missed the point, Ettle divorced his wife because she was not a Nazi and married a woman twenty years his junior, who was more in keeping with his political tastes.[114] Though the Ettles were poor in 1933, they certainly were not by 1939. The Ettles' career was typical of many others who followed a similar "career path."

The Ettles formed a close working relationship with the police president of Frankfurt, Adolf Beckerle, who later became the Nazi ambassador to Bulgaria. Through his connections, Ettle was appointed by the Reich Ministry for Public Enlightenment and Propaganda as an expert advisor on the removal of Jewish goods for the Frankfurt Foreign Currency Office.[115] Ettle's goal was to "de-Judaise" the art trade of Frankfurt. His techniques were simple, but effective. Ettle would discover the location of Jewish collections and offer to buy these items from their owners. After the events of November 1938, many Jews were desperate to get out of Germany. They could not take their property with them, and often they were strapped for funds. Ettle convinced these individuals that he was an honorable fellow and sincerely wanted to help. He used this approach on the family of Max Brings, a Jew the Nazis had banished to Poland.[116] The next step, which he used with the Brings family, was to haggle and offer an outrageously low price that was rejected. Then he went to the Gestapo, turned in the Jews, and obtained the right to auction off the property. Ettle automatically pocketed part of the

---

[112] Report, "Case of Wilhelm and Anni Ettle," File "Wilhelm Ettle, Investigative Reports and Correspondence, 1945–1954," Restitution, Research and Reference Records, 1900–54, Records Concerning the Central Collecting Points, Records of the Wiesbaden Central Collecting Point, RG 260.

[113] Ibid.

[114] 1st Lt. Ira Ball, "Report of Investigation Concerning Wilhelm Ettle and Wife, 31 January 1946," File "Wilhelm Ettle, Investigative Reports and Correspondence, 1945–1954," Restitution, Research and Reference Records, 1900–54, Records Concerning the Central Collecting Points, Records of the Wiesbaden Central Collecting Point, RG 260.

[115] Report, "Case of Wilhelm and Anni Ettle."

[116] Ibid.

proceeds and turned the rest over to the Nazis. As his profits on Jewish art treasures became too obvious, even members of the Nazi Party attacked his cupidity. He was expelled from the party in 1942.[117] Despite this setback, the Ettles survived the war and retained a great deal of their ill-gotten gains, which included a number of outstanding paintings. As we shall see later, this audacious pair attempted to reestablish their business during the occupation.

As the Nazis expanded beyond the Alt-Reich and Austria, their looting practices went with them. The case of Franz Petschek is illustrative of Nazi methods and attitudes. Petschek was a Czech industrialist who fled the Sudetenland after the Munich Agreement. Petschek first went to Switzerland and eventually entered the United States, where he later became a citizen.[118] Petschek had a valuable stamp collection consisting of 500 volumes and 100,000 items. The stamp collection, along with the rest of Petschek's property, was seized in September 1938. The Nazis brought the stamps to Germany in 1941 or 1942 and sold them to Dr. Otto Krause and Dr. Hans Masel for RM35,000, a mere fraction of their value.[119] We will meet Dr. Masel again later in our story, where we will find him in the employ of the American military government and trying to hang onto his share of the stamps.

Hermann Göring, in alliance with a reluctant Alfred Rosenberg, utilized a number of operatives. He controlled Rosenberg, who intensely disliked Göring's role in the looting operation, but could not stop him. Because of his own poor standing with the Nazi leaders and the military, he was boxed in by Göring's agents.[120] Göring's chief henchman was Walter Andreas Hofer, a second-rate art critic, who became a specialist in rock-bottom price schemes at the expense of desperate people. Hofer, like Frau Almas-Dietrich, had a skeleton in the closet. In the 1920s, he had worked as a salesman in the art firm of his Jewish brother-in-law. He originally came to Göring's attention by selling him art. By 1937, he had insinuated himself into the Nazi leader's good graces and became his art advisor. Hofer still maintained his own business on the side and kept whatever Göring did not want.[121] From such a privileged position, Hofer reaped great financial benefits. Göring and Hofer were ably assisted by the two top ERR officials in Paris: Baron Kurt von Behr and Dr. Bruno Lohse. Von Behr, the black sheep of an old Mecklenburg family, saw the opportunity for his own advancement if he assisted Göring with his obsession for art collecting. At von Behr's secret request, Göring ordered

---

[117] Ibid.

[118] Claims Report J0141, File "Jewish Claims, 1938–1951," Restitution Claims Records, 1945–47, Records Concerning the Central Collecting Points, Records of the Munich Central Collecting Point, RG 260.

[119] Ibid.

[120] James S. Plaut, "Loot for the Master Race," *Atlantic Monthly* (September 1946): p. 60.

[121] Ibid., p. 61.

art historians serving in the Luftwaffe transferred to Paris to assist the ERR with its inventory and evaluation work. Göring also supplied the shippers, photographers, packers, drivers, trains, and planes needed to ship the seized treasures to Germany.[122] In effect, Göring, with the connivance of von Behr and his deputy, Lohse, took control of the ERR in France.

The ERR, and also the German Embassy and the high command, were so assiduous in seeking out Jewish art collections that even the Vichy government was moved to protest. In response, Dr. Hermann Bunjes, director of the Franco-German Art Historical Institute and one of Göring's purchasing agents, drew up a reply titled "French Protests Against the Safeguarding of Ownerless Jewish Art Properties in Occupied France."[123] This document is practically peerless in its duplicity. Bunjes claimed that the French wanted to retain this art in order to sell it themselves and use the money against Germany. The Nazi writer also asserted that French protests were a stratagem to cloud the issue of German claims for return of cultural materials destroyed by French soldiers in Germany after 1918.[124]

The Nazis had techniques other than outright seizure. One of the most common was to pay for works of art with money previously paid to the German government by a defeated nation to defray occupation expenses. For example, Hitler bought 262 signed and dated Flemish and Dutch masterpieces for 50 million francs.[125] Originally, though, the money was paid by the Vichy government to cover German expenses. In essence, Hitler paid nothing. Another technique, which often was combined with the one just described, was to force owners to sell their collections at only a fraction of their real value. Göring was a master at this. A classic example is the handling of the Goudstikker estate. Jacques Goudstikker was a wealthy Jew who died while attempting to flee to London in May 1940. Goudstikker left a fabulous collection in his art shop and valuable pieces of property. Göring soon moved in for the kill. Walter Hofer selected six hundred of the choicest items, including Rubens's *Diana at the Bath*, Bronzino's *Portrait of a Young Lady*, and four small Memling altar panels, while Alois Miedl, a shady German businessman and banker active in the Netherlands, purchased the Goudstikker firm and three private residences.[126] This deal among thieves of course did not involve giving any of the proceeds to Goudstikker's widow and daughter, who had made it to Canada after numerous harrowing experiences.[127]

The master of the Reich was certainly not adverse to this sort of maneuver, as his involvement in the Fritz Mannheimer story illustrates. Mannheimer

[122] Ibid., p. 60.
[123] Ibid., p. 57.
[124] Ibid.
[125] Flanner, *Men and Monuments*, p. 225.
[126] Nicholas, *The Rape of Europa*, pp. 104–7, 110.
[127] Ibid., pp. 84–5.

was a Jew and a financial genius who was an ardent foe of the Nazis. He fled Berlin shortly before Hitler took power and went to Amsterdam.[128] He formed a syndicate of Dutch and Swiss bankers to underwrite short-term French government issues. The Nazis sought to undercut his financial moves, and he died mysteriously on 9 August 1939.[129] He left a widow and many creditors. Among his assets, Mannheimer left a mansion in Hobbemastraut and a chateau near Paris filled with works by Rembrandt, Vermeer, Fragonard, and Watteau. After the conquest of Holland, Posse, working with Mühlmann, forced the creditors and Mannheimer's widow to accept a ridiculously low bid for the art collection.[130] He had ful-filled Hitler's directive to obtain for him one of Europe's premier private collections.

Posse found the Netherlands a very profitable locale for his acquisitions. Using foreign currency at his disposal, he purchased from the widow of Otto Lanz, a former Swiss consul in the Netherlands, a collection of Italian paintings, sculpture, and furniture.[131] Posse also acquired valuable paintings and drawings from the collection created by Franz Koenigs, a German banker resident in the Netherlands since the early 1920s. As was the case with Fritz Mannheimer, Koenigs had hit difficult times with the Depression and had put his drawings up as collateral for a loan, and then they were placed in the Boymans Museum in 1933 for safekeeping. As war approached, the director of the museum got coal broker D. G. van Beuningen to buy the collection and keep it for the Netherlands.[132] After the invasion of May 1940, Posse worked assiduously to get the best of the Italian and Northern works. After months of haggling, he bought 525 of the paintings from van Beuningen for the Linz collection. Though the director of the Boymans Museum deeply regretted van Beuningen's action, he was delighted to receive the more than two thousand drawings from the Koenigs collection, which van Beuningen donated to the museum.[133] Although the van Beuningen transaction seemed reasonable on its face, in reality the coal merchant had little choice in the deal if he wished to keep his business, and himself, alive and well.

Hitler and Göring were not the only ones to profit from the upheaval in art ownership. Those further down in the hierarchy often reaped great rewards as well. Holland and Belgium, for example, were under German civil government, and the ERR had only small branch offices in Amsterdam and Brussels. Art owned by Jews and Christian anti-Nazis was confiscated

[128] Roxan and Wanstall, *The Rape of Art*, p. 78.
[129] Ibid.
[130] Ibid., p. 80.
[131] Nicholas, *The Rape of Europa*, p. 108.
[132] Ibid., pp. 110–11.
[133] Ibid.

by Enemy Property Control units. Receipts from forced sales were put into Foreign Currency Control, with a 15 percent cut for the Nazi sales agent.[134] Often, officials of the Enemy Property Control units pocketed up to 85 percent of the proceeds from a sale. Artur Seyss-Inquart, Nazi high commissioner for the Netherlands, kept $3.4 million from the sale of banker Fritz Mannheimer's collection of *preziose*, a life-sized bird carved from one huge emerald.[135]

The case of Italy, Germany's erstwhile ally, provides further insight into Nazi methods. As Mussolini and Hitler grew closer in 1937, an art acquisition commission from the German government arrived in Rome in search of new finds. The team, headed by Prince Philip of Hesse, first requested permission to obtain the *Discobolus of Myron*.[136] This famous work was the property of Prince Lancellotti and was registered as a national treasure in accordance with provisions of a 1909 law, which barred the export of masterpieces of Italian culture. Despite determined opposition from art authorities, Foreign Minister Galeazzo Ciano forced compliance, and thirty-four unopened crates were sent to Germany.[137] The Fascists permitted other exports, such as Leonardo's *Leda* and Tintoretto's version of *Leda and the Swan*.[138] After Italy deserted the Germans in September 1943, theft similar to that occurring in the rest of Europe became commonplace. Items from the Naples National Museum were spirited away to please Göring.[139] Among other things, he received sculptures from Pompeii, the armor of Charles V, and paintings such as Titian's *Danse*. The cream of Florentine galleries was taken by the German 62nd Division and taken to South Tyrol.[140] Lack of fuel fortuitously prevented the trucks from going further, and all but one case were quickly recovered. An estimated 1,941 items were taken from museums in Naples, Florence, and Venice; seized from individuals; or illegally exported.[141]

## The Cost

As the war drew to an end, the Allies sought to estimate the value of the looted art that so disfigured the cultural landscape. The British Ministry

---

[134] Flanner, *Man and Monuments*, p. 227.
[135] Ibid.
[136] Rodolfo Siviero, *Second National Exhibition of the Works of Art Recovered in Germany* (Florence: Sansoni, 1950), p. 13.
[137] Ibid., p. 14.
[138] Ibid.
[139] "International Treasure Hunt: Italian Efforts to Trace Works of Art Missing Since the War," *New York Times*, 6 March 1963.
[140] Ibid.
[141] Siviero, *Second National Exhibition of the Works of Art Recovered in Germany*, p. 7.

of Economic Warfare estimated the loss at £36 million ($144 million).[142]
Francis H. Taylor of New York's Metropolitan Museum of Art estimated
for the U.S. Foreign Economic Administration that the losses were in the
$2 billion to $ 2.5 billion range.[143] But who really knew? Who could calculate
all the damage?

Had anyone tried to stay this swath of destruction and preserve European
culture? Let us turn now to those who sought to preserve and restore a
welcome respite from the predators whom we have so painfully just revisited.

[142] Memorandum, "Looted Art in Occupied Territories, Neutral Countries and Latin America –
Preliminary Report, 5 May 1945," File "Safehaven," Records of the Office of the Director,
Bureau of Areas, European Branch, RG 169, Records of the Foreign Economic Administration, National Archives at College Park, Maryland.
[143] Ibid.

# 3

## Preservers and Restorers

### Response to Crisis

### American Detachment

Intelligence reports from Europe clearly revealed to the exiled governments the disaster caused by Nazi looting. Émigrés from the various countries pored over reports received from their homelands and detailed what was taken and, often, where the items were sent. One of these émigrés, Professor Charles Estreicher, the noted Polish art historian, later played an important role in Allied efforts to recover lost property and punish the Nazis. During 1942, discussions took place in two main forums: a subcommittee of the main committee of the exiled governments, the Comité Interallie pour l'Étude de l'Armistice, and periodic meetings of finance ministers, presided over by the British.[1]

While the Continental Allies focused on the recovery of lost property, British interests differed somewhat. Except for the occupied Channel Islands, the British had not suffered from Nazi looting. They were, nonetheless, acutely aware of European sensitivities in this area and realized that victory would raise complicated questions regarding the identification and restitution of tens of thousands of items. The British understood that they had to deal with this issue to preserve amicable relations with their allies. In addition, the British realized the need to protect the good name of their army when fighting on enemy-held territory. In 1941, the Italians charged that the British had committed depredations on ancient Roman ruins in North Africa. This led to the eventual appointment of Sir Charles Leonard Woolley, a prominent scholar, as archeological advisor to the director of civil affairs in the War Office.[2] So the British were concerned not only with the eventual

---

[1] Richard A. Johnson, "Protection, Restitution and Reparation of Objets d'Art, and other Cultural Objects, 17 November 1944," File "Restitution Background Material," London Files, 1943–5, RG 239.

[2] Sir Charles Leonard Woolley, *A Record of the Work Done by the Military Authorities for the Protection of the Treasures of Art and History in War Areas* (London: His Majesty's Stationery Office, 1947), p. 5.

restitution of cultural items but also with their protection during combat, particularly for propaganda purposes. Sir Leonard felt the raison d'être of the whole cultural preservation effort was to protect the good name of the army. This attitude surfaced later as one of the motivating factors for the postwar restitution program.[3]

Because the military defeat of the Germans rested solely with the Big Three Allies – the United States, the Soviet Union, and Great Britain – the exiled governments planned for the surrender at the end of hostilities, the point at which they hoped to exert some influence. Much of their armistice planning revolved around restitution and reparations. The exiled finance ministers in London frequently discussed the German policy of forced transfers of property. In the summer of 1942, they debated the text of a proposed declaration reserving the right to invalidate all transfers of property rights and interests in territory occupied by the Axis. Although this proposal eventually resulted in the issuance of the 5 January 1943 Inter-Allied Declaration Against Acts of Dispossession Committed in Territories under Enemy Occupation or Control, the United States was not involved in the meetings of the finance ministers. The State Department belatedly requested that the American Embassy in London send a representative to a crucial 24 July 1942 meeting on the proposed declaration. State Department instructions included an expression of American sympathy and a request for a ten-day postponement until the American government formulated a policy on the declaration.[4]

Throughout the war, this pattern, stemming from a strong American reluctance to make any postwar political commitments, repeated itself over and over. Even as late as October 1944, President Franklin D. Roosevelt wrote to Secretary of State Cordell Hull, "I dislike making plans for a country we do not yet occupy."[5] Throughout the war years, American policy makers focused almost exclusively on military operations. High-level Allied conferences at Cairo and Quebec revolved around mostly military matters, with meetings at Casablanca and Tehran focusing on military and political topics. During the war, political affairs claimed the lion's share of attention only at Yalta.

American emphasis on military factors created difficulties with Great Britain. As early as December 1941, Foreign Secretary Anthony Eden discussed with Soviet leader Joseph Stalin postwar boundaries and spheres of influence. This drew an outraged cry from Cordell Hull, an old Wilsonian liberal who disliked secret diplomacy. Roosevelt, fascinated by his role as

---

[3] Ibid., p. 9.
[4] U.S. Department of State, *Foreign Relations of the United States: Diplomatic Papers, 1942*, vol. 1, *General* (Washington, D.C.: U.S. Government Printing Office, 1960), p. 72.
[5] Franklin M. Davis, *Come as a Conqueror: The United States Army's Occupation of Germany, 1945–1949* (New York: Macmillan, 1967), p. 107.

commander-in-chief, pushed off postwar concerns to the State Department for study. Considering the department's peripheral involvement in the major diplomatic and military decisions of the war, its efforts in postwar policy planning were compensatory and ineffectual. Early State Department efforts were narrowly focused on personnel and postwar studies. The president in late December 1941 approved Hull's proposal to organize a committee to study and prepare postwar American foreign policy. This body, known as the Advisory Committee on Postwar Foreign Policy, initially included only State Department officials, a few academics, and some representatives from the foreign policy establishment.[6]

Gradually, the scope of the advisory committee broadened to include representatives from the White House and the War and Navy departments and members of Congress. The Committee created a subcommittee structure to study in depth questions relating to security, boundaries, international organizations, and economic policy.[7] But this effort was only in an embryonic stage by the summer of 1942. Certainly, restitution had received little or no attention. It is interesting to note that eventually there existed very elaborate interdepartmental machinery that created reams of studies and reports. But the end of the war found the United States without firm, concrete policies in any number of sensitive areas. Restitution was one of these areas.

## The Declaration

At the 24 July 1942 London meeting of the exiled continental finance ministers, the American representative raised questions regarding issuing the declaration by all the United Nations and clarifying language on property confiscated from persons not resident in occupied territory. The finance ministers were generally enthusiastic about the proposed text and referred the matter to their governments for instruction. The ministers did express concern that the Russians participate in issuing the declaration.[8] The question of Russian involvement in restitution planning, as well as in other postwar issues, played a significant role in determining the final shape and effectiveness of Allied policies.

The British officials who headed the 24 July meeting met later with embassy representatives in an effort to understand American thinking. The British team included Nigel Bruce Ronald, as the Foreign Office representative, and Sigismund Waley and Arthur Ronald Fraser from the Treasury and

---

[6] U.S. Department of State, *Post-War Foreign Policy Preparation, 1939–45*, in General Foreign Policy Series 15, Publication 3580 (Washington, D.C.: U.S. Government Printing Office, 1949), p. 65.

[7] Ibid., p. 72.

[8] *Foreign Relations, 1942*, vol. 1, *General*, p. 72.

the Board of Trade, respectively. John Maynard Keynes, the economic advisor to the British government, also joined in the discussion. Keynes and his associates stressed the British view that only the United Nations members directly involved should issue the declaration. They believed that adding other nations would lengthen the period of negotiations and confuse the issue.[9] In the face of Axis successes, the Continental Allies wanted a declaration as soon as possible. Despite the sense of urgency, it took five more months to conclude the negotiations. The difficulties and conflicts involved reveal some of the underlying tensions that later prevented a unified Allied restitution effort.

One contentious point was the effort waged by the Belgians and several other small nations to insert a statement of obligation on all signatories to assist in the recovery of property. The British opposed this move because, in their opinion, the declaration would then in reality be a treaty with legal obligations. The argument the British used was that this would require a lengthy ratification process in each country and thus hinder the goal of an early issuance to inhibit forced transfers of property.[10] In reality, the British were reluctant to bind their hands with mandatory obligations to the smaller powers. They wanted a free hand in all matters relating to postwar settlement. We will see that this reliance on general statements of principle, while maintaining maximum operational flexibility, also characterized the stance of the United States and the Soviet Union on other issues that arose. This pattern is a major theme in all the wartime negotiations, including those over restitution. In the face of British opposition, the Belgians withdrew their proposed statement and accepted a general reference in the final text to the solidarity of the signatories.[11]

Although the United States had few specific opinions regarding the issues involved in the proposed declaration, the State Department did urge the British Foreign Office to eliminate the warning to neutral governments about trafficking in looted property. Secretary Hull and his advisors feared that neutral governments, particularly Spain and Sweden, might resent this warning and harm the Allied cause in other areas.[12] The Foreign Office accepted the American suggestion and forced through a watered-down warning to all persons in neutral countries. The Continental Allies always wanted some sort of provision forcing neutral nations to surrender any loot found within their borders. The Big Three, for diplomatic reasons of their own, repeatedly rejected this type of approach.

Besides wishing not to offend certain neutral states and avoiding binding obligations, the only other firm American position was on the necessity

---

[9] Ibid., p. 74.
[10] Ibid., p. 78.
[11] Ibid.
[12] Ibid.

to include Soviet Union and China in the negotiations. The State Department instructed the American ambassador in London, John G. Winant, to see to it that the Chinese received as much information as the Russians on the development of the declaration.[13] This reflected Roosevelt's aim of gaining recognition for China as one of the Great Powers. In October, Winant proposed rewording the text from stating the declaration related to the "Axis Powers and their associates" to "the governments with which the signatories are at war."[14] This allowed the Russians, who were not at war with one of the Axis Powers, Japan, to sign the declaration.

The final draft of the Inter-Allied Declaration Against Acts of Dispossession Committed in Territories under Enemy Occupation or Control, issued on 5 January 1943, announced the determination of the sixteen governments and the French National Committee to defeat any methods of dispossession, whether or not they had the appearance of legality.[15] While this principle was firmly proclaimed, the brief text avoided any mention of concretely implementing the declaration. Throughout the history of Allied negotiations on restitution, laboriously developed agreements on principles were usually unaccompanied by specific procedures for implementation. The debate on implementing the 5 January declaration set an early example.

## Compromise and Avoidance

The Belgians, Dutch, and, to some extent, Norwegians wanted a subcommittee of experts established in order to make recommendations on implementing the declaration in various countries. The British, in particular, were opposed to this idea and succeeded in restricting the subcommittee to a fact-finding role.[16] The subcommittee began working several weeks after the issuance of the Inter-Allied Declaration. It specifically gathered data on existing legislation in Allied countries that invalidated forced property transfers and Axis methods of disposition, and it prepared a report for the signatories to the 5 January declaration.[17]

Even this modified approach failed to prevent conflict. Each looted nation submitted reports on depredations experienced on its territory. The Polish government-in-exile submitted information on events in eastern Poland, occupied by the Soviet Union as a result of the Nazi–Soviet Non-Aggression Pact of August 1939. The Russians were furious and demanded either the suppression of the Polish memorandum or deletion of all references to

[13] Ibid., p. 75.
[14] Ibid., p. 80.
[15] U.S. Department of State, *Foreign Relations of the United States: Diplomatic Papers, 1943*, vol. 1, *General* (Washington, D.C.: U.S. Government Printing Office, 1963), p. 444.
[16] *Foreign Relations, 1942*, vol. 1, *General*, p. 83.
[17] *Foreign Relations, 1943*, vol. 1, *General*, p. 446.

Poland in the final report.[18] The British chairman of the subcommittee, H. S. Gregory, director of the Trading Department, groped desperately for a solution. The conflict had nothing to do with restitution, but everything to do with postwar boundaries and territory. Because the Poles refused to withdraw their report, Gregory proposed that the Soviets append a statement at the end of the report disassociating themselves from the Polish memorandum. The Soviets rejected the proposal in no uncertain terms.[19] The Foreign Office instructed Gregory not to force the issue and to seek a solution. The other signatories wanted the Soviets to sign the report.

Nigel Bruce Ronald of the Foreign Office expressed the British view that inter-Allied collaboration on the technical level would collapse if political disputes were not eliminated from technical committees.[20] The Soviet attitude on technical and operational cooperation seriously impeded reaching agreements on any number of issues relating to Germany and the resolution of the war. By the end of 1943, Gregory, with great effort, worked out the draft of the final report that did not mention eastern Poland or the memorandum submitted by the Poles. Again, Great Power wishes dominated, and the Poles reluctantly submitted.[21] The pattern that frustrated many Europeans on the restitution issue, among others, was thus set. It is interesting to note the practically nonexistent role played by the American government. In the first part of the war, at least, the British dominated in formulating Allied policy on restitution and property.

## The Art World Responds

Though the U.S. government expressed little interest in the early stages of the war in cultural protection or restitution, private groups and individuals in the United States were very concerned about the fate of Europe's cultural heritage. Factors heightening concern over cultural preservation included the increasingly intense Anglo-American aerial bombardment of Europe and the certainty of an eventual Allied landing on the continent. In the fall of 1942, leaders of the art world met to discuss their fears and plan possible action. Participants included the president of the Archeological Institute of America William B. Dinsmoor, the director of New York's Metropolitan Museum of Art Francis Henry Taylor, the associate director of the Fogg Museum of Fine Arts of Harvard University Paul J. Sachs, and the director of the National Gallery of Art in Washington, D.C., David Finley.[22]

---

[18] Ibid., p. 454.
[19] Ibid., p. 453.
[20] Ibid., p. 457.
[21] Ibid., p. 456.
[22] *Report of the American Commission for the Protection and Salvage of Artistic and Historic Monuments in War Areas* (Washington, D.C.: U.S. Government Printing Office, 1946), p. 1.

As Francis Henry Taylor explained to Charles A. Thompson, chief of the State Department's Cultural Relations Division, a series of proposals and a strategic plan evolved from these meetings. The group discussed the twin goals of cultural preservation and restitution and decided the active involvement of the American government was imperative. Paul Sachs, a successful banker who had become a noted art educator and philanthropist, later gave George Stout the credit for first articulating the idea of an independent, government-sponsored commission at a meeting at the Metropolitan Club in New York City shortly after Pearl Harbor. Stout, a pioneer in art conservation and head of the conservation laboratory at the Fogg Museum, assisted Sachs, Taylor, and the others while also on active duty with the Navy at the Patuxent Naval Air Station in southern Maryland.[23] Clearly, an autonomous body created with a presidential mandate held the greatest promise. Placing a culturally oriented program with either the State or War departments risked its submersion in bureaucratic warfare.

The small group of planners, joined by Archibald MacLeish, the Librarian of Congress, decided to make a direct approach to President Roosevelt. After debating various methods, the group designated David Finley, along with his colleague John Walker, chief curator at the National Gallery of Art, to seek the aid of Chief Justice Harlan F. Stone in getting their concerns directly to the president. Stone was a logical choice, not only because of his independent status as head of the nation's judiciary but also because of his position as chair of the board of directors of the National Gallery. Finley and Walker met with the chief justice a few days after Thanksgiving and outlined for him the strategy envisioned by the art leaders. The chief justice, in agreement with the proposed strategy and moved with a sense of urgency because of the recent Allied landings in North Africa, sent a letter to the president on 8 December 1942. As drafted by Dinsmoor, Taylor, MacLeish, and their colleagues, Stone's letter asked Roosevelt for a statement of policy supporting the protection of fine arts and monuments. Stone also urged the creation of a committee "for the protection and conservation of works of art and of artistic or historic monuments and records in Europe."[24] In a bid to increase support for this idea, Stone noted the proposed commission's potential usefulness in combating enemy propaganda and in assisting with the eventual restitution of stolen objects.

Stone expanded on his initial proposal in a further letter to the president. The chief justice, utilizing the ideas of those who drafted the original letter,

---

[23] Francis Henry Taylor to Charles A. Thompson, 13 March 1943, 1940–4 Decimal File (840.403/4), RG 59, General Records of the Department of State, National Archives at College Park, Maryland; Craig Hugh Smyth, *Repatriation of Art from the Collecting Point in Munich after World War II* (The Hague: Maarssen, 1988), pp. 10, 14, 16.

[24] *Foreign Relations*, 1943, vol. 1, *General*, p. 469.

strongly suggested that the American government urge the Soviet Union and Great Britain to create national commissions similar to the one proposed for the United States.[25] During the war, Stone saw the three national commissions working with the Allied armies in providing the qualified personnel and information necessary to protect works of art.[26] Another aspect of this plan featured the creation of a subcommittee of experts operating under the three national commissions and assigned the task of collecting data on looted property and receiving restitution claims. At the time of the Axis surrender, the data collected by the subcommittee of experts would serve as the starting point for Allied restitution efforts.[27]

The most interesting aspect of the expanded proposal is the sketchy outline it provides of an international system. By the end of 1942, the Allies agreed to oppose Nazi looting tactics and to return stolen property at the conclusion of the war. The question of how to achieve these goals remained. The State Department, from 1942 onward, considered the feasibility of an international organization focusing on cultural relations, as well as social and cultural reconstruction.[28] During the rest of the war, the Continental Allies proposed several forums as the nucleus for such an international organization. Though many Americans and Europeans favored an international approach to cultural matters, including restitution, this proved a very elusive goal.

## Delays

In view of the diplomatic and political ramifications, President Roosevelt referred Stone's letter to Secretary of State Cordell Hull for a draft reply. Hull responded on December 24 that the idea had a great deal of merit. Hull sought the president's consent to contact the Joint Chiefs of Staff (JCS) and obtain their approval, given the fact that any program to protect fine arts and monuments during combat operations involved the military. Hull particularly noted the advantage of proclaiming concern for protecting the symbols of civilization and giving the Allied cause a moral boost.[29] In light of Hull's affirmative response and his own predilections, the president wrote Stone on 28 December that he had referred the proposal to the appropriate agencies for comment, and he expected unanimous agreement with the objectives involved.

[25] Ibid., p. 470.
[26] Ibid., p. 471.
[27] Ibid., p. 472.
[28] *Postwar Foreign Policy Preparation, 1939–45*, p. 236.
[29] Cordell Hull to Franklin D. Roosevelt, 24 December 1942, 1940–44 Decimal File (840.403/5-7/3), RG 59.

Interested citizens and private groups, meanwhile, decided not to wait for governmental action. Francis Henry Taylor, the erudite, energetic, and volatile director of the Metropolitan Museum of Art, met with William B. Dinsmoor, professor of Greek at Columbia University, to discuss how the critical issue of protecting fine arts and monuments could go forward as the government deliberated what it should do. Dinsmoor and Taylor agreed that a private group had to be created to further the cause. George Stout provided Taylor and Dinsmoor with the draft of a memorandum that was sent to the American Council of Learned Societies for consideration. The council, at its annual meeting on 29 January 1943, formed a committee on the Protection of Cultural Treasures in War Areas with Dinsmoor as chair (known as the Dinsmoor Committee). This committee received grants from the Rockefeller Foundation and began preparing lists of cultural institutions in Europe with the purpose of transmitting them to the War Department for use by the military. Scholar-refugees from Europe aided the Committee in preparing lists, maps, and catalogues.[30]

In the spring, Paul Sachs helped form another private organization, a special subcommittee of the American Defense–Harvard Group, which began a collaborative venture with the military that set the pattern for the rest of the war years. The Office of the Provost Marshal General of the Army (PMGO), which organized and operated the newly created School of Military Government in Charlottesville, Virginia, felt that at least certain of the officers training for civil affairs work in future liberated or occupied countries needed additional information on the protection of art objects and monuments. On 10 March 1943, Lieutenant Colonel James H. Shoemaker requested assistance from the American Defense–Harvard Group, and by 20 March, a special subcommittee was preparing lists of institutions and monuments needing protection and writing manuals on conservation for implementation in the field.[31]

Though the American Defense–Harvard Group and PMGO project showed increasing civilian-government interaction, professionals in the academic and museum worlds expressed growing concern over the government's lack of a substantive response to Chief Justice Stone's proposal for a national commission. Inquiries at the State Department uncovered the fact that Roosevelt's approval for an approach to the JCS had not made its way back to Hull. Belatedly, the acting chief of the European Affairs Division, Ray Atherton, wrote on 5 March 1943 to Admiral William Leahy, Roosevelt's chief of staff, seeking JCS concurrence.[32] Leahy responded promptly on 9 March that the Joint Chiefs saw no military advantage to the idea of a

[30] *Report of the American Commission*, p. 34; Smyth, *Repatriation of Art*, p.18.
[31] Ibid.
[32] Ray Atherton to William Leahy, 5 March 1943, 1940–44 Decimal File (840.403/11), RG 59.

national commission for the protection of cultural items. The JCS did con-
cede the eventual desirability of this idea and agreed to cooperate as long as
there was no hindrance to military operations.[33] The military's lack of enthu-
siasm for cultural preservation limited the effectiveness of these efforts.

In the midst of pressing war-related business, President Roosevelt informed Chief Justice Stone on 24 April, that the Joint Chiefs agreed to cooperate with the proposed commission, provided it did not interfere with their
military operations. Roosevelt also stated that the State Department would
query the Soviet Union and Great Britain on their interest in this matter.[34] The
reappearance of high-level interest prompted two significant events. The first
occurred when representatives of the War Department (Civil Affairs Division
and Operations and Plans Division) and the National Gallery of Art met on
27 April to consider protective measures for cultural treasures. All agreed
on the need for a national commission to carry on this work in conjunction
with the School of Military Government.[35]

The second significant occurrence began in early May when Ernst Posner,
a distinguished German archivist, presented a paper at the National Archives
entitled "Public Records under Military Occupation." Posner showed his-
torically how the records of occupied territories were important tools for
the conquering forces.[36] Fred Shipman, chief of the Roosevelt Presidential
Library in Hyde Park, N.Y., heard the talk and immediately sent a memorandum to the president on the subject. Roosevelt, obviously impressed
with Posner's point of view, read Shipman's memorandum to his cabinet on
8 May and asked the department heads to protect records in war zones. In
addition, the president sent a cable to the Mediterranean Theater of Operations expressing concern for local Sicilian records.[37] Roosevelt's intervention
prompted General Dwight Eisenhower, on the eve of the invasion of Sicily,
to issue an order protecting cultural objects as much as possible. This was
the first instance during the war of an official American statement regarding
cultural preservation.


## Getting Started

As a result of the president's continued interest, Secretary Hull sent him a
lengthy letter on 21 June summarizing action taken on the proposed commission. Hull said that the new organization, which he titled the American

---

[33] William Leahy to Ray Atherton, 9 March 1943, 1940–44 Decimal File (840.403/11),
RG 59.

[34] *Foreign Relations, 1943*, vol. 1, *General*, p. 473.

[35] William B. Dinsmoor to Franklin D. Roosevelt, 17 May 1943, 1940–44 Decimal File
(840.403/5-2/3), RG 59.

[36] Oliver W. Holmes, "The National Archives and the Protection of Records in War Areas,"
*American Archivist* 9 (April 1946): 110.

[37] Ibid., p. 111.

Commission for the Protection and Salvage of Artistic and Historic Monuments in Europe, would work with the School of Military Government and subsequent organizations of a civilian character to care for artistic and historic objects and to gather information for a post-hostilities restitution program.[38] The secretary also offered a list of commission members and suggested the use of volunteer experts to gather information on items that needed protection. Hull defined the functions of the new commission in the same terms as used by Stone in his 23 December 1942 letter. The secretary of state did not refer to the proposed Soviet and British commissions or to the subcommittee of experts.[39]

The president swiftly approved Hull's outline on 23 June.[40] The time-consuming task of gathering acceptances from the proposed commission members took until 20 August, when the State Department officially announced the establishment of an advisory panel to assist the government in formulating policies for the protection of fine arts and monuments during the war in Europe and for the return of any looted cultural items after the war. Because Chief Justice Stone declined to head the new commission, Justice Owen J. Roberts assumed the chairmanship. The group was generally referred to as the Roberts Commission. Other commission members came from interested private organizations or federal agencies. Members from the private sector included William B. Dinsmoor, Francis Henry Taylor, Dr. Paul J. Sachs, and former governor of New York Alfred E. Smith. Government representatives included David Finley and Huntington Cairns of the National Gallery of Art; Herbert Lehman, chief of the Foreign Relief and Rehabilitation Corporation; and Archibald MacLeish, the Librarian of Congress.[41] Finley was selected to serve as the commission's vice chair.

The first meeting of the Roberts Commission highlighted problems and areas of concern that persisted, not only during the war but also in the postwar period. Huntington Cairns, assistant director of the National Gallery, noted that the British, in response to the State Department proposal that they create an organization similar to the Roberts Commission, raised the question of what exactly was covered in the phrase "works of art." Archibald MacLeish recognized the need for agreement on a basic definition before an international approach to cultural preservation had a chance for success. He proposed creating a special subcommittee to prepare a working definition.[42] The other members unanimously agreed. The matter of definitions, whether

---

[38] *Foreign Relations*, 1943, vol. 1, *General*, p. 477.
[39] Ibid.
[40] Ibid., p. 480.
[41] *Report of the American Commission*, p. 3.
[42] Minutes of Commission meeting, 25 August 1943, File "August 25, 1943 Meeting," Minutes of Meetings, RG 239.

for works of art or restitution, consumed great amounts of time and energy, particularly at the level of Allied negotiations.

Spirited debate over the inclusion of private property within the purview of the commission occupied much of this first session. Francis Henry Taylor urged that the subcommittee compiling information on public property appropriated by the Axis also consider looted private works of art. Huntington Cairns dissented because he felt this was an extra and unnecessary burden. Taylor promptly responded that Secretary Hull's letter establishing the parameters of the commission's responsibilities included private property. Justice Roberts intervened by observing that he could not see why private property was not added to the work of the subcommittee.[43] This decision helped in laying the groundwork for a broad restitution effort, which later burdened American military authorities in Germany.

Another area of concern, one that dominated the commission's first year, involved protection of fine arts and monuments in war zones. Dr. Paul Sachs discussed the private group's compiling lists of endangered objects and preparing atlases that highlighted cultural sites. Sachs moved that private groups channel their works through the commission to ensure proper distribution. All readily agreed on the necessity for this approach.[44]

## Obstacles and Problems

The Roberts Commission in 1944 and 1945 focused on restitution; nevertheless, its experiences and difficulties with cultural protection in 1943 foreshadowed later problems. Before the war ended, the Roberts Commission coordinated the preparation of over seven hundred maps of important cultural centers and regions in both Allied and enemy countries. Lists often accompanied the maps and provided information on various cultural repositories, monuments, and archives.[45] The War Department distributed the maps to the Allied air forces in an attempt to prevent damage to historic or cultural places. The supply process, though, was fitful at best, and many air units never received maps. For instance, lists that might have aided air force intelligence in 1944 and 1945 were later discovered in Army historical archives at Cheltenham, England.[46] Lack of strong support from the military at the operational level continued to hinder the cultural preservation program.

In the fall of 1943, the War Department's Civil Affairs Division (CAD), at the urging of the Roberts Commission, established a Monuments, Fine Arts, and Archives branch. Because the CAD was a staff office in Washington, it exercised only weak control over policy matters in the various theaters of

43 Ibid.
44 Ibid.
45 *Report of the American Commission*, p. 4.
46 Ibid., p. 19.

operation.[47] Army commanders had the paramount role, and for many of them civil affairs, particularly the concerns of the MFA&A (Monuments, Fine Arts, and Archives, were not a high priority. As we shall see later in this study, American military government was in reality quite independent of its nominal head, the CAD. The Roberts Commission's early hopes of an effective conduit through which it could influence policy making in the military were doomed to disappointment. Despite the weaknesses in the CAD, and later in MFA&A operational units, the Roberts Commission members keenly felt the importance of these units in serving the national interest. As William Dinsmoor put it, "The effects of the creation of such an organization, if properly publicized, would be to form a powerful implement supplementing the military and relief efforts, and helping to win the confidence and cooperation of the conquered peoples."[48]

Another continual area of frustration for the Roberts Commission and the Civil Affairs Division was the recruitment and assignment of experienced fine arts and archival professionals for service in the field. Even though elaborate MFA&A organizations were developed for the Mediterranean and European theaters of operations, these remained mostly paper organizations owing to lack of personnel. For instance, in Sicily and Italy the United States and Great Britain operated joint civil affairs programs. However, only two British archivists were assigned to Italy, and the first American was not sent until September 1944![49] The fine arts received only slightly better consideration. During operations in Italy and northwest Europe, there were rarely more than a dozen monuments and fine arts officers in the field.[50] The situation improved somewhat when the war ended, but then added restitution responsibilities actually caused further deterioration. This problem resulted from rigid War Department personnel policies. The department would not directly commission civilian experts as officers nor direct assignments made by the theater commanders. When the Roberts Commission recommended the transfer of a curator, art historian, or archivist, the Civil Affairs Division could not initiate the action. Because the CAD was a staff and not an operational division, it could only make recommendations to commanders in the field. Operational units were very reluctant to lose personnel, so little progress was made in resolving this conflict.[51] The lack of thorough-going military support, the absence of a strong policy-making center, and a dearth of qualified personnel severely handicapped the MFA&A program. After

[47] Earl F. Ziemke, *The U.S. Army in the Occupation of Germany, 1944–46* (Washington, D.C.: Center of Military History, United States Army, 1975), p. 54.

[48] David Findley to Harlan F. Stone, 30 November 1942, File "Commission for the Protection of Artistic and Historic Monuments in Europe – Proposal," Roberts Commission, RG 17, World War II Records of the Chief Curators, Gallery Archives, National Gallery of Art, Washington, D.C.

[49] Holmes, "National Archives and Protection of Records," p. 117.

[50] *Report of the American Commission*, p. 128.

[51] Ibid., p. 18.

the war, these problems continued and affected the restitution effort in a detrimental fashion.

Yet, despite these obstacles, the Roberts Commission helped recruit a talented cadre of men and women for service in the MFA&A. Young curators from the National Gallery already serving in the war effort were recruited into MFA&A work. Among them, Charles Parkhurst, Lamont Moore, Craig Hugh Smyth, and Theodore Rousseau, would perform heroic feats in saving and helping to restore Europe's looted treasures. In casting its net, the commission found other talented professionals, including Edith Standen, secretary to the Widener Collection prior to the war; James Rorimer; James Plaut; Thomas Carr Howe, Jr.; and S. Lane Faison, Jr., among others. These men and women, future leaders in the American art and museum world, helped track down Nazi plunder, preserved what was uncovered, and formed the backbone for American restitution efforts.

By the spring of 1944, the Roberts Commission and its affiliated groups had completed most of the handbooks, lists, atlases, and guides necessary for distribution to the military. As the invasion of Europe drew nearer, the emphasis in the Roberts Commission shifted to restitution and the posthostilities period. To understand American restitution policy properly, we must view it within the tangled diplomatic and military context of general Allied policy making during the last two years of the war.

# 4

## Wartime Frustrations

### *Great Power Diplomacy and Cultural Restitution*

The last two years of the war brought to the fore the sharp ideological, national, and personal rivalries that afflicted the crusade against Nazism. Postwar restitution, a goal generally accepted by all the Allies, became embroiled in the diplomatic and political conflicts of the Great Powers. As the Allies and the Axis powers struggled for domination, rifts within the respective alliances affected the course of the war and shaped the outlines of the world to come. It is important to understand the strategic context of these geopolitical clashes, for this affected restitution issues at the time and in the subsequent decades.

### Strategic Context

From mid-1942 onward, the battlefield situation for the Allies, though difficult and still precarious, began to stabilize. The Russians on the eastern front had halted the Nazi offense, though by no means had they rolled it back. The U.S. Navy had blocked the Japanese advance in the Pacific at the Battle of Midway but was faced with the bloody task of retaking Japanese-occupied territory. By late in the year, the Allies had invaded North Africa, weakening the Italians and forcing the Germans to redirect troops from other battle fronts to confront the invaders. The year 1943 was also the year that began to reveal the splits in the Grand Alliance.[1]

The Allies were supposedly committed to the common goal of defeating Hitler, the unconditional surrender of Germany, and eradicating Nazism. The Soviets opened their first summer offensive of the war in 1943 and fought to drive the German invaders from their territory. Yet Soviet leader Joseph Stalin had a double strategy. On the one hand, his forces fought the Germans, and he hounded his allies to open a second front in Western

---

[1] Gerhard L. Weinberg, *World in the Balance: Behind the Scenes of World War II* (Hanover, N.H. and London: University Press of New England, 1981), p. 25.

Europe and provide greater material support to the Soviets. Yet he secretly put out feelers to the Germans to see if a separate, compromise peace could be made. This ambivalence was further underscored by Soviet support, at the same time, for the League of German Officers and the National Committee for a Free Germany, which had the goal of ultimately securing communist domination of Germany after Hitler's defeat.[2]

The British and the United States also had differing war aims, though theirs were far more compatible than they were with those of the Soviet Union. Early on, Winston Churchill wanted to accede to Stalin's demand for the guaranteed restoration of the Soviet Union's pre–June 1941 borders, along with Soviet control of the Eastern European invasion route the Germans used.[3] Franklin Roosevelt and the American government resisted making firm political and territorial commitments throughout the war. Churchill, aware of British weakness, clearly understood that the immense manpower resources of the Red Army were needed to defeat the Germans, and this meant the projection of Soviet power into Eastern and Central Europe. Churchill wanted to tie down the Soviets as soon as possible with political arrangements and deals.[4] Roosevelt, as a matter of principle and because of his deep repugnance for the secret treaties of World War I, sought to avoid what he regarded as premature agreements. Furthermore, Roosevelt understood that American power would take time to build, but ultimately would have a serious impact. When American power was fully projected in Europe and Asia would be the time to arrange postwar political settlements.[5]

Though the British and Americans differed on the future of the British Empire and the need for free trade, both were deeply committed to defeating Hitler first and then the Japanese. Both parties also expected a relatively rapid American withdrawal from Europe after the war and thus saw the need to restore France as a partner with Britain to balance Soviet power on the continent.[6] Roosevelt was the primary champion of a new postwar international organization designed to foster cooperation among the victors. In conferences at Moscow, Tehran, and Cairo during 1943, the British and Americans sought to keep Russia engaged in the war. These conferences also aided in temporarily resolving differences among the Allies.[7]

The Axis powers were never as united as their foes. Ebbing Italian support for the war effort collapsed with the spring and summer 1943 invasions

---

[2] Gerhard L. Weinberg, *A World at Arms: A Global History of World War II* (New York: Cambridge University Press, 1994), pp. 288–9, 306.

[3] Ibid., p. 731.

[4] Ibid.

[5] Ibid.

[6] Weinberg, *World in the Balance*, pp. 33–4.

[7] Ibid., pp. 34, 44.

of Sicily and the Italian mainland.[8] Mussolini's government fell, and the Germans had to pull needed troops from the eastern front to block the Allies in Italy. Despite his goal of fighting on only one front at a time, Hitler now had to confront a multifront war.[9] The Japanese urgently pleaded with Berlin to reach a separate peace with the Soviet Union, thus hopefully preventing the Soviets from entering the war in the Far East on the side of Britain and the United States. Hitler, always clear on his basic goal of land in the east, knew the Soviets would not agree to the loss of the Ukraine, so he never seriously contemplated a negotiated end to the war in the east.[10] Thus, the Allied policy of unconditional surrender remained intact.

One of the ongoing conflicts within the Grand Alliance was over what to do about German power and the status of Germany after its final defeat. As noted, Stalin hedged his bets by simultaneously exploring the possibility of a negotiated settlement and planning for the occupation of Germany and its ultimate refashioning along Soviet lines.[11] The British and the Americans likewise debated the merits of pacification versus punishment of the Germans. This debate occurred not only between the two governments but also within each government. The U.S. State Department basically favored a less punitive approach with an emphasis on rehabilitation, reconstruction, and the reintegration of Germany into the family of nations. Secretary of the Treasury Henry Morgenthau and the leaders of the War Department favored a much harsher approach urging denazification, deindustrialization, a lengthy period of democratic tutelage, and potential dismemberment.[12] Morgenthau swayed Roosevelt to his view, and at the Quebec Conference in September 1944 Roosevelt and Churchill agreed to deindustrialize Germany and to take other harsh measures.[13]

By this point, the Allies had successfully landed in Normandy and were moving inexorably toward the Rhine. With the failure of the German counteroffensive in the Battle of the Bulge in the closing days of 1944, Germany lay open to the Allies in the west while the Soviet winter offensive pushed in from the east. By this time, Stalin had abandoned any idea of a separate peace with Hitler and was focused on Soviet security needs in Eastern and Central Europe. By early 1945, Roosevelt and Churchill had begun to move away from the harshest elements of the Morgenthau plan. Yet the American president still hesitated to make any firm postwar commitment.[14] So the policy issued by the U.S. Joint Chiefs of Staff (JCS 1067) at

---

[8] Weinberg, *A World at Arms*, p. 603.

[9] Ibid.

[10] Weinberg, *World in the Balance*, p. 43.

[11] Weinberg, *A World at Arms*, pp. 288–9, 306.

[12] John Lewis Gaddis, *We Now Know: Rethinking Cold War History* (Oxford: Clarendon Press, 1997), p. 117; Weinberg, *A World at Arms*, p. 730.

[13] Weinberg, *A World at Arms*, p. 730.

[14] Ibid., pp. 765, 796–7.

the end of March 1945 for the military occupation of Germany reflected the stern approach of Morgenthau and the War Department. After much urging from Churchill, Roosevelt did agree to dividing Germany into zones of occupation and to the basic terms of the surrender to be imposed on the Germans.[15] At Yalta, the final Big Three conference of the war, held in February 1945, the leaders agreed to the zonal concept and boundaries, carving out a zone for the French from territory allocated to Britain and the United States.[16]

Little else was settled about the postwar treatment and management of Germany, beyond denazification and demilitarization. Much time was devoted at Yalta to debates about the need for democracy in Poland and the role and place of the Polish government-in-exile in the postwar era. Concessions granted by Stalin for free elections and the inclusion of democratic leaders in the provisional government were repudiated soon after the conference.[17] The overwhelming presence of the Red Army in Poland and the other Eastern European states meant that the Western Allies had little say in what happened. Thus, as the Allies closed in for the final battles with the Germans, there was much distrust and disillusionment lurking beneath the façade of the Grand Alliance. Among the many military, political, diplomatic, and economic issues that engaged Allied diplomacy during the war, restitution proved to be a tenacious and difficult problem. The two focal points for these debates were London, the site of ongoing Allied discussions, and Washington, where American policy struggled to emerge from the complex world of interdepartmental committees.

### The Big Four Debate

In London, the main arena for negotiations was the European Advisory Commission (EAC). Created at the Moscow Foreign Ministers' Conference in October 1943 and expanded to include the French in November 1944, the EAC was the forum where the Big Four attempted to thrash out the political questions surrounding the defeat of Germany.[18] From the EAC's inception, its terms of reference or purpose of the EAC provoked controversy among the Allies and within the American government. Certain aspects of these disagreements illustrate some of the difficulties encountered in negotiations specifically related to restitution. Briefly stated, the three governments had different views on the role of the EAC. The British wanted to refer a wide

---

[15] Ibid., p. 730.
[16] Ibid., pp. 803–4.
[17] Marc E. Trachtenberg, *A Constructed Peace: The Making of the European Settlement* (Princeton, N.J.: Princeton University Press, 1999), pp. 7–8.
[18] U.S. Department of State, *Foreign Relations of the United States: Diplomatic Papers, 1944*, vol. 1, *General* (Washington, D.C.: U.S. Government Printing Office, 1966), p. 1.

variety of topics and proposals to the EAC, many of which did not relate exclusively to surrender terms or control machinery. The British particularly wanted to discuss policy recommendations for liberated Allied territory.[19] Secretary of State Cordell Hull, much to the chagrin of Ambassador John G. Winant, who also served as the U.S. representative to the EAC, insisted on a strictly limited role for the EAC. This flowed from the administration's desire to postpone political decisions during the war as much as possible.[20] The Soviet views on the EAC and its role were similar to those of the American government. Basically, the Soviets wanted to avoid any commitments that interfered with their long-range security goals in Eastern Europe. During the EAC discussions, the Russians and Americans often found themselves opposing detailed and specific proposals put forth by the British.

Major issues included the text of an Instrument of Surrender and whether to consult with the other Allies, the principles for governing defeated Germany, and the structure of military government machinery. Foreign Secretary Anthony Eden and the Foreign Office consistently failed in efforts to achieve agreements on detailed political, economic, and military clauses proposed for the Instrument of Surrender and the principles on which to govern Germany. The best the EAC could achieve in 1944 and 1945 were agreements on a brief surrender document restricted only to military matters, zonal boundaries for the future zones of occupation, and a barebones structure for the future military government. The approved governing structure included an Allied Control Council (ACC) composed of the commanders-in-chief from each zone and a coordinating committee to implement ACC decisions.[21] All this structure was ratified at the Yalta Conference, but no agreement on principles by which to govern Germany was ever reached.

## Continental Concerns

While the Great Powers struggled to reach agreement on postwar cooperation, the smaller European nations had their own concerns. Restitution was one area in which the Continental Allies pushed their views and feelings forward. After the 5 January 1943 declaration on looting, the Conference of Allied Ministers of Education appointed the International Books and Periodicals Commission to study the replenishing of libraries. The conference, composed of the conquered European states and Great Britain, wanted to keep up the momentum generated by the inter-Allied agreement on looting. The International Books and Periodicals Commission drew up several proposals for reviving damaged libraries and archives and for recovering stolen

[19] Ibid., p. 2.
[20] Ibid., p. 13.
[21] Ibid., p. 1.

articles.[22] At the same time, two other groups, the London International Assembly and the International Committee of the Central Institute of Art and Design, drew up restitution plans for cultural objects. Both urged the United Nations to establish a special office for cultural restitution.[23] This marked the beginning of a concerted effort by the smaller powers to create a cultural restitution body.

The Conference of Allied Ministers of Education referred these plans to its International Books and Periodicals Commission, which created two subcommittees to study the proposals in detail. Throughout the summer and fall, the subcommittees labored to reach a consensus. In early 1944, the International Books and Periodicals Commission adopted, in principle, two schemes: one the *Restitution of Objets d'Art, Books and Archives* and the other the *Recovery of Scientific Equipment from Enemy Territory in Europe.*[24] Two features in these schemes guaranteed future conflicts with the Great Powers. Both schemes urged the early establishment of an inter-Allied body for cultural restitution. This proposed organization was to have extensive powers to control property in Germany, recover looted items stored in neutral countries, and settle claims.[25] Obviously, conflicts would ensue if an inter-Allied group attempted to exercise authority in neutral, sovereign territories. Also, the Big Three were not likely to favor any competing machinery apart from that created by the EAC.

The invasion of Normandy spurred the Europeans to greater efforts in trying to influence the major Allies. The Inter-Allied Commission for the Study of the Armistice worked with the Conference of Allied Ministers of Education to create a united front. The conference, at a special meeting in April 1944, formed an Inter-Allied Commission for the Protection and Restitution of Cultural Materials – known as the Vaucher Commission after its French chairman, Professor Paul Vaucher – to work on the joint project.[26] The two groups drafted schemes that were essentially similar to those already adopted by the International Books and Periodicals Commission. The revised schemes were part of a general effort by the European Allies to gain a voice in deciding on the final surrender terms for Germany. A new feature of these schemes was the call for special restitution machinery for persecuted

---

[22] William B. Dinsmoor, Memorandum No. 4, "Restitution of Art Objects and Other Cultural Materials," 25 May 1944, File "Restitution Background Material," London Files, 1943–5, RG 239.

[23] Ibid.

[24] Ibid.

[25] Ibid.

[26] Richard Johnson, "Explanatory Note on Restitution Scheme of the Conference of Allied Ministers of Education, 15 December 1944," File 134.4, Decimal Files, 1943–1945, Records Relating to the European Advisory Commission (Records of Philip E. Mosely), RG 43, Records of International Conferences, Commissions, and Expositions, National Archives at College Park, Maryland.

minorities.[27] The Europeans foresaw that restitution to governments only would cause problems if undeviatingly followed. This problem eventually caused Allied military authorities in Germany an endless series of headaches. In the face of these pressures, the three major Allies had differing responses. The Russians ignored the schemes and the organizations behind them. The United States and Great Britain were divided regarding the principles and machinery for cultural restitution. Serious conflicts over international control and the scope of cultural restitution were on the horizon.

## British Disarray

In the summer of 1944, problems in Europe forced the Roberts Commission directly into the restitution minefield. One significant problem involved British efforts to develop machinery comparable to the Roberts Commission and establish a definitive position on restitution. The State Department's query in May 1943 on British interest in creating a special commission to deal with war-related cultural matters provoked an intense debate. The Foreign Office favored an overall Reconstruction Commission under a United Nations agency. Any national committees were viewed, at best, as subordinate to the Reconstruction Commission. The Foreign Office was not favorably inclined toward creating special machinery for cultural restitution and rehabilitation.[28] The Board of Education, supported by private groups such as the Conference of Directors of National Museums and Galleries, strongly dissented. These groups wanted a commission similar to that created in the United States, with responsibilities for the war and postwar periods. In addition, these Britons advocated inter-Allied machinery specifically for cultural affairs.[29]

A bitter debate in the House of Lords in mid-February 1944 illustrated British divisions. Lord Cosmo Gordon Lang, the former Archbishop of Canterbury, submitted a motion inquiring about the measures taken by the government for the preservation of historical and art treasures. Lang also asked if the government intended to appoint a commission similar to the Roberts Commission. Lord Latham attacked Lang and heatedly accused the clergyman of showing more concern for old buildings than for British servicemen.[30] Both Viscount Samuel and the Lord Chancellor, Viscount John Allse Simon, felt Latham was responding to an earlier speech by the Bishop of Chichester, George Bell, advocating suspension or modification of Britain's blanket

[27] Ibid.

[28] Appendix 1 to Minutes, 27 July 1944, File "July 27, 1944 Meeting," Minutes of Meetings, RG 239.

[29] Ibid.

[30] Great Britain, Parliament, *Hansard's Parliamentary Debates* (Lords), 5th series, vol. 130 (1943–4): 814–62.

bombing policy. Samuel and Simon sought to separate Lang's motion from the bombing debate by stressing the War Cabinet's agreement with General Eisenhower's directive on protecting Sicilian art treasures and the need to protect the nation's reputation. This debate, and others like it, hampered British involvement in cultural protection and restitution. John Maynard Keynes, among others, deplored that "public discussion" of cultural preservation in combat areas had "started off on the wrong foot, and people are getting badly confused about it."[31] Prime Minister Churchill did not create a national commission until May 1944 and restricted its scope to general discussions on restitution and reparations policy for the postwar period. This group, known as the Macmillan Committee after its chairman, Lord Hugh Macmillan, the Minister of Information, did not have the right to work with military authorities during the period of operations and carried little weight.[32] Consequently, the British MFA&A program during the war was as limited as the American one in size and impact, though for different reasons.

### Entering the Fray

Given the pressures from the European Allies concerning cultural restitution and the evident impasse in the British government, the Roberts Commission decided to act. Archibald MacLeish urged his colleagues to act swiftly. At a 27 July 1944 commission meeting, he stressed the urgency of the situation. In his view, both the Foreign Office and the State Department viewed paintings and books in the same category as locomotives.[33] The members then agreed to send a letter from Justice Roberts to the Secretary of State, offering their advice on restitution and soliciting any decisions already made by the State Department. Secretary Hull's response to the Roberts Commission in early September revealed the gap between State Department views and those in the art and museum world. Hull noted that the department had formulated certain statements of policy on reparations, restitution, and property rights in some ways applicable to works of art. The Secretary of State enclosed these statements, approved by the Executive Committee on Economic Foreign Policy, along with his wish to receive the recommendations of the commission.[34]

---

[31] Ibid. Also, John Maynard Keynes to John Walker, 23 February 1944, File "American Commission for the Protection and Salvage of Artistic and Historic Monuments in Europe, June 1943–June 1944," Roberts Commission, RG 17, Records of the Chief Curator, National Gallery of Art.

[32] Appendix 2 to Minutes, 27 July 1944, File "July 27, 1944 Meeting," Minutes of Meetings, RG 239.

[33] Minutes, 27 July 1944, File "July 27, 1944 Meeting," Minutes of Meetings, RG 239.

[34] U.S. Department of State, *Foreign Relations of the United States: Diplomatic Papers, 1944*, vol. 2, *General: Economic and Social Matters* (Washington, D.C.: U.S. Government Printing Office, 1967), p. 1036.

It is significant that the Executive Committee, created in April 1944, did not have a Roberts Commission representative on it, nor did it consult the commission when drafting restitution principles. This confirmed MacLeish's view that the State Department did not differentiate between a Rembrandt and a diesel engine.[35] Many of the Executive Committee's principles were noncontroversial and were included in later Roberts Commission recommendations to the State Department. These included restricting restitution to identifiable items in existence prior to enemy occupation, returning items to the government of the territory from which looted, restoring property in the condition found, and not considering restitution as a credit toward meeting Germany's reparations obligations.[36] Other principles created anxiety within the Roberts Commission.

The most seriously debated principles related to restitution-in-kind and the restricted nature of the restitution effort. Restitution- or replacement-in-kind was a very divisive and tricky concept that later caused no end of Allied disagreements. MacLeish again led the way by expressing his fear that if this principle were widely implemented, Germany might emerge a cultural desert.[37] At first examination, the idea of replacing a looted item that was lost while under enemy control with an analogous object seemed just and fair. A closer look at the idea revealed numerous complications. For instance, who was to decide what was an analogous object? Would items selected for replacement-in-kind come from German public or private collections? What types of looted items qualified for replacement-in-kind? These were only a few of the major questions associated with the principle of restitution-in-kind. The commission was also disturbed by the generally restrictive tone of the Executive Committee's principles. These principles strongly implied a restitution effort limited to relatively few kinds of property, lasting for a relatively brief period. The Roberts Commission, through its European contacts, realized the enormity of Nazi looting. Clearly, any restitution effort, even if somewhat limited, was a potentially extensive operation. Also, the commission understood the special efforts required for cultural restitution.

## Debates in London

While the Roberts Commission struggled to define cultural restitution principles, events in London accelerated the restitution debate. One significant move was the creation in August 1944 of British and American planning groups for the eventual occupation of Germany. The American group,

---

[35] U.S. Department of State, *Post-War Foreign Policy Preparation, 1939–45*, in General Foreign Policy Series 15, Publication 3580 (Washington, D.C.: U.S. Government Printing Office, 1949), p. 217.

[36] *Foreign Relations, 1944*, vol. 2, p. 1037.

[37] Minutes, 11 October 1944, File "October 11, 1944," Minutes of Meetings, RG 239.

formally designated the U.S. Group, Control Council (Germany), referred to hereafter as the USGCC, had a Monuments, Fine Arts and Archives branch. This branch eventually evolved into the dominant organizational factor in postwar American military government, as far as restitution policy was concerned.[38] Another important factor was the increasing cooperation between the London representative of the Roberts Commission, Francis Henry Taylor, and the American advisors to the European Advisory Commission. Both felt strongly the need for an inter-Allied approach to restitution. As a result, Alan Lightner, the secretary to the American delegation to the EAC, asked Taylor and Mason Hammond, an MFA&A officer, to prepare a draft EAC directive on the control of monuments, works of art, and other cultural materials.[39] This document, revised somewhat by the American advisors, was tentatively titled "Draft Directive No. 2: Control of Works of Art and Monuments." The directive provided a brief definition of the phrase "works of art and other cultural materials" that included "archives, records or documents of historic or cultural importance and scientific exhibits, specimens or equipment of a research or educational character or pertaining to cultural history."[40]

Responsibility for conservation and restitution was placed in the Control Council, the planned governing body for occupied Germany.[41] This feature showed the strong view of Americans in London on the necessity for united Allied policies on restitution. The directive also provided for strict controls on any cultural material found in Germany and for interzonal access in postwar Germany to qualified art experts.[42] This "international" approach reflected the agreement of many Americans in London with the plan proposed by the Vaucher Commission. The European Allies in early September urged adequate military efforts to prevent the removal of cultural material from Germany and the establishment of an inter-Allied body to coordinate all restitution activities during the occupation.[43]

At the same time the draft EAC directive was formulated, other negotiations regarding cultural property took place in London. These were prompted by the imminent occupation of territory in western Germany.

---

[38] In November 1944, the internal structure of the USGCC was reorganized. Several divisions were created, one of which was for reparations, deliveries, and restitution (RDR). The MFA&A Branch was put in the RDR Division and remained there through the rest of the war. The USGCC structure paralleled the later organizational arrangement for the ACC.

[39] Francis Henry Taylor, Report, 6 September 1944, File "August 25, 1943 Meeting," Minutes of Meetings, RG 239.

[40] Draft Directive No. 2, File 134.1, Decimal Files, 1943–1945, Records Relating to the European Advisory Commission, RG 43.

[41] Ibid.

[42] Ibid.

[43] Memorandum, "Upon the Measures to Be Taken Immediately upon the Occupation of Germany, 6 September 1944," File "August 25, 1943 Meeting," Minutes of Meetings, RG 239.

One important question was how to control German and non-German-owned property. Allied authorities were concerned that the Nazis might transfer assets abroad to fund a resurgence. Cultural items such as paintings, sculpture, and rare books were particularly valuable. Military authorities in Supreme Headquarters, Allied Expeditionary Forces (SHAEF), consulted with Francis Henry Taylor, Mason Hammond, and others involved with the EAC in formulating an appropriate measure. SHAEF decided the best temporary measure was a "freeze" on property movement in German territory as it came under Allied control.[44] After gaining British concurrence, SHAEF issued Military Government Law No. 52 on 26 September 1944. Any transaction involving a work of art or cultural material of value or importance, regardless of ownership or control, was expressly forbidden.

In addition to the draft EAC directive and Military Government Law No. 52, American officials in London during September were involved in yet another project. This was the effort by Mason Hammond in the MFA&A Branch of the USGCC, in conjunction with the U.S. military advisors to the EAC and Francis Henry Taylor, to draft a military directive for American armed forces. This draft military directive on "Monuments, Fine Arts and Archives" was adopted by the Army in December 1944, as paragraph 1186, Chapter 16, in Part 3 of the *Handbook for Military Government in Germany Prior to Defeat or Surrender*. The directive expressly stated that "It is the policy of the Supreme Commander to take measures to facilitate the eventual restitution of works of art and objects of scientific or historical importance which may have been looted from United Nations Governments or nationals."[45]

## American Divisions

These American efforts in London reflected pressures from the Continental Allies, as well as looming responsibilities in soon-to-be-occupied Germany. The draft EAC directive and the draft military directive for the American armed forces were forwarded to Washington for approval, along with other draft directives, where they fell into the deep intragovernmental disputes over European and German policy.[46] As mentioned earlier, fierce disputes wracked the American government over the future treatment of Germany. Secretary of State Hull and his successor Edward R. Stettinius (1944–5)

---

[44] *Report of the American Commission for the Protection and Salvage of Artistic and Historic Monuments in War Areas* (Washington, D.C.: U.S. Government Printing Office, 1946), p. 12.

[45] Supreme Headquarters, Allied Expeditionary Forces, *Handbook for Military Government in Germany Prior to Defeat of Surrender*, pt. 3, chap. 16, par. 1186(a) (London, December 1944).

[46] U.S. Department of State, *Foreign Relations of the United States: Diplomatic Papers, 1945*, vol. 3, *European Advisory Commission; Austria; Germany* (Washington, D.C.: U.S. Government Printing Office, 1968), p. 446.

sought in various forums, such as the cabinet, the Committee of Three Secretaries, and personal meetings with the president, to soften the harsher aspects of the Morgenthau Plan and JCS 1067. The State Department's failure was clear when Stettinius instructed Ambassador Winant to accept JCS 1067 as representing U.S. views with respect to policy.[47] The only slight concession gained by the diplomats was a begrudging acceptance by the War Department to revise slightly JCS 1067 in order to present it to the EAC as a basis for tripartite discussions.[48]

In the midst of disputes on pastoralization, denazification, and centralized control of Germany, restitution received little attention. Cultural restitution policy received even less attention. In light of American experiences after World War I, Roosevelt opposed a large-scale cash reparations program, though he did favor restitution of looted property.[49] Winant, despite his entreaties, failed to receive any detailed instructions on the reparations and restitution issues, though the European Allies expressed tremendous concern.[50] This was the result of bitter divisions within the American government over postwar policies. An American position on reparations and restitution slowly emerged in 1945, but Allied consensus was never achieved. Keenly aware of this conflict and chaos, the Roberts Commission studied the principles recommended by the Executive Committee on Economic Foreign Policy, the draft directives prepared in London, and a memorandum received from the Macmillan Committee. The commission, at its 11 October 1944 meeting, approved most of the principles proposed by the Executive Committee. At the urging of Archibald MacLeish, the members voted for a limited restitution-in-kind program, that specifically exempted objects used in religious ceremonies or connected with buildings under ecclesiastical ownership prior to 1938.[51] The commission's decisions reflected a desire to return all identifiable looted objects, while not robbing Germany of its cultural heritage. The commission forwarded its recommendations at the end of October to the secretary of state, along with copies of the draft U.S. military directive on monuments and fine arts and the Macmillan Committee memorandum.

The concern felt in the London Embassy over cultural restitution prompted Third Secretary Richard Johnson to prepare a report to complement the Roberts Commission's recommendations and designed to stimulate interest and awareness in the State Department. Johnson noted the pressure from the small European powers for an inter-Allied restitution office, with broad authority to decide claims, control cultural objects found in enemy territory, and take possession, with consent, of the property of one

[47] *Foreign Relations, 1944,* vol. 1, *General,* p. 418.
[48] Ibid.
[49] Ibid., p. 414.
[50] Ibid., p. 357.
[51] Minutes, 11 October 1944, File "October 11, 1944," Minutes of Meetings, RG 239.

United Nations member found in that of another.[52] The third secretary also explained the British proposal of a small, provisional cultural objects commission restricted to receiving information and aiding the military in property control.[53] In the midst of these conflicting pressures, Johnson told the department it was faced with several difficult choices: whether to move bilaterally or multilaterally; if multilaterally, whether the United States should join a Western European group before the defeat of Germany or wait for one to cover all Europe; how to include the Soviets in a European or international agency; whether the United States should support Britain's idea of a group formed by the Great Powers to settle restitution questions.[54] In Johnson's opinion, the department also had to wrestle with the complexities involved in the jurisdiction of an international body. For instance, was jurisdiction limited to objects frozen by the Allied Forces in Germany, or could governments of the United Nations surrender to the proposed international group objects frozen by their forces or civilian agencies elsewhere in Europe?[55]

The general governmental lack of interest in cultural restitution is evident from the fact that the State Department did not reply to the Roberts Commission until January and never returned a substantive response to the London Embassy. The only reason that the Roberts Commission received a reply was because of the "collusion" between Archibald MacLeish, newly appointed assistant secretary in January 1945, and his former colleagues on the commission. Sumner McKnight Crosby, a professor of medieval art history on leave from Yale University and serving as the Roberts Commission's representative in London, wrote MacLeish urging American backing for an inter-Allied restitution commission.[56] He stressed that Philip Mosely, the political advisor to Ambassador Winant, thought that an advisory body was urgently needed to represent the Big Four and the European Allies. Crosby pointedly noted that Mosely believed the department should inform the Roberts Commission of any decision regarding cultural restitution.[57]

MacLeish met with his former colleagues on the Roberts Commission to formulate a response to Crosby. They decided that MacLeish would respond by asking the commission for its views on the need for a restitution commission.[58] This was designed to create outside pressures on the

[52] Richard Johnson, "Protection, Restitution and Reparation of Objets d'Art and Other Cultural Objects, 17 November 1944," File "Restitution Background Material," London Files, 1943–1945, RG 239.

[53] Ibid.

[54] Ibid.

[55] Ibid.

[56] Sumner McKnight Crosby to Archibald MacLeish, 9 January 1945, 1940–4 Decimal File (840.403/1-945), RG 59.

[57] Ibid.

[58] Minutes, 18 January 1945, File "January 18, 1945, Meeting," Minutes of Meetings, RG 239.

State Department bureaucracy. Justice Roberts kept the momentum going by answering MacLeish promptly on 3 February. He told the assistant secretary that his group favored an overall restitution commission with an advisory branch on art and cultural property. The commission felt adjudicatory powers properly belonged in another section of the commission.[59] In this aspect, the Roberts Commission's proposal was closer to that of the British than to those put forth by the Conference of Allied Ministers of Education.

This orchestrated pressure induced a long, delayed response from the State Department to the Roberts Commission's proposed principles of 30 October 1944. Acting Secretary of State Grew wrote Justice Roberts on 27 February approving most of the Roberts Commission's revisions of the principles formulated by the Executive Committee on Economic Foreign Policy.[60] The department also approved recommendations from the Roberts Commission concerning a "freeze" by all European countries on art movement, German responsibility for cultural items destroyed during Allied military actions, and a limited restitution-in-kind policy.[61] The department demurred from any opinion on the formation of a United Nation's committee to hold in trust the cultural resources of Germany. The department favored, in principle, restricting restitution-in-kind, but it also had no clear guidance on this contentious issue.[62] Basically, the State Department refused to take a clear stand on any contentious issues involving cultural restitution. Therefore, attention shifted once again to London.

### An International Body?

The focus in late 1944 and early 1945 was on the creation of an international restitution body. Sumner McKnight Crosby was in the thick of events. He urged the commission to support the Macmillan Committee's call for an inter-Allied commission for the restitution of art treasures. Both Crosby and Philip Mosely agreed with the Europeans that rapidly unfolding events on the Continent required an expert body for a very technical field.[63] The Americans in London were delighted when the British government formally presented the Macmillan Committee's proposal to the EAC, even though when Ambassador Winant presented the U.S.-proposed Draft Directive No. 2 on the "Control of Works of Art and Monuments," he could not proclaim U.S. adherence to the creation of an international

---

[59] Owen J. Roberts to Archibald MacLeish, 3 February 1945, File "January 18, 1945, Meeting," Minutes of Meetings, RG 239.

[60] Joseph C. Grew to Owen J. Roberts, 27 February 1945, File "London File: Restitution Background Material," London Files, RG 239.

[61] Ibid.

[62] Ibid.

[63] Sumner McKnight Crosby to Archibald MacLeish, 9 January 1945, 1940–4 Decimal File (840.403/1-945), RG 59.

body.[64] Crosby also kept in close contact with the Vaucher Commission, even though the United States had only observer status with the Conference of Allied Ministers of Education. Crosby, Mosely, and members of the Roberts Commission and the Macmillan Committee wanted the Vaucher Commission to serve as the nucleus for an international cultural restitution organization. Such an organization would administer as a trust all cultural property in Germany and could balance the resources.[65] This was logical for several reasons. The Vaucher Commission had accumulated an enormous amount of information on cultural looting. Also, the commission had the solid support of the Europeans, with the major exception of the Soviet Union. The French, though generally supporting the Vaucher Commission and the idea of an international restitution group, dissented from the idea of a trusteeship. The stifling of this initiative for an international cultural restitution body vividly illustrates the difficulties that were to beset the cultural restitution effort. Despite the Roberts Commission's enthusiastic support for the idea, the State Department, as we saw, refused to take a stand.

The major obstacles to a cultural restitution commission remained in Europe. Though the British government officially proposed a cultural restitution commission, in reality it was divided. The Foreign Office wanted to keep reparations and restitution issues solely in its bailiwick.[66] It was suspicious of both the Vaucher Commission and the Macmillan Committee. The British military, encouraged by Sir Leonard Woolley, wanted no civilian interference, certainly not during wartime.[67] American and British military officials also feared that sharing information with the Vaucher Commission would cause security leaks. The fatal obstacle, though, was the Soviet Union. Throughout EAC deliberations, the Russians desired only generalized agreements (the Instrument of Surrender, Control Council machinery) that did not hinder Soviet actions. At no point did they present a restitution plan, something done by the other Allies. Events showed that the Russians had their own plans for property control in Germany. In addition, the Soviets refused to recognize the Conference of Allied Ministers of Education. It was, therefore, not feasible for the Vaucher Commission to serve as the nucleus for some kind of international understanding. American timidity, British internal divisions, French objections to the trusteeship concept, and Russian lack of cooperation prevented any agreement on an international body of experts to handle cultural restitution. Failure to reach

---

[64] Draft Directive No. 2, File "134.1," Decimal Files, 1943–5, Records Relating to the European Advisory Commission, RG 43.

[65] Minutes, 11 October 1944, File "October 11, 1944," Minutes of Meetings, RG 239.

[66] Appendix 2 to Minutes, 27 July 1944, File "July 27, 1944 Meeting," Minutes of Meetings, RG 239.

[67] Ibid.

an agreement during the war decreased the prospects of any postvictory accommodation.

## Lost in the Collapse

For the rest of the spring of 1945, cultural restitution was lost amidst the great Allied debates on the future of Germany. At the Yalta Conference, the Big Three agreed to establish a reparations commission. Also, the conference agreed to discuss the Russian suggestion that Germany's reparations bill be set at $10 billion, with half reserved for the Soviet Union. The reparations commission was to settle the scope and methods for the program. The few months prior to Germany's collapse were spent in futile efforts by the four powers on the EAC to agree on a general directive for the Allied commanders. Debate continued in the United States over the tone and substance of America's German policy. By the end of March, Roosevelt approved a revised JCS 1067, which still stressed political and economic decentralization.[68] When Ambassador Winant submitted this plan to the EAC, it went nowhere.

The Russians, based on their political traditions, favored a strong centralized approach in governing Germany. The French, again based on political traditions, favored encouraging German particularism tendencies. The British wanted a moderate approach, while the American position actually contained elements from all three positions. The British and French felt that if the Control Council could not agree, then action should be suspended while the governments settled the dispute. Ambassador Winant, at State Department direction, stressed the controlling influence of the zonal commanders.[69] The State Department only reluctantly advocated this position, and then because of pressure from the War and Treasury departments.

The French were the only EAC power that focused actively on cultural restitution in the final two months of the war. Ambassador Renè Massigli submitted a paper on cultural restitution that stressed the need for an extensive replacement-in-kind effort and the need for an international body.[70] The former issue roused little support from the other three powers on the EAC, and the latter, in part because of French opposition to an international trusteeship, was already a dead issue. The only other EAC activity relating to cultural restitution was the British critique of the American-proposed Draft Directive No. 2.

---

[68] U.S. Department of State, *Foreign Relations of the United States: Diplomatic Papers, 1945*, vol. 3, *European Advisory Commission; Austria; Germany* (Washington, D.C.: U.S. Government Printing Office, 1968), p. 473.

[69] Ibid.

[70] Statement by Ambassador Massigli, 12 April 1945, File "134.4," Decimal Files, 1943–5, Records Relating to the European Advisory Commission, RG 43.

In April, the British responded to the American-proposed "Draft Directive No. 2: Control of Works of Art and Monuments." The draft directive, originally prepared by the Joint U.S. Advisors to the EAC and left substantially unchanged by the bureaucracy in Washington, proposed a strong role for the ACC in establishing policies on restitution and conservation. The draft also stated that the ACC could demand transfer of title to looted objects hidden anywhere in the world.[71] Though the American proposal was submitted in November 1944, it took the British five months to comment. It is interesting to note that the other two EAC delegations never directly commented. This shows the relatively low priority that cultural restitution occupied on the agenda of the EAC. The British urged softening the mandatory provisions involving the ACC and eliminating reference to foreign experts operating in the zones of occupation. They also wanted to exclude all possibilities of using cultural material for reparations, once claims for replacement-in-kind were satisfied.[72] They also advocated setting a time limit for filing restitution claims and giving Germans two years from the filing of a claim to turn over the item or face the possibility of restitution-in-kind.

The British comments caused a stir among the Americans in London, the Roberts Commission, and the State Department. Sumner McKnight Crosby agreed with the British that some time limit was necessary, lest restitutions go on indefinitely.[73] Crosby, Mosely, and the Roberts Commission strongly resisted the British enhancement of the zonal commanders' role at the expense of the ACC. They believed this would hinder a unified Allied cultural restitution program.[74]

Several important facts and problems concerning cultural restitution emerge from our review of Allied wartime diplomacy. First of all, restitution was a vital concern to only one of the Big Four: France. The British and Americans had only a peripheral interest, and the Russians had their own ideas on how to recoup their losses. Second, the great cost of the war inevitably meant a scramble for precious resources. In this kind of environment, any activity that did not directly aid the war effort received little support. The fate of nations did not hinge on cultural conservation or restitution. Third, serious Allied disagreements on postwar policy for Germany inhibited the

---

[71] Draft Directive No. 2, File "134.1," Decimal Files, 1943–1945, Records Relating to the European Advisory Commission, RG 43.

[72] Planning Committee Comments on EAC (45) 35: "Comments by the U.K. Delegation on U.S. Directive No. 2, 'Control of Works of Art and Monuments,'" File "134.4," Decimal Files, 1943–1945, Records Relating to the European Advisory Committee, RG 43.

[73] Sumner McKnight Crosby, "The Acting Secretary of State's Letter to Justice Owen J. Roberts, February 27, 1945, re the restitution of works of art, books, archives, and other cultural property," File "134.4," Decimal Files, 1943–1945, Records Relating to the European Advisory Commission, RG 43.

[74] Minutes, 26 April 1945, File "Special Meeting – April 26, 1945," Minutes of Meetings, RG 239.

development of a coherent approach to handling cultural objects. Cultural restitution was lost in the maze of other, and greater, conflicts. Finally, many issues revolving around cultural restitution were in themselves very complex. Issues, such as the scope of the entire effort, restitution-in-kind, returning property to refugees, and the disposition of heirless property were very difficult to resolve. In the aftermath of the German collapse, all of these factors affected the restitution effort that the conquerors had to face. But even though the diplomats debated restitution concepts and policy, action on the battlefield brought matters to a head.

### The MFA&A in Action

From D Day onward, Allied forces fought their way from the Normandy beaches across France to break the German western front. Several MFA&A officers were assigned to American units, beginning an almost unrelieved period of danger and difficult work leading to the German surrender and the custody of millions of precious cultural items. The MFA&A men were selected by the War Department based on the advice and guidance of the Roberts Commission's Committee on Personnel. Committee Chairman Paul Sachs, regarded as the dean of the American museum community, could identify those with the right skills and talents for the difficult MFA&A challenge.[75] A number of these individuals were already in the armed services, and Sachs worked with the War Department to get them reassigned to MFA&A duties. L. Bancel La Farge was the first MFA&A officer to serve in France, arriving a week after D Day. In civilian life a New York architect, La Farge was stationed at SHAEF headquarters. He played a leading role in planning and coordinating MFA&A work during the war and in the early phases of the occupation.[76] As we shall see, he also played a crucial role in one of the most traumatic moments for MFA&A officers during the occupation: the transfer of 202 German masterpieces to the United States in late 1945.

Other MFA&A officers the Roberts Commission recommended included George Stout, who served with the U.S. First Army; Robert Posey, with the Third Army; Ralph Hammett, with the Communications Zone of the U.S. Army's European Theater of Operations; and First Lieutenant James J. Rorimer, who began with the Advance Section of the Communications Zone in Normandy, transferred to the Seine Section in Paris, and ended up with the U.S. Seventh Army in the U.S. Zone of Occupation in Germany.[77] Rorimer, one of a few MFA&A officers to write memoirs about his wartime

---

[75] James J. Rorimer, *Survival: The Salvage and Protection of Art in War* (New York: Abelard Press, 1950), p. xi.
[76] Lynn Nicholas, *Rape of Europa: The Fate of Europe's Treasures in the Third Reich and the Second World War* (New York: Alfred A. Knopf, 1994), p. 283.
[77] Rorimer, *Survival*, pp. xi, 5.

and occupation experiences, was a former curator at the Cloisters in New York City responsible for planning the housing of the Metropolitan Museum's medieval collections in the facility. He enlisted in the Army as a private in 1943 but was soon detailed to Europe as an officer doing MFA&A work. Like the other MFA&A officers, Rorimer labored to prevent Allied troops from entering churches, museums, and other historic sites and pilfering or damaging property. All the officers worked with local French authorities to shore up and repair damaged buildings.[78] With so few officers and such extensive territory to cover, the MFA&A officers labored under extremely difficult and exhausting conditions.

But it was Rorimer's assignment in Paris that was to figure prominently in uncovering Nazi loot and revealing the scope of what was to become the U.S. Army's burden with cultural restitution. His job in Paris was to obtain intelligence about German looting and the location of art removed from France. In Paris, he met the key person in tracking down Nazi looters and loot, the Jeu de Paume curator Rose Valland. Rorimer described her as a "rugged, painstaking scholar."[79] Another MFA&A officer, Thomas Carr Howe, Jr., remembered her as "a robust woman with gray hair and the most penetrating brown eyes I have ever seen."[80] In any event, Valland, at first mistakenly accused by French authorities of being a Nazi collaborator, was wary and trusted no one with her information. She did tell Rorimer soon after the liberation of Paris on 15 August 1944 that she estimated the Germans had taken one third of the privately owned art of France.[81]

Rorimer realized that Valland had worked with Jacques Jaujard, director of the National Museums, to get information to the French Resistance about German transfer of loot out of the country. It was Valland who had alerted the Resistance to German plans to take a final shipment of fifty-five boxcars of loot out of Paris before the city fell to the Allies. The Resistance blocked the move, and, as Rorimer compared the contents with the lists that Valland had kept, he realized Valland's value.[82] Rose Valland understood that her knowledge of where the loot was taken in Germany was critically important. Better than anyone else, she appreciated the value of what had been taken, and she feared that the SS would destroy the art or that the Americans and others would steal the artistic patrimony of her country. Rorimer worked assiduously to gain her trust, and from time to time she dangled leads in front of him, telling him about Göring's twenty visits to the Jeu de Paume and the visits of other Nazi bigwigs as well. Finally, after

---

[78] Nicholas, *Rape of Europa*, p. 275–305.
[79] Rorimer, *Survival*, p. 108.
[80] Thomas Carr Howe, Jr., *Salt Mines and Castles: The Discovery and Restitution of Looted European Art* (Indianapolis and New York: Bobbs-Merrill, 1946), p. 24.
[81] Rorimer, *Survival*, p. 108.
[82] Ibid., p. 109.

months of effort, Valland's Christmas gift of a bottle of champagne signaled to Rorimer that she felt they could work together.[83]

Though he often found Valland difficult, moody, and not above some manipulative scheming, Rorimer never doubted her integrity or loyalty to France. Finally, during Rorimer's visit to her apartment, Valland began to reveal all she knew. She told Rorimer that she had lists of the treasures exported to Germany. She explained that each night she had taken the negatives of photos taken during the day of seized art and had prints made, returning the negatives to the files in the morning. She showed him photos of Rosenberg and his officials and explained in detail how the confiscations had been carried out. She showed Rorimer photos of the stolen art and of two castles in southern Bavaria where Valland claimed much of the ERR loot had gone.[84] After much prodding, Rorimer got Valland to give a set of her photos, lists of stolen art, and other information to SHAEF headquarters. Reluctantly, Valland agreed to go through channels. As an experienced bureaucrat, she had little faith in bureaucrats. As she told Rorimer, "Channels? I call it bureaucracy. It is nothing more than wheels within wheels. Inefficiency. One fellow is thick-headed and smug, and poof... nothing happens."[85] She put her trust in Rorimer and wanted him to go to Germany and save the treasures.

As events proved, Valland was correct in her distrust of the bureaucracy. Rorimer later found Valland's information filed away at headquarters and unused.[86] By early April, with Allied armies in western Germany, the news broke about the first big find of stolen loot. A salt mine at Merkers in Thuringia, about seventy miles west of Weimar, contained art from the Kaiser Friedrich Museum, as well as gold reserves.[87] Shortly thereafter, a discovery was made at a salt mine at Heilbronn that held, among other items, stained-glass windows taken from Strasbourg Cathedral, 830 paintings, 147 sculptures, and 3,600 cases of books from various German collections.[88] As April turned into May, Allied forces found numerous other hiding spots – monasteries, castles, mines, barns – filled with both German cultural property and items stolen by the Nazis. Not everything, though, was hidden in the country. In Nuremberg, Mayor Liebl had built bunkers under the eleventh-century Kaiserburg to store the treasures that he considered ought to belong to his city. In the climate-controlled chambers, he put the Veit Stoss altarpiece, Nuremberg's city museum collection, and the coronation regalia of the Holy Roman Emperors. Liebl committed suicide on 19 April, as the city fell to

[83] Ibid., pp. 108–10.
[84] Ibid., pp. 111–14.
[85] Ibid., p. 112.
[86] Ibid., p. 113.
[87] Ibid., p. 133.
[88] David Roxan and Ken Wanstall, *The Rape of Art: The Story of Hitler's Plunder of the Great Masterpieces of Europe* (New York: Coward-McCann, 1965), p. 152.

Allied forces. After some probing by MFA&A Lt. Walter Horn, a German-speaking investigator, Liebl's treasures were uncovered.[89]

By mid-April, Rorimer, fueled by his own and Valland's impatience, was ordered to the U.S. Seventh Army to investigate the salt mine at Heilbronn. After working for weeks to stabilize the situation in the mine to prevent water damage and to ensure the security of the items stored in the mine, Rorimer next went to Neuschwanstein, the Bavarian castle Rose Valland identified as one of the primary sites of ERR loot. There, Rorimer found behind a hidden steel door records of the ERR. The shipping books, the eight thousand photographic negatives, and the twenty thousand catalogue cards testified to the accuracy of Rose Valland's records and memory. The castle contained Bavarian artwork, paintings stolen from France, the Rothschild jewels, and one thousand pieces of silver from the David-Weill collection. Another castle, Herrenchiemsee, and the Carthusian monastery at Buxheim contained hundreds of crates of paintings and furniture.[90]

In the frantic early days of May, as Germany collapsed and U.S. forces poured into the soon-to-be American zone and beyond, Rorimer received a verbal message from the captured Hermann Göring. He was concerned about his abandoned train at Berchtesgaden, which was filled with art and Renaissance furniture. Rorimer hurried there to save what had not been looted by local Germans and freed Nazi prisoners and slave laborers.[91] Rorimer then went to Munich, where Rose Valland had told him that the Führerbau contained stolen French art. Mobs had looted much of the art, but Rorimer and U.S. troops protected what remained and eventually obtained much of what had been stolen.

While Rorimer worked in Munich to begin managing the influx of what was starting to pour in from newly discovered repositories, another salt mine yielded the greatest treasures of all: the Linz collection. MFA&A Captain Robert Posey had learned from an art dealer in Luxembourg that *The Adoration of the Mystic Lamb* was in a salt mine. Posey was told by a young German scholar that the salt mine was at Alt Aussee, in the mountains southeast of Salzburg, Austria.[92] He was greatly relieved when the U.S. Third Army reached the mine before the Russians. Posey and MFA&A Private Lincoln Kirstein arrived at the mine after the Austrian resistance had prevented the SS from destroying the mine and the priceless art. The two MFA&A men found a series of chambers, connected by tunnels, with a miniature rail system. To their amazement, they found 10,000 paintings (over 6,700 from Hitler's Linz collection), 230 drawings, 1,039 prints, coins, armor, cases of books, and the Gordon Craig theater archives stolen from France.[93]

---

[89] Nicholas, *Rape of Europa*, pp. 349–50.
[90] Ibid., pp. 340–2.
[91] Rorimer, *Survival*, pp. 198–9.
[92] Roxan and Wanstall, *The Rape of Art*, p. 159.
[93] Ibid., pp. 155–6.

FIGURE 5. Lt. James J. Rorimer displays jewelry looted from the Maurice Rothschild collection, Neuschwanstein. *Credit:* Courtesy National Archives, Photo no. III-SC-204827-S.

Even more amazing were the world masterpieces stored in the mine. *The Adoration of the Mystic Lamb* had first gone to Neuschwanstein after its seizure in Pau, France. As Allied bombing intensified and the threat of danger loomed larger, the Germans took the altarpiece to Alt Aussee for safekeeping. Also in the mine were the Dirk Bouts altarpiece from Louvain and Michelangelo's *Madonna* from the Church of Our Lady in Bruges.[94] Posey and Kirstein coordinated with Rorimer the transfer to Munich of the contents from Alt Aussee. Laboriously, Posey and Kirstein worked with Army troops and local residents to pack the treasures, haul them up using the rail system, and load them into U.S. Army trucks. This was followed by a hair-raising trip over the mountains to Munich. Slowly, the work went forward here and across devastated Germany. The dimension of the U.S. Army's problem in protecting, storing, and returning all that had been stolen was as yet not fully defined. But clearly, major burdens and responsibilities lay ahead for the Army and the MFA&A.

[94] Ibid.

PART TWO

# FIRST EFFORTS

# 5

## Restitution Imbroglio

### The American Dilemma in the First Six Months of Occupation

The German collapse in early May 1945 found the Allies without a clear policy on how to govern the vanquished enemy. As historian Franklin Davis has put it, "[M]ilitary occupation is a transition, a connective, an operation aimed at shaping the potentials of victory to the purposes of war."[1] Varied war aims of different Allies created an impasse in the EAC during the final months of its existence.

### Conflicted Aims

At the time of the surrender, the EAC had only agreed on the surrender terms, zonal boundaries, and administrative machinery for the Allied Control Council. In the late spring, the delegates struggled to agree on a general directive that encompassed military, political, and economic terms for governing Germany. The French and British were in fairly close agreement, with the Soviet Union at the opposite end of opinion and the United States somewhere in between. The U.S. draft general directive stressed economic and political decentralization, with wide powers allocated to the commanders-in-chief in the four zones.[2] This reflected the dominance of the Treasury and War Departments over the views of the State Department. The British government favored a more centralized approach to governing the four zones, and both they and the French favored intergovernmental negotiations if the ACC could not agree on any action.[3] The United States – at the urging of the American military, particularly General Lucius D. Clay, deputy military

---

[1] Franklin M. Davis, *Come as a Conqueror: The United States Army's Occupation of Germany, 1945–1949* (New York: Macmillan, 1967), p. xiv.
[2] U.S. Department of State, *Foreign Relations of the United States: Diplomatic Papers, 1945*, vol. 3, *European Advisory Commission: Austria; Germany* (Washington, D.C.: U.S. Government Printing Office, 1968), p. 473.
[3] Ibid., p. 505.

governor for the U.S. Zone – held that the commanders-in-chief could act if the ACC did not reach an agreement on an issue, without waiting for their governments to settle the matter.[4] American Army officials feared interference from the other three powers in the internal affairs of the U.S. Zone.

The Soviet Union, as clearly revealed in a letter from diplomat Robert Murphy to H. Freeman Mathews, director of the State Department's Office of European Affairs, wanted unilateral control over its zone. The Russians were uncooperative in planning for the ACC and sought to exclude their allies from any say in the occupations of Romania and Bulgaria.[5] The general Russian demeanor in the EAC discussions was to say little and agree to nothing. We will see this amply demonstrated when we turn to EAC discussions on restitution.

The British wanted to exert maximum pressure on the Soviets in order to force a change in their tactics in Eastern Europe and to compel greater cooperation in Germany. On VE Day, American and British forces were deep in the assigned Soviet Zone of Occupation. British officials, such as Prime Minister Churchill and the minister-counselor in Washington, Roger Makins, urged no Anglo-American withdrawals from the Soviet Zone until relations with the Russians were settled.[6] The new Truman administration, at this point bent on continuing the Roosevelt policy of cooperation with the Soviet Union, would have none of it. State Department officials, including Secretary of State James Byrnes, who succeeded Edward Stettinius in December 1945 and served until 1947, and H. Freeman Mathews, as well as the head of American forces in Europe, Dwight D. Eisenhower, advocated a swift withdrawal and issuance of a proclamation establishing the ACC.[7] At American insistence, the British agreed to withdraw into their zone, and the ACC was established on 5 June. In light of these differences, the EAC reached no overall agreement on the treatment of Germany. Decision making was referred to the Big Three conference, scheduled to meet in Berlin in midsummer.

EAC discussions on restitution clearly reflected overall Allied divergences on the aims of the occupation and treatment of the Germans. In this situation, the Americans and British were in fairly close agreement, with the Soviets and French at two extremes from the Anglo-American position. In the late spring and early summer, the discussions in the EAC on restitution revolved around general policy principles and establishing an international commission. Progress on these matters was thwarted because of Allied disagreement over the related issue of reparations. As a result of the Yalta Conference, the Allies established a reparations commission to allocate and determine

[4] Ibid.
[5] Ibid., p. 243.
[6] Ibid., p. 312.
[7] Ibid.

the form of reparations. The United States favored reparations from existing German property and produce. The Americans adamantly opposed monetary reparation payments out of fear that the post–World War I situation, where American loans floated German reparation payments to the Europeans, would recur.[8]

Reparations discussions took place in Moscow between 11 June and 14 July and ended in an impasse. The Western Allies wanted an agreement that set limits on Soviet removals from their zone and coordinated industrial reparations among the four zones in order to prevent an economic imbalance. The Russians had the bulk of Germany's prewar industry in their zone, and the United States, which had a primarily agricultural zone, wanted to limit what its zone had to contribute. Cultural items were not on the agenda during these talks. With a stalemate in Moscow, the reparations issue was referred to the Big Three meeting in Berlin.

## America Proposes

Because of the deadlock on reparations, President Truman ordered the American EAC delegation to abstain from any discussions on restitution.[9] In reality, this primarily meant no cultural restitution because the reparations dispute revolved around factories, industrial equipment, and transportation stock. Therefore, the Americans did participate to some extent in EAC discussions on cultural restitution, as well as continue the intragovernmental U.S. debate. In Washington, disagreements on cultural restitution principles are best seen in the light of the ongoing German policy disputes described earlier in this study. The State Department and Roberts Commission wanted a strong ACC role in restitution, particularly within the framework of an international body. Military leaders were suspicious of an international group operating in the American Zone.

The reparations issue also created some conflict. Certain members of the American delegation to the reparations commission, particularly chairman Edwin Pauley and member Isador Lubin, leaned toward using cultural items for reparations. They opposed accepting the proposed British prohibition against cultural objects for reparations purposes.[10] We will see that this issue came up at the Berlin Conference and created a serious conflict within the American military government. The whole question of cultural restitution was enmeshed in the reparations question, debates over the extent of continued Allied cooperation, and the nature of Allied controls in Germany. There

---

[8] Ibid., p. 1222.

[9] Ibid., p. 1236.

[10] U.S. Department of State, *Foreign Relations of the United States: Diplomatic Papers, 1945*, vol. 2, *General: Political and Economic Matters* (Washington, D.C.: United States Government Printing Office, 1967), p. 945.

were intergovernmental divisions as well as splits within the U.S. government. In light of these irreconcilable conflicts, the State Department sent
Ambassador Winant on June 7 a draft, "Agreement on Principles Governing
Restitution of Cultural Property," that essentially attempted to compromise
where possible and evade where necessary.

The American proposal reaffirmed the Declaration of 5 January 1943 on
the German obligation to restore looted items and the assumption that all
property transferred during the occupation was done under duress.[11] Roberts
Commission suggestions on no restitution-in-kind involving German religious objects in use prior to 1938 and the restricting of this form of restitution so as not to deprive Germany altogether of its historic or artistic
materials were incorporated.[12] Another idea from the Roberts Commission,
put forward by Sumner McKnight Crosby, prohibited restitution-in-kind
claims for looted items already accepted by a claimant nation. This eliminated the possibility of complicated multiple claims over an item.[13] The draft
avoided issues hotly debated within the American government by making no
reference to an international restitution commission and stitching together
compromise wording on the use of art objects for reparations. Items in public or private German collections were exempt from reparations, pending the
determination of claims for restitution-in-kind. This left open the theoretical
possibility of using art objects for reparations but, in effect, froze these items
pending resolution of the complex restitution-in-kind issue.[14] Those favor-
ing the use of art objects for reparations were mollified by a provision that
restituted items would not count as credit against Germany's reparations
obligations.[15]

British counterproposals to the U.S. position, as put forth in Draft Directive No. 2, were met in a similar fashion of compromise and evasion. The
idea of a two-year limit on a restitution claim, before a claim for restitution-
in-kind was filed, was accepted. The proposed weakening of the ACC role in
restitution was met by not mentioning the ACC![16] The draft agreement, the
product of extensive Roberts Commission, State Department, and Allied
negotiations since the summer of 1944, failed to elicit from the EAC a
response commensurate with the labor involved. Special Advisor Crosby
reported to the Roberts Commission that, even though the British were generally favorable, the French had a much different approach. The French wanted
to use restitution-in-kind as a threat to force the Germans to divulge the locations of looted property. The French wanted not only restitution-in-kind

---

[11] Ibid., p. 944.
[12] Ibid.
[13] Ibid., p. 940.
[14] Ibid., p. 944.
[15] Ibid.
[16] Ibid.

using analogous German objects but also a monetary form of compensation.[17] In other words, if they did not take an analogous object, then they could assess and collect the monetary value of the looted item. This sounded suspiciously like reparations.

Basically, the conflict between the French and the Americans was rooted in differing views on the entire reparations/restitution issue. The United States favored reparations limited to certain industrial and agricultural categories, with restitution restricted to works of art, securities, and certain types of capital goods. Restitution-in-kind, for the Americans, if it took place at all, was strictly limited to unique objects, such as works of art. The French favored a broad approach that allowed restitution-in-kind for all cultural and noncultural items from German assets.[18] As a result of their historic and wartime experiences, the French had a much harsher attitude than the Americans concerning the treatment of Germany. EAC agreement on the American proposal was improbable given French disagreement with the American approach and Russian silence. With agreement on principles impossible, attention next turned to creating an international restitution commission. At this point, the Americans played the silent role.

## The Restitution Commission – Again!

Robert Murphy, political advisor to SHAEF, informed General Clay on 26 June 1945 of heated EAC debate concerning a previous proposal for the creation of a restitution commission. The Soviet delegate said his country viewed the proposed commission as a violation of the authority of the four powers. The Soviets suggested that the Occupying Powers file their claims through the ACC and its Directorate of Reparations, Deliveries and Restitution (DRDR). Other Allied governments could present their claims to the ACC through accredited military missions.[19]

The French and British pointedly noted the possible impropriety of the Big Four judging their own claims and the resentment the other powers would feel at being excluded from the process. Both countries saw the need for a restitution commission to receive claims from Allied governments and to adjudicate conflicts.[20] The French suggested a commission with permanent representation of the Four Powers, with the ad hoc membership of Allied

---

[17] Report, 23 June 1945, File "Sumner McK. Crosby – Special Advisor Report of," Minutes of Meetings, RG 239.

[18] *Foreign Relations, 1945*, vol. 3, *European Advisory Commission: Austria; Germany*, p. 1172.

[19] Robert Murphy, "EAC Delegations on Restitution, 30 June 1945," File "EAC Directive No. 2 and Pertinent Papers," General Records, 1938–1948, Records Concerning the Central Collecting Points, Records of OMGUS Headquarters Relating to the Central Collecting Points, RG 260.

[20] Ibid.

governments in cases concerning them.[21] The British had a slight variation on the French proposal, and they urged the membership of all interested Allied governments. Both France and Great Britain viewed the commission as an intergovernmental, semijudicial body transmitting its findings to the ACC, which would issue any orders.[22] The American delegate was silent in the face of all this, because his government could not reach a decision on the idea of a restitution commission. With the cultural restitution issue stalemated, the EAC delegates had no choice but to refer the matter to the ACC, which held its first meeting in Berlin on 29 June.

Strong views on cultural restitution were the norm, not only among the EAC members but throughout Europe. The Foreign Offices of Belgium, Luxembourg, and the Netherlands spoke for the other small states when they submitted identically worded aide-memoirs to the British government to forward to the EAC. They urged the immediate creation of an inter-Allied organization to supervise cultural restitution under the authority of the ACC.[23] The three countries proposed a freeze on the movement of all cultural articles, the return or replacement of all looted cultural items, and the agreement that restitution-in-kind take place within six months of the signing of the Instrument of Surrender.[24] Obviously, these proposals were most compatible with the French position. Exclusion of the smaller European states from any control over restitution machinery or principles created a great deal of resentment and suspicion, just as the French and British delegates foresaw.

## American Interests

The failure to settle restitution policy at the EAC level meant that military authorities in Germany had to settle the issue. To understand the development of cultural restitution policy in the U.S. Zone of Occupation, we must first look at general American policies followed in Germany. The general historical interpretation of American occupation policy is that it was unclear, fraught with internal conflicts, and operated in a vacuum until 1947. Revisionists view American policy through the lens of ideology and the East-West conflict of the Cold War. Perhaps the more realistic view is that of occupation policy enmeshed within the evolution of American foreign policy vis-à-vis the former Allies. This perspective, most persuasively presented by John

---

[21] Ibid.

[22] Ibid.

[23] Memorandum by the United Kingdom representative to the EAC, 5 May 1945, File "EAC Directive No. 2 and Pertinent Papers," General Records, 1938–1948, Records Concerning the Central Collecting Points, Records of OMGUS Headquarters Relating to the Central Collecting Points, RG 260.

[24] Ibid.

Gimbel, views American actions and policies governed by a broad range of interests.[25] Some interests, particularly those revolving around the anti-Nazi purge elements of American policy, were given high priority only during certain periods. Other interests were often more important. These included concern for American security, the economic rehabilitation of Germany and Europe, the growth of the free enterprise system, and the containment of communism.[26] American cultural restitution policy, never a matter of overriding importance to top policy managers, is best understood within the context of a continuity of American interests underlying the course of the U.S. occupation.

The immediate problem confronting the American military was how to keep the Germans in the U.S. Zone alive. The devastation in Germany was unbelievable. Cities were in ruin, industry was at a halt, and agricultural output was minimal. The Army, in many ways a reluctant occupying force, wanted to provide only the minimum assistance necessary and hasten the moment when it could turn its responsibilities over to civilian authorities, either American or German. Military Governor Dwight Eisenhower and his successors, Joseph T. McNarney and Lucius D. Clay, consistently sought to turn over the Army's duties to American civilians or a revamped German civil administration.[27] The fact that they were not successful until 1949 is attributable to State Department reluctance to assume total responsibility for the occupation and diplomatic difficulties with erstwhile allies.

## MFA&A Struggles to Cope

With millions of refugees and displaced persons requiring assistance and supervision, the military was not overly concerned with cultural items. But, in fact, the situation regarding these items was quite serious. During the war, in order to prevent destruction the Germans had dispersed much of their cultural holdings throughout the countryside. When they did this, they were unaware of future Allied zonal partitions. For example, famed archival and library collections, such as those of the Collegio Rabbinco Italiano, Bibliotheca Rosenthaliana, Yivo, Spinoza, and Rothschild, were dispersed in at least six repositories.[28] In the American Zone alone, there were fourteen hundred of these repositories.[29] As already noted, these hiding places were often in deep salt mines because salt absorbs water and thus provides an

[25] John Gimbel, *The American Occupation of Germany: Politics and the Military, 1945–49* (Stanford, Calif.: Stanford University Press, 1968), p. xiii.
[26] Ibid.
[27] Robert Murphy, *Diplomat Among Warriors* (New York: Doubleday, 1964), p. 230.
[28] Leslie I. Poste, "Books Go Home from the War," *Library Journal* 13 (December 1948): 1700.
[29] Leslie Poste, "The Development of U.S. Protection of Libraries and Archives in Europe During World War II," 2 vols. (Ph.D. dissertation, University of Chicago, 1958), vol. 2, ch. 9, p. 1.

excellent atmosphere for preserving paintings. At one such location, the mine at Bernterode, the Americans found where the German high command had hidden the coffins of Frederick the Great and his father, Marshal von Hindenberg, and his wife; the Hohenzollern crown jewels; and numerous Army regimental banners![30] Approximately 15 million items, which included priceless art treasures, the collections of 40 of prewar Germany's 100 largest scientific museums, and 144 important archival collections – were eventually located in the repositories.[31] An important difficulty was that a great deal of looted material was interspersed in the repositories. Though 75 percent of the contents were eventually judged as legitimately German, this left about 3.75 million items eligible for restitution.[32]

The MFA&A staff in the American Zone had few resources at its command. Transportation was limited, and materials for cultural restoration were nonexistent. Yet the seeds of a strategy to cope with the increasing volume of cultural items requiring protection, preservation, and return had already been sown. Major Mason Hammond, a professor of the classics at Harvard University before his wartime service in the military, had suggested the collecting-point concept as a management strategy for handling cultural property coming into the hands of the U.S. Army. Hammond made this suggestion in late 1944, while he served as the head of MFA&A policy at SHAEF headquarters.[33] Hammond had great credibility because he had been the Army's advisor on fine arts and monuments in the North African campaign, the first such specialist to serve in the field.

Major L. Bancel La Farge, the Army's MFA&A chief in the field, picked up on Hammond's idea and obtained consent to implement the concept. The idea was to gather all the items from the various repositories uncovered by U.S. forces and to bring them to centrally located sites where they could be protected, preserved, and organized for eventual return. In the devastation pervasive throughout Germany, it was not realistic to build a protected environment at each repository. Rather, a few central collecting points stood a far better chance of getting the housing, coal, and security needed for protecting artworks, books, and archives. La Farge, a tall, slender man in his early forties, was known for his energy, strength of character, and good judgment. At his direction, the few MFA&A officers in the field began to establish collecting points.[34] Though about a half dozen were initially created, only three would last throughout the occupation period and became known as central

---

[30] John Walker, "Europe's Looted Art," *National Geographic* (January 1946): 41–9.

[31] Poste, "U.S. Protection of Libraries," vol. 2, ch. 6, p. 19.

[32] Ibid., ch. 9, p. 1.

[33] Craig Hugh Smyth, *Repatriation of Art from the Collecting Point in Munich after World War II* (The Hague: Maarseen, 1988), pp. 19, 23.

[34] Ibid., p. 26; Thomas Carr Howe, Jr., *Salt Mines and Castles: The Discovery and Restitution of Looted European Art* (Indianapolis and New York: Bobbs-Merrill, 1946), p. 33.

collecting points. Most of the MFA&A's work during the occupation would revolve around the collecting points.

A small art-looting investigation unit was created in late November 1944 in the Office of Strategic Services, the World War II predecessor of the Central Intelligence Agency. Francis Henry Taylor of the Roberts Commission recommended three art historians to serve as the principal investigators. These men – James S. Plaut, S. Lane Faison, Jr., and Theodore Rousseau – were on the ground in Germany by April 1945 and began interrogating dozens of individuals, from Göring on down, implicated in massive art looting. The art-looting investigators worked closely with MFA&A officers, and both sides freely shared information. The unit head, James Plaut, was formerly at the Fogg Museum at Harvard and was proficient in French and German. He ardently hoped to see art dealers, museum directors, and other Nazi collaborators brought to justice for their roles in looting. Rousseau, also linguistically gifted, and Faison conducted many of their interrogations at Alt Aussee and in Munich. Though the men worked on gathering evidence from May through October 1943, in the end only two (Göring and Rosenberg) were prosecuted, at least in part, for looting.[35] Prominent henchmen, such as Kajetan Mühlmann and Karl Haberstock, were never prosecuted, though Rousseau reported that Haberstock was "one of the individuals most responsible for the policies and activities of this group, which dominated official German purchasing and confiscation of works of art from 1939 through 1944."[36] But in a series of interrogation reports, they were able to document the scope and nature of Nazi looting and to provide details on specific works of art. Records found at Alt Aussee and in the Führerbau provided assistance in identifying what was stolen by the ERR, the Linz project team, and "purchased" by the Dienststalle Mühlmann in the Netherlands.[37] But the fact that Allied prosecutors determined that looting was not a first-tier crime was disheartening and allowed almost all of the guilty to go free.

Effective military government, in general, was hindered by a complex structure that had two different, and often competing, fonts of authority. Overall command was in the hands of General Eisenhower, who wore two hats. He was the military governor of the U.S. Zone and commander-in-chief of SHAEF and its American successor (as of 28 June 1945), U.S. Forces European Theater (USFET). Eisenhower's deputy military governor, Lucius Clay, headed the relatively small policy-making body for the zone, the USGCC (Germany).[38] Policy implementation was in the

[35] Anne Rothfeld, "Project ORION: An Administrative History of the Art Looting Investigation Unit (ALIU): An Overlooked Page in Intelligence Gathering" (unpublished M.A. thesis, University of Maryland, 2002), pp. 47–8, 77, 80–1.
[36] Ibid., p. 95.
[37] Ibid.
[38] Murphy, *Diplomat Among Warriors*, p. 249.

FIGURE 6. James S. Plaut (l) and S. Lane Faison (r), summer of 1945 at Alt Aussee, Austria, during interrogations of Nazi art personnel. *Credit:* S. Lane Faison Papers, National Gallery of Art, Gallery Archives.

hands of USFET, organizationally parallel to, and thus not subordinate to, the USGCC (Germany). Such a confusing and diffuse structure was not conducive to orderly and effective policy.

The carrying-out of the MFA&A function is an excellent example of the structural difficulties in American military government. During the first four months of the occupation, the MFA&A branch in the policy-making arm of American military government, the USGCC (Germany), developed policies relating to the conservation of Germany's cultural heritage and the restitution of looted cultural items. Yet, operational responsibility for inspecting repositories, protecting cultural objects, and implementing restitution procedures resided with MFA&A officers stationed with local military government detachments (E teams) scattered throughout the zone.[39] These detachments were under the direct control of USFET and not the USGCC (Germany). Preserving public order, not caring for art objects, was the top priority for USFET.

Organizational changes in the fall of 1945 only made matters worse for MFA&A. General Eisenhower, in keeping with the Army's desire to turn over its responsibilities, established states (*Länder*) in the American Zone. The three *Länder*, operated by American-approved German administrators, assumed responsibility for most day-to-day routine operations in the U.S. Zone. German authorities took over primary responsibility for cultural matters, though this did not include restitution. Increased German self-government set the stage for Eisenhower's reorganization of military government in mid-October. He reduced the size of the USGCC (Germany) and renamed it the Office of Military Government for Germany (U.S.).[40] Because of increased German activity in cultural affairs, the MFA&A function was downgraded from branch to section status and placed in the restitution branch of the newly created Economics Division.

Eisenhower continued the split in military government structure by retaining operational responsibilities in the military government section of USFET, though he renamed it the Office of Military Government (U.S. Zone).[41] Military government offices were created for the new *Land* of Bavaria, Württemberg-Baden, Greater Hesse, and the enclave of Bremen.[42] Though Eisenhower's successor, Joseph T. McNarney, merged the Office of Military

[39] *Report of the American Commission for the Protection and Salvage of Artistic and Historic Monuments in War Areas* (Washington, D.C.: U.S. Government Printing Office, 1946), p. 124.

[40] Memorandum, "Reorganization of Military Government Control Channels in Order to Develop German Responsibility for Self-Government, 5 October 1945," File "SMR US Group CC," General Records, 1938–48, Records Concerning the Central Collecting Points, Records of OMGUS Headquarters Relating to the Central Collecting Points, RG 260.

[41] Ibid.

[42] Ibid.

Government for Germany (U.S.), popularly known as OMGUS, and the Office of Military Government (U.S. Zone) in the spring of 1946, he continued the *Länder* military government offices. Each of these regional military governments had MFA&A offices, and so throughout the occupation there never was a unified MFA&A structure.

In practical terms, this affected cultural restitution, the major American MFA&A function remaining after the fall of 1945. As previously mentioned, a number of collecting points were established during the summer, in an effort to centralize and control the millions of displaced cultural objects and remove them from unsafe repositories.[43] By early 1946, only three collecting points remained. Two of them, at Munich and Wiesbaden, were under the operational control of the Bavarian and Greater Hesse military governments. The third one, the Offenbach Archival Depot, was governed directly by OMGUS. The sensitive nature of Offenbach's holdings, looted Jewish cultural objects, certainly required direct OMGUS control. Wiesbaden, on the other hand, held items from the Prussian state museums in Berlin and other German-owned objects.[44] Why was this material deemed fit for local military control? The Munich Collecting Point contained priceless looted paintings discovered in Germany and Austria. Why was central control not necessary for these objects?

The answers are not clearly stated in the documents. Several factors probably created this situation. Americans were used to a political situation at home that emphasized strong local governments. A primary American aim in Germany was to create solid, democratic practices at the local level, and so the *Land* governments received increasing autonomy and responsibility. The *Land* military governments were supposed to strengthen their German counterparts. Many of the holdings at the Wiesbaden and Munich Collecting Points were German in origin, and so, perhaps, control at the local level seemed natural. At the end of the occupation, as we will see, the *Land* assumed control of the remaining items in the collecting points. Another factor was probably diplomatic. The occupying powers never reached an agreement on the ultimate disposition of Berlin or the property of the former state of Prussia. OMGUS, with headquarters in Berlin, perhaps felt placing sensitive museum items in Wiesbaden would provide less ground for conflict.

The *Land* military governments not only administered the two collecting points and implemented restitution but also had the final say in allocating personnel for the MFA&A function. In OMGUS, at General Clay's insistence, only about six people were assigned to the MFA&A section. In the *Land* military governments, a high point of fifteen officers was reached in

---

[43] *Report of the American Commission*, p. 134.
[44] Robert S. Giles, *Archival and Library Restitution in the United States Zone of Germany: A Preliminary Study* (Washington, D.C.: American School of Social Sciences and Public Affairs, 1947), p. 8.

August 1945.[45] Thereafter, there were usually no more than two or three individuals assigned in each *Land* to MFA&A work. The chief of the *Land* military government could decide how many individuals, if any, would do MFA&A work. Clay's insistence on a small American policy staff and restricted resources at the local level meant immediate trouble for cultural restitution.

In late May and June of 1945, General Clay and his top staff were pre-occupied with getting the ACC operational. They wanted to postpone any cultural restitution activity until there was an Allied agreement, which, given the impasse on the EAC, was highly unlikely. Clay did not want to divert limited American resources to what he regarded as a nonessential area, and he wanted to avoid diplomatic problems that unilateral action might cause.[46] The cultural advisor in the USGCC (Germany), John Nicholas Brown, was alarmed at the potential for harm to valuable items and to America's rep-utation. Brown, a scion of an old and wealthy Rhode Island family and a noted patron of the arts, worked assiduously to focus attention on cultural items.[47] At the end of May, Brown wrote Clay that an exception to the ban on cultural restitution was necessary. Internationally recognized master-pieces, such as *The Adoration of the Mystic Lamb*, required prompt return, lest harm come to them while under American protection. This would create not only a cultural loss but also a wave of severe criticism from the Euro-peans.[48] Clay did not directly respond to Brown, which Colonel Henry J. Newton, onetime head of the OMGUS Division for Reparations, Deliveries and Restitution, interpreted as due to the general's lack of interest.[49] Newton also noted Clay's inclination to include art as an allowable item for German reparations payments, a source of disagreement between the two men.

## Bitter Conflict

This ominous news marked the beginning of a bitter conflict. In preparation for the forthcoming Allied Conference in Berlin, the USGCC (Germany) prepared a memorandum for the president on policy regarding art objects.

[45] Bulletin No. II: "Monuments, Fine Arts, and Archives, 10 August 1945," File "Plans – MFA&A," General Records, 1938–48, Records Concerning the Central Collecting Points, Records of OMGUS Headquarters Relating to the Central Collecting Points, RG 260.

[46] Sumner McK. Crosby, "Comments on Lt. Col. Woolley's Report re: 'Ad Interim Restitution,' 12 July 1945," File "Crosby, Sumner McK. Trip (2d) 1945," Correspondence, 1943–6, RG 239.

[47] J. Y. Smith, *Washington Post*, 11 October, 1979, p. C4.

[48] John N. Brown, "Ad Interim Restitution of Important Works of Art, 28 May 1945," File "London File: Restitution: London 1944–45, EAC Discussions," London Files, RG 239.

[49] Memorandum for the Files, "Conference with Lt. Col. Harris, RD&R Division, U.S. Group Control Council for Germany, 21 August 1945," File "Newton, Colonel Henry J.," Corre-spondence, RG 239.

By midsummer, the number of cultural objects in the U.S. Zone was growing daily. This forced Clay to move from his initial no-restitution stance. Newton regarded his successor in the RDR Division, Colonel Leslie Jefferson, as the instigator of the unsatisfactory plan.[50] This memorandum, formally titled "Art Objects in the U.S. Zone," divided works of art into three categories: Category A, easily identified looted works of art; Category B, looted art for which the Germans alleged making payment; and Category C, German art stored in the American Zone for safekeeping.[51] The USGCC (Germany) staff proposed the immediate return of Category A items; the restitution of Category B objects, with a proviso that reserved for future Allied agreement whether or not these items were accountable as reparations payments; and the transfer of Category C items to the United States. According to Sumner McKnight Crosby, Clay explained that the United States did not intend to claim industrial reparations but might want at some point intangibles such as art.[52] Clay stated in his memo that the Category C works "might well be returned to the U.S. to be inventoried, identified and cared for by our leading museums." Clay made two other points about the Category C art – that they "be placed on exhibit in the United States, but that an announcement be made to the public, to include the German people, that these works of art will be held in trusteeship for return to the German nation when it has reearned its right to be considered as a nation."[53]

At the Berlin Conference, which met from 18 June until 15 July, the entire reparations issue was thoroughly aired. Disagreements over economic and political matters were so deep, decisions were referred to a council of foreign ministers, created at the conference by the three Allied leaders. Restitution was not extensively discussed, and, once again, this contentious subject was put off to a later date and a different forum. In light of the continuing impasse over restitution, Edwin Pauley and General Clay sought President Truman's approval for the interim cultural restitution plan devised by the USGCC (Germany). Pauley, head of the American delegation to the Allied Reparations Commission, wanted control over both reparations and restitution matters. He did not favor separating the two subjects, a position strongly advocated by the British. The British also absolutely opposed the use of art in reparations. Clay wished to relieve the U.S. Army of some of its unwanted responsibilities. Truman approved Clay's memorandum and granted Pauley the responsibilities he desired.[54] Pauley immediately informed

[50] Ibid.
[51] U.S. Department of State, *Foreign Relations of the United States: Diplomatic Papers, 1945*, vol. 1, *The Conference of Berlin* (Washington, D.C.: U.S. Government Printing Office, 1960), p. 924
[52] Telephone interview with Sumner McK. Crosby, 16 April 1981.
[53] Lynn Nicholas, *Rape of Europa*, p. 385.
[54] *Foreign Relations, 1945*, vol. 1, *The Conference of Berlin*, p. 513.

General Eisenhower of Truman's order and that his representative would coordinate restitution and reparations activities.[55] Then Pauley and Assistant Secretary of State for European Affairs William Clayton changed the trusteeship concept in Clay's memo and agreed that for Category C "their eventual disposition will be subject to Allied decision."[56] This was the language sent to the British and the Soviets. Within the framework of these events, the American government announced the transfer of 202 German paintings from the Kaiser Friedrich Museum in Berlin to the United States for safekeeping.

The uproar resulting from the president's order on restitution and the announced transfer of the 202 paintings forced a different American approach. British Foreign Secretary Ernest Bevin urged Secretary of State James Byrnes to reconsider shipping German art to the United States. Bevin thought the American move would create ill-will among the Germans and make Allied control more difficult.[57] Bevin stressed that the European Allies, who favored a strong restitution-in-kind policy, would object to American control of German art objects. The foreign secretary pointedly exposed the flimsiness of the official American explanation for the proposed transfer, which was the lack of adequate facilities in Germany to safeguard the works of art. Bevin noted the dangers of transatlantic shipping, and he insisted there were adequate facilities in Germany.[58] Soviet Foreign Minister VyacheslavMolotov also expressed coolness to the Category C idea. He felt this was contrary to the spirit of the 5 January 1943 declaration. Byrnes told the American ambassador in Moscow, Averell Harriman, that the Russians must not have understood that Category C items were German, not looted Allied property.[59] It is unlikely that the astute Molotov misunderstood. Perhaps Secretary Byrnes did not grasp the allusion to Nazi looting tactics.

MFA&A officers reacted with shocked surprise and bitter opposition. Major Mason Hammond obtained a meeting with General Clay and debated the propriety and necessity of the whole venture. But Hammond "failed to move" Clay and was told by an obviously irate general to keep his opinions to himself until he left the Army. Thirty-two of the thirty-five MFA&A officers met in early November and drafted what came to be known as the "Wiesbaden Manifesto."[60] In passionate terms, the officers argued against the policy of "protective custody" as "establishing a precedent which is

[55] Ibid.
[56] Nicholas, *Rape of Europa: The Fate of Europe's Treasures in the Third Reich and the Second World War* (New York: Alfred A. Knopf, 1994), p. 386.
[57] *Foreign Relations, 1945*, vol. 2, *General: Political and Economic Matters*, p. 949.
[58] Ibid., p. 950.
[59] Ibid., p. 947.
[60] Mason Hammond to John Walker, 17 October 1945, File "American Committee for the Protection and Salvage of Archive and Historic Monuments in Europe, March 1945–January 1953," Roberts Commission, RG 17, National Gallery of Art.

neither morally tenable nor trustworthy." They argued that the depots created for displaced art were fully functional and able to protect the German cultural heritage in its custody. Bluntly put, these officers believed that the U.S. government and its army had put them in a position similar to former German military personnel soon to be prosecuted for "the crime of sequestering, under the pretext of 'protective custody,' the cultural treasures of German occupied countries." Though promising to carry out orders, the officers stated, "We are thus put before any candid eye as no less culpable than those whose prosecution we affect to sanction."[61] Faced with the Army command's intransigence, the MFA&A staff prepared to implement what they referred to with bitter irony as the "Westward Ho, Watteau" project.[62]

Colonel Henry McBride, administrative officer at the National Gallery, met a frosty reception when he inspected the Munich collecting point to see if any artworks should be transferred to the United States. The officer in charge, Craig Hugh Smyth, told McBride in no uncertain terms that one item that particularly interested the colonel, the Czernin Vermeer, was not going anywhere. As Smyth put it, "This picture is not in danger. You can see exactly. It's guarded as well as it could be guarded anywhere!" McBride did not take the *Vermeer*. Smyth's suspicious attitude toward McBride reflected the belief prevalent among MFA&A officers that the National Gallery saw the transfer policy as an opportunity to expand its collection.[63] McBride had an equally unpleasant encounter with another MFA&A officer, Charles Parkhurst, who stormed out of a heated discussion. Parkhurst felt that McBride had threatened him with possible court martial if the MFA&A officer did not back away from the "Wiesbaden Manifesto" and become more pliable. After debating what Parkhurst termed the higher morality of not obeying the order to transfer the masterpieces, McBride told him, "You can't afford to do this." In response to Parkhurst's query "Why not?" McBride replied, "Because you have a wife and two children." Parkhurst's enraged response was to walk out. He never saw McBride again.[64]

Art and academic circles in the United States actively lobbied against the idea. Former MFA&A officer Charles L. Kuhn, from Harvard University, published a broadside against the transfer of the 202 paintings in the *College Art Journal*. Kuhn charged that U.S. representatives on the Reparations Commission and General Clay wanted to use these paintings, which were in Category C, for reparations. Kuhn refuted the government's claim

[61] "Protective Custody," *Magazine of Art* 2 (February 1946): 42, 73–5.

[62] Oral history interview with Charles Parkhurst by Alfred C. Viebranz, 10 November and 6 December 1988, p. 53, National Gallery of Art.

[63] Oral history interview with Craig Hugh Smyth by Alfred C. Viebranz, 1 March 1993, pp. 30, 33, National Gallery of Art.

[64] Oral history interview with Charles Parkhurst, p. 64.

that conditions in Germany justified the move. He asserted that the MFA&A had refurbished a museum in Wiesbaden that was perfectly adequate for the paintings. Petitions and protests poured into Washington from art and academic circles opposed to the transfer of art.[65] Andrew C. Ritchie of the Albright Art Gallery put his finger on the most troubling implication of the unilateral action. As he wrote, "If the United States has seen fit to act only on its own responsibility in this matter, the way is clear for the other three occupying powers, Britain, France and Russia, to take action." Ritchie feared that "to divide her museum collections among the four powers with no definite assurance that each of the parts will be returned at the same time is to present Germany with an uncertain, if not chaotic, situation as regards one of the instrumentalities of her rebirth – her cultural patrimony."[66]

Cultural organizations also entered the contentious fray. The American Anthropological Association passed a resolution stating that "scientific documents and specimens and works of art, legitimately acquired in the first instance by public institutions in enemy countries, be not made subject to seizure or to alienation by the United States as reparations and that as soon as possible such materials be restored to institutions originally housing them." The College Art Association of America wrote a brief tart letter to the State Department closed with "We would therefore urge that the Department of State clarify this action, and would strongly recommend that assurances be given that no further shipments are contemplated."[67]

In view of the firestorm, a hasty policy retreat began. Both the Roberts Commission and Chief Justice Stone, chair of the National Gallery's board of trustees, hastened to defend the Army and begin to de-escalate the controversy. A press release from the National Gallery asserted that "the Chief Justice added that he felt the United States Army deserved the highest praise for the care exercised in salvaging these great works of art and in making provision for their safety until they can be returned to Germany." The Roberts Commission expressed similar sentiments.[68]

Domestic and British opposition were probably the key factors in producing a new approach. Byrnes wrote Ernest Bevin that after reconsideration the United States felt it was safe for the bulk of the contested art objects to remain in Germany.[69] Nonetheless, the secretary of state insisted that there was not quite room for all the items, and so a small number (202) required storage in the United States. This was undoubtedly to save face for General Clay, the foremost advocate of the "safekeeping" explanation. In his

[65] Charles L. Kuhn, "German Paintings in the National Gallery: A Protest," *College Art Journal* 5 (January 1946): 78–81.
[66] "Protective Custody," pp. 42, 73–5.
[67] Ibid.
[68] Ibid.
[69] *Foreign Relations, 1945*, vol. 2, *General: Political and Economic Matters*, p. 955.

memoirs, Clay presents this as the only reason for the proposed transfer.[70] To conform with the British position, the United States moved to reseparate the reparations and restitution issues and have them dealt with primarily by the ACC. Pauley's triumph was short-lived. Never again was there a realistic possibility that the United States would place art in the same category as factories and ships. The knotty issues of property control and disposition were now left in the hands of four military men.

## Restitution Imperative

OMGUS authorities faced a difficult situation when the delegates at the Berlin Conference referred the restitution question to the Conference of Foreign Ministers, which was not scheduled to meet until October. Allied nations were clamoring for the return of industrial items necessary for their economic recovery. In addition, the Allies wanted their cultural treasures returned immediately. With no international agreement in sight, American officials faced the question of whether to implement a unilateral restitution policy or wait for an agreement with the other Occupying Powers. Circumstances in the American Zone forced General Clay to change his earlier stance on no restitution without an Allied agreement. As he reported to General Eisenhower, American troops had already located five hundred repositories filled with valuable cultural items.[71] Undoubtedly, many more would appear. Eisenhower, in light of President Truman's approval of the OMGUS memorandum on disposition of art objects in the U.S. Zone, directed the immediate return of artworks in Categories A and B.[72] Given the heated reaction to Category C, only token moves were ordered for these items.

Lucius Clay immediately issued restitution instructions that covered cultural items, as well as industrial, agricultural, and transportation equipment. Clearly, the United States wanted to relieve the genuine economic hardship of its Allies and lift from itself expensive and troublesome responsibilities with cultural preservation. Clay's instructions, in keeping with earlier American proposals submitted to the EAC, provided for Allied restitution missions to work in the American Zone, after OMGUS reviewed the initial lists of items submitted by the Europeans.[73] Despite these moves, the Americans clearly understood the need for a comprehensive agreement that covered all the

---

[70] Lucius D. Clay, *Decision in Germany* (Garden City, N.Y.: Country Life Press, 1950), p. 309.

[71] Indorsement to memorandum, "Art Objects in U.S. Zone, 29 September 1945," File "Misc. Correspondence RD&R Div. USGCC 1945," General Correspondence, 1944–9, Records of the Economics Division, RG 260.

[72] Memorandum, "Restitution Policy and Procedure, 24 September 1945," File "Plans – MFA&A," General Records, 1938–48, Records Concerning the Central Collecting Points, Records of OMGUS Headquarters Relating to the Central Collecting Points, RG 260.

[73] Ibid.

zones of occupation. The British, also under pressure from their Continental Allies for assistance, submitted an interim restitution plan to the ACC that covered noncultural items.[74] The ACC referred the proposal to the Coordinating Committee (CORC), which consisted of the four deputy military governors responsible for making recommendations to the ACC. Immediate conflict broke out in the CORC, and this delayed the entire restitution program throughout the fall.

## The Struggle to Agree

The Russians first of all insisted that restitution was under the jurisdiction of the Council of Foreign Ministers and thus was not a subject the ACC or the subordinate group of deputy military governors, the CORC, could discuss.[75] When the foreign ministers decided they could not settle the knotty restitution question and referred it to the ACC, the Russians no longer had a basis for their objection. The Russian delegate, General Vassily Sokolovsky, next blocked matters by stating that the Soviet Union could not agree to any restitution actions until an overall definition of the term *restitution* and the property covered by the term was settled.[76] This very point had eluded the EAC, the delegates at the Berlin Conference, and the Council of Foreign Ministers.

Because of these Soviet objections, the CORC instructed the DRDR of the ACC to work on an acceptable definition and an interim plan. This was consistent with the CORC's responsibilities in implementing ACC decisions, supervising German administrative units, and supervising interzonal transactions. In studying interim restitution, the DRDR prepared separate papers for cultural and noncultural items, although they worked on an overall definition covering both categories. Consideration of cultural restitution was delayed while the members of the CORC and DRDR wrangled over the definition and sensitive issues primarily relating to noncultural property.

The Soviet Union wanted to restrict restitution only to those items removed by force.[77] The French delegate on the CORC, General Louis Koeltz, noted that the 5 January 1943 Declaration included dispossession by any means whatever. While his two Western colleagues supported Koeltz,

74 CORC/P(45)36 (Revise), 10 September 1945, File "CORC/P(45) 1-60," Allied Control Council Documents, 1945–9, Records of the Allied Control Council, Germany, 1941–50, RG 43.

75 *Foreign Relations, 1945*, vol. 3, *European Advisory Commission: Austria; Germany*, p. 1345.

76 "CORC/P(45)167 (Revise), 30 November 1945," File "CORC/P(45) 116–176," Allied Control Council Documents, 1945–9, Records of the Allied Control Council, Germany, 1941–50, RG 43.

77 *Foreign Relations, 1945*, vol. 3, *European Advisory Commission: Austria; Germany*, p. 1426.

General Sokolovsky caustically commented that the Russians were not interested in assisting French industrialists who had collaborated with the German war effort.[78] The French were odd men out in debates focusing on replacement-in-kind. They wanted this to apply to noncultural and cultural items. The Soviets would accept replacement-in-kind only for unique cultural works that were not recovered.[79] Long-held American and British views on this subject coincided with the Russian position.

With the CORC deadlocked throughout October and November on the definition and scope of restitution, the DRDR focused its efforts on reaching an agreement for the interim restitution of cultural works. M. Glasser, the French representative in the DRDR, confronted his Soviet colleague, Colonel I. I. Volegov, with a request to reaffirm General Sokolovsky's agreement to restitute cultural items.[80] Volegov, in view of the French–Soviet impasse on restitution, would only repeat the position of his superiors that restitution had to wait until an agreement was reached on the definition. The Russians did agree to the establishment of a Cultural Works Committee that was supposed to resolve cultural restitution issues.[81]

This committee drew up an interim plan designed to avoid most of the controversies that plagued efforts to settle the overall restitution question. Restitution was restricted to easily identifiable items of well-known ownership, which were taken during the occupation.[82] The interim plan provided for a broadening of the terms at a later date. The idea behind this was to begin cultural restitution in all four zones, without bogging down in the question of whether the Germans had legitimately paid for any items or if the seller had acted voluntarily. All movable goods of religious, artistic, documentary, scholarly, or historic value, "the disappearance of which constitutes a loss to the cultural heritage of the country concerned," were included in the definition.[83] The plan also provided procedures for claimant nations to follow. These included submitting descriptive lists of missing items and establishing panels of experts to review claims.[84] Though the DRDR approved the plan, nothing further could be done until the CORC and the ACC finally decided the scope of the restitution program.

The deadlock over the restitution issue reflected the broader Allied disagreements over reparations and the future economic development of

---

[78] Ibid.

[79] "CONL/P(45)65, 4 December 1945," File "CONL/P(45)," Allied Control Council Documents, 1945–9, Records of the Allied Control Council, Germany, 1941–50, RG 43.

[80] Minutes of the Seventh Meeting, Reparations, Deliveries and Restitution Division, 18 October 1945, File "DRDR/M(45)," Allied Control Council Documents, 1945–9, Records of the Allied Control Council, Germany, 1941–50, RG 43.

[81] Ibid.

[82] *Foreign Relations, 1945*, vol. 2, *General: Political and Economic Matters*, p. 955.

[83] Ibid.

[84] Ibid.

Germany. The Russians were not interested in any restitution program because they viewed German industrial equipment as the needed replacements for their own devastated economy. Not only did the Russians feel desperate economically, but they also had contributed most to the defeat of Hitler. Sokolovsky's sarcastic comment to Koeltz about French collaboration with the Germans indicates the depth of feelings. The Russians were simply not interested in returning equipment belonging to the Western Allies or in sharing the economic products of their zone with the other three Occupying Powers.

The situation was similar in regard to cultural items. While paying some lip service to the principle of returning the cultural heritage of other nations, British MFA&A officers already reported that the Russians were running the German fine arts program as an adjunct to its military command.[85] Foreign restitution missions were not allowed in the Soviet Zone. During discussions in the ACC, CORC, or DRDR, the Russians gave little evidence of interest in expediting cultural restitution. In fact, the Russians had already removed many priceless treasures from their zone of occupation. Treasures seized included the Pergamum Altar, stored in a Berlin factory by the Germans; more than nine hundred paintings from the Kaiser Friedrich Museum; and the art and sculpture of the Sans Souci Palace in Potsdam.[86]

The issues of reparations payments, interzonal exchanges of goods, and restitution confounded the Council of Foreign Ministers and the control machinery in Germany. In light of this impasse, General Clay presented a compromise proposal at the twenty-third CORC meeting designed to achieve some progress, at least, with the restitution program. The United States wanted to satisfy the demands of its Allies on restitution and, at the same time, hoped for movement toward an agreement that determined which German property was eligible for reparations, how much each ally received, and the terms for interzonal economic exchanges.

Clay's 27 November 1945 proposal defined property liable to restitution as everything taken by force, with property obtained through other means eligible for return if consistent with reparations and the minimum economy necessary for Germany.[87] This was to satisfy the Russian complaint that designating too much property as eligible for restitution would hinder reparations owed the Soviet Union. Also, this definition met Western objections

---

[85] Monthly MFA&A Report, September 1945, File "Monthly MFA&A Reports of British Zone – Field Reports, April–October, 1945," General Records, 1938–48, Records Concerning the Central Collecting Points, Records of OMGUS Headquarters Relating to the Central Collecting Points, RG 260.

[86] John H. Scarff to Huntington Cairns, January 1946, File "American Commission – Mr. Cairns' Personal Correspondence 1944–1949," Subject Files, 1938–79, RG 4, Records of the Office of the Secretary-General Counsel and Its Predecessors, Gallery Archives, National Gallery of Art, Washington, D.C.

[87] *Foreign Relations, 1945*, vol. 3, *European Advisory Commission: Austria; Germany*, p. 1426

that the 5 January 1943 declaration covered property taken by other than forceful means.

The Russians added a proviso to Clay's proposal at the 12 December CORC meeting. The Russians accepted Clay's definition, with the understanding that any replacement-in-kind was limited to unique cultural objects.[88] They would not tolerate any threat to their reparations shipments. The French, who ardently desired a comprehensive replacement-in-kind provision, reluctantly agreed to the Russian position. The Americans and British, skeptical of replacement-in-kind even for unique objects, insisted that detailed implementation wait for a separate paper.[89] With the deadlock broken, the CORC adopted a final definition for the term *restitution* and forwarded it to the ACC for a decision.

The final definition provided for restitution of noncultural and cultural items, with Clay's compromise on the return of everything taken by force with return of all property removed by other means contingent on reparations agreements and maintaining the minimum German economy. The CORC also approved and sent to the ACC the interim cultural restitution deliveries plan drawn up by the Cultural Works Committee.[90] This plan did not draw a distinction between various means of dispossession and assumed all cultural objects were removed by force. In effect, this interim agreement was the program initiated by General Clay and USGCC (Germany) in September. It is clear that from the first debates in the EAC onward, agreement on cultural restitution was held back by deep differences on noncultural restitution and reparations. Even though all the Allies supposedly shared similar principles regarding cultural property, the reader should not assume the program went smoothly from this point forward. Incredibly complex problems arose concerning heirless property, items belonging to Eastern European refugees, restitution-in-kind of unique objects, and the extent of the entire cultural restitution effort. As we will see, many of these problems reflected fundamentally different Allied approaches on the treatment of Germany and the future development of Europe itself.

The Paris Conference on Reparations, which met in November and December 1945, was a harbinger of future conflicts. The Soviet Union boycotted the conference and refused to acknowledge the Inter-Allied Reparations Authority (IARA) set up by the conference.[91] The Russians insisted that reparations agreements were a subject only for the Council of Foreign

---

[88] Ibid.

[89] Minutes of the Thirteenth Meeting, Reparations, Deliveries and Restitution Division, 26 November 1945, File "DRDR/M (45) 1-17," General Records, 1945–8, Records of U.S. Element, Allied Control Authority, Records of the Reparations, Deliveries and Restitution Division, RG 260.

[90] *Foreign Relations, 1945*, vol. 3, *European Advisory Commission: Austria: Germany*, p. 1463.

[91] *Foreign Relations, 1945*, vol. 2, *General: Political and Economic Matters*, p. 1281.

Ministers, which had already met failure in this regard. In an annex to the final declaration of the conference, Albania, Belgium, Czechoslovakia, Denmark, France, Greece, India, Luxembourg, the Netherlands, and Yugoslavia stated their interpretation of restitution in light of the 5 January 1943 Declaration. They argued for complete restoration or replacement by equivalent objects for items of an artistic, religious, cultural, historic, or scientific nature.[92] Clearly, this clashed with the American hesitancy concerning replacement. American doubts were clearly expressed in the DRDR, when a U.S. representative described how difficult it was to decide what object was unique, which German museum had a proper equivalent, and how to conduct removals while preserving democratic principles in Germany.[93] The small states also called for restitution missions to operate in each zone of occupation and to search for missing objects.[94] This would obviously antagonize the Russians, who had no intention of letting anyone roam freely in their zone. The United States, for that matter, was not enthusiastic about this idea. The French were already pressing for the right to investigate freely in the American Zone.

Though formal agreement on restitution would come early in 1946, in many ways the basic patterns of restitution were already set. Allied agreements on restitution were limited in scope, extremely difficult to implement on a quadripartite basis, and subject to recriminations and breakdowns. Simply put, there was no effective Four Power governance in Germany. Beyond war crimes prosecutions, demilitarization, and the dismantling of the Nazi Party, there was little Allied agreement. All the wartime diplomatic strife about the future of Germany and the question of German power continued in new venues. The problems with restitution reflected the broader clashes of Great Power interests and ideologies. In the cultural restitution arena, as in everything else, there were four distinct approaches. American efforts were focused on shedding responsibility for cultural loot and German property in U.S. custody as quickly as possible. Clay's interim cultural restitution strategy, the creation of the collecting points, and the shipping of unopened crates back to the country of origin, all indicate America's desire to meet – and complete – its responsibilities in the briefest period of time feasible. That this effort took four years was not the result of the military's desire to retain custody over Europe's cultural patrimony. It is a testament to the difficulty of the task.

The strategy developed by Lucius Clay and the USGCC (Germany) in the summer of 1945, with the exception of handling German-owned art, lasted

92 Ibid., p. 1445.
93 Minutes of the Thirteenth Meeting, Reparations, Deliveries and Restitution Division, 26 November 1945, File "DRDR/M (45) 1-17," General Records, 1945–8, Records of U.S. Element, Allied Control Authority, Records of the Reparations, Deliveries and Restitution Division, RG 260.
94 *Foreign Relations*, 1945, vol. 2, *General: Political and Economic Matters*, p. 1445.

until the end of the occupation period. Issues that slowed the task arose, but returning cultural loot to the countries of origin was the basic pattern. Deviations from this approach – heirless Jewish property and property of refugees from communism – were the rare exceptions. In the first months of occupation, the "factory" approach to implementing the strategy was well underway. The "factories," the central collecting points, were managed by MFA&A officers who were experts in their fields and staffed by German art and museum specialists. Items were inventoried and catalogued and then shipped out. In this early period, the pattern was set for returning clearly identifiable German property to the institutions or individuals who had title to the property. Nothing fundamental changed in the American approach until the end of the occupation.

It can also be said that nothing fundamental changed in the Russian approach. The "trophy" brigades scoured the Soviet Zone and removed millions of artworks, drawings, prints, sculptures, books, and archives to the Soviet Union. No heed was paid to whether the items were Soviet property, belonged to other nations and stolen by the Nazis, or were legitimate German property. All were destined to replenish Soviet cultural institutions, to create a new "Linz-style" museum, or for exploitation for intelligence purposes. Consistent with their wartime pattern, the Soviets never meaningfully engaged their Allies and other states in resolving restitution issues. Their zone was a forbidden area to the Allies, and they provided little to no information concerning cultural restitution matters. From the beginning, the Soviets considered Stalin's decrees as providing the legal justification for their actions in Germany. This pattern and attitude has remained in place until the present time. Later discussions in this book about cultural restitution and the Russian Federation will take us directly back to the immediate postwar period.

The French and British likewise demonstrated consistent patterns lasting until the end of the occupation. The French did not engage in wholesale removals of property along the Soviet model, but they insisted much more vociferously than the British or Americans that the Germans compensate for lost or destroyed cultural property. Experiencing two wars on its soil in a generation, the French were determined that the Germans must pay. Consistently, the French fought for restitution-in-kind on a broad basis, not just for so-called unique items. Though doomed to eventual disappointment, the French always sought the most extensive compensation possible. The British policies and attitudes were closer to those of the Americans than were the French, but neither the British nor the French had particularly robust or large-scale restitution programs. In great part, this was the result of the unanticipated consequences of the zonal boundaries. As luck would have it, the Germans had put their repositories mostly in what became the American Zone. This required the Americans to run a high-volume, high-profile operation. The British and French were not faced with the political and practical issues that confronted the United States. But overall basic restitution policies and procedures were quite similar among the three Western powers. Patterns formed by national self-interest, interpretations of international law, and operational realities set the cultural restitution policies and programs of the four powers.

# 6

## The Allies Agree on Restitution

### Struggling to Agree

Despite the CORC recommendation on the definition *restitution*, Allied debate and divisions continued. At the sixteenth ACC meeting, General Vasily Sokolovsky proposed amendments to the CORC proposal. He did this in spite of the fact that the Soviets had accepted the CORC definition, which was based on a compromise originally presented by General Clay. The Soviets insisted on a new clause that permitted any of the United Nations to receive compensation from Germany for any of its items used in the reparations program.[1] According to the CORC definition, any items removed by means other than force were eligible for restitution only if this did not interfere with reparations. The Soviets wanted to ensure that they received compensation for any of their property found in Germany, whether or not force was used in the original transfer.

The CORC debated the Soviet amendment and the proposed definition at its weekly meeting on 17 January. The British representative, General Brian Robertson, expressed concern that there was no mention in the proposed definition for retaining a minimum level of economy for Germany.[2] The British feared that massive restitution and reparations programs would leave Germany a wilderness and create a dangerous vacuum in central Europe. General Clay assured his British colleague that his original proposal to expand the definition to property obtained by means other than force was not intended to cause starvation or chaos in Germany.[3] The Soviet delegation brusquely rejected the British concerns and refused to permit any reference to the German economy in the definition. The committee,

---

[1] U.S. Department of State, *Foreign Relations of the United States: Diplomatic Papers*, 1946, vol. 2, *Council of Foreign Ministers* (Washington, D.C.: U.S. Government Printing Office, 1970), p. 483.
[2] Ibid., p. 486.
[3] Ibid.

therefore, decided to accept the Soviet addition to Clay's original proposal. Though the Western Allies forced the U.S.S.R. to broaden the general categories for restitution beyond acquisition by force, the Soviets successfully insisted on provisions that limited restraints on their obtaining reparations.

The debate over restitution-in-kind was a cultural matter. Throughout the fall, the Soviets insisted that any restitution-in-kind or replacement program pertain only to unique objects. From the Soviet point of view, unique objects were outstanding artistic or historic items. The French wanted a replacement program for both cultural and noncultural items. The United States and Great Britain would have none of this. They correctly perceived that the French favored using cultural items in the reparations program. By this point, the opinion of the Roberts Commission on keeping art out of reparations was the official American position. This was certainly the result, in part, of the heated reaction to the removal of German art to the United States.

Not only did General Lucius Clay support the Soviet position on restricting restitution-in-kind to unique works of art, but he categorically stated "he would not commit the United States to replacement of objects of art item for item."[4] With the British supporting the Soviets and the Americans, the French reluctantly agreed to a provision that put the issue off a bit longer. The CORC revision, to which the ACC agreed, read: "As to goods of a unique character, restitution of which is impossible, a special instruction will fix the categories of goods which will be subject to replacement, and the conditions under which such goods could be replaced by equivalent objects."[5] So the restitution agreement ratified by the ACC on 21 January did not authorize an immediate restitution-in-kind program. It merely provided for the preparation of a "special instruction" to define the parameters of such an effort.

In light of the CORC compromises, the ACC accepted the proposed definition for restitution on 21 January with little debate. The definition is most interesting for what it did not say. There was no indication on how the restitution and reparations efforts were to interact, no precise delineation of the various methods of dispossession, and silence on such issues as restitution to ex-enemy nations, restitution of property taken from German citizens, and the disposition of heirless property. Now the ACC, as well as the EAC and the Council of Foreign Ministers, had proved unable to resolve substantively the difficult legal, political, and economic problems relating to property control.

---

4 Minutes of the Seventeenth Meeting of the Allied Control Council (CONL/M(46/2)), 21 January 1946, File "CONL/M(46)," Allied Control Council Documents, 1945–9, RG 43, Records of the Allied Control Council, Germany, 1941–50.

5 Minutes of the Thirty-Second Meeting of the Coordinating Committee, 17 January 1946, File "CORC/M(46)," Allied Control Council Documents, 1945–9, RG 43, Records of the Allied Control Council, Germany, 1941–50.

Most of the issues the ACC sidestepped or ignored never were resolved at the quadripartite level, eventually forcing unilateral decisions by the zonal commanders.

## Germany's Future

The debate over Germany's future was at the heart of Allied disagreements that prevented effective quadripartite government and the managing of Germany as a single unit. The Soviets and the French feared a resurgence of German power. Delays in creating a second front during the war in Western Europe meant that Red Army troops had swept through Eastern Europe. Now, Stalin was determined to maintain political, economic, and military control over Romania, Bulgaria, and especially Poland. Poland was the primary invasion route for another German thrust eastward and the route for Soviet control of its zone in Germany.[6] The Western Allies, in turn, were bitterly disappointed by the failure of the Soviets to live up to agreements made at Yalta to allow free elections in Poland.

Serious doubts about the continued efficacy of Allied cooperation was already evident at the Potsdam Conference. By December 1945, the Western Allies realized that cooperation with the Soviets in Eastern Europe and in the economic and political management of Germany was highly unlikely.[7] Stalin, in turn, feared the American nuclear monopoly (which he would end) and followed Tsarist expansionist policies in Iran and Turkey, which greatly concerned the Americans and British.[8] But Germany's future was the fundamental line of division. The Soviets wanted a unified Germany that was under the ideological sway of Moscow. In their zone, the Soviets merged the communists and Social Democratic parties to form a political front that would hopefully appeal to social democrats in the other zones. Barring success in controlling a unified Germany, the Soviets were intent on retaining sole control in their zone.[9] Economically, the Soviet Union did not implement the Potsdam agreement to deliver agricultural produce to the other zones, stripped German factories and mines in their zone of any useful equipment, and demanded extensive reparations from the other zones of occupation.

The French, also concerned about the resurgence of German might, sought to have the Ruhr and Saar regions stripped from German control and worked

---

[6] Marc Trachtenberg, *A Constructed Peace: The Making of the European Settlement* (Princeton, N.J.: Princeton University Press, 1999), p. 4.

[7] Ibid., p. 14.

[8] David Reynolds, *One World Divided: A Global History since 1945* (New York and London: W. W. Norton, 2000), p. 15. Trachtenberg, *A Constructed Peace*, p. 19.

[9] John Lewis Gaddis, *We Now Know: Rethinking Cold War History* (Oxford: Clarendon Press, 1997), p. 116.

to prevent the development of any central German government organs as called for at the Potsdam Conference. Because the French had not been invited to the conference, they did not believe that they were bound by its decisions.[10] The Americans and the British were distrustful of the Soviets, wanted to restore the German economy, and intended to block any further westward expansion of Soviet power and influence. Though officially committed to eventual reunification, both governments in the course of 1946 came to the conclusion that the best way to achieve their goals was in an economic merger of their zones.[11] By this point, the de facto partition of Germany was apparent.

Even though the diplomats in Washington and London were increasingly skeptical about cooperation, General Clay sought to implement the Potsdam agreement to treat Germany as an economic unit. Clay became increasingly frustrated as the ACC remained embroiled in disputes over the minimum level for the German economy, Soviet demands for advance reparations payments, and Western complaints that the Soviets were removing too many factories and plants from their zone and using properties for reparations in which foreign citizens had significant interests.[12] When the Soviets blocked developing an all-German peace economy industrial plan, Clay halted reparation payments in May 1946. In July, Secretary Byrnes announced that the United States was prepared to merge its zone economically with any other zone. Only the British responded favorably, and a bizonal agreement was reached 5 September. The next day, the secretary of state delivered an address at Stuttgart to American and German officials, which had long-term implications. Byrnes cautiously announced American interest in future German self-government.[13] The bizonal arrangement and the Stuttgart speech were the first steps toward the eventual creation of a West German state.

By this point, according to Marc Trachtenberg, Byrnes had given up on his original idea of an "amicable divorce" with the Soviets and the Americans operating independently in their spheres of influence. Like others in the U.S. government, he was alarmed about perceived Soviet expansionist tendencies. Byrnes also wanted to block Soviet propaganda that sought to encourage Germans toward a unified state under Soviet influence or a neutral state between the two blocks.[14] In this diplomatically divisive year, previously divided elements in the American government united behind the strategy of containment articulated by State Department official George Kennan.[15]

---

[10] *Foreign Relations, 1946*, vol. 2, *Council of Foreign Ministers*, p. 565.
[11] Reynolds, *One World Divided*, p. 25.
[12] Trachtenberg, *A Constructed Peace*, pp. 43–4.
[13] Ibid., pp. 45–8.
[14] Ibid., pp. 25–34.
[15] Gaddis, *We Now Know*, p. 117.

Not surprisingly, the restitution program was caught up in the general strife. The 21 January definition was simply too vague for effective implementation. The ACC was forced to issue a clarification in early March. This clarification noted that forceful dispossession included requisitioning, physical force, and legal instruments negotiated under duress. The inclusion of requisitioning as a means of forceful dispossession resolved a point in favor of the French, who had originally raised the question. The clarification noted that if force was used, the right to restitution was absolute.[16] The deep Allied divisions over Germany's future would continue to affect adversely efforts to make restitution work.

## Making Restitution Work

With an agreement on restitution in hand, the ACC instructed the CORC to prepare the necessary procedures. The procedures, issued on 17 April, reflected the general Allied inability to operate programs on a quadripartite or unified basis. The responsibility for implementing the procedures, and thus controlling restitution, was squarely placed on the zonal commanders. Their duties included locating looted property, the custody and preservation of this property, and providing assistance to Allied restitution missions.[17] The procedures did not spell out the method of handling claims when they were received nor the parameters for the functioning of the restitution commanders. The commanders were required only to prepare periodic reports for the ACC. Clearly, four restitution programs, not one, were in the offing.

The effort to draw up a "special instruction" for restitution-in-kind illustrates, in a small way, the unbridgeable gulf that separated the Occupying Powers. This effort consumed a great deal of time in the CORC and the DRDR over many months. The French presented a paper in the DRDR on 22 January, making any looted item not found eligible for restitution-in-kind. Replacement was on an item-for-item basis, with an object of comparable value provided.[18] In a subsequent DRDR meeting, the French proposed preparing a list of all German-owned objects removed from each zone

[16] "Summary of the Restitution Program in the U.S. Occupied Zone of Germany," File "Final Reports – Reparations and Restitution," Reports and Related Records Re: Restitution, 1945–50, Records of the Reparations and Restitution Branch, Records of the Property Division, RG 260.

[17] Quadripartite procedures for Restitution (CORC/P(46)143), 17 April 1946, File "CORC/P (46)76-150," Allied Control Council Documents, 1945–49, RG 43, Records of the Allied Control Council, Germany, 1941–50.

[18] DRDR/P(46)6, 22 January 1946, File "ACA, DRDR P/46, 1-30," General Records, 1945–8, Records of the U.S. Elements of Inter-Allied Organizations, Records of U.S. Element, Allied Control Authority, Records of the Reparations, Deliveries and Restitution Directorate, RG 260.

after 9 May 1945. Restitution-in-kind would take place from this pool of objects. Negative reactions were swift and sharp. At the CORC meeting of 4 March, the American delegate, General Oliver P. Echols, once again emphatically rejected the idea of a general restitution-in-kind effort. He reiterated the American belief that this was really reparations.[19] The French delegate heatedly responded that nine nations at the Paris Conference on Reparations supported his country's stand.[20]

Soviet intransigence almost totally derailed the negotiations for a "special instruction." The Soviets adamantly refused to accept one proposed article, agreeable to the other three powers, which required:

In cases where the request for replacement is submitted by one of the Occupying Powers, the Allied Control Council will require the Commander of the Zone of that Occupying Power to submit a list of all similar or equivalent German-owned property removed from its zone by the Occupying Power submitting the request and the basis on which such removals were made.[21]

The Soviets claimed that it was impossible to compile a list of German objects removed from its zone. After all, early in the occupation other armies were in the Soviet Zone, and the Germans had removed many items. This was consistent with the general Soviet refusal to allow any investigation into activities carried out in its zone. This was entirely consistent, also, with Soviet lack of cooperation in economic matters, and with reports that they used German cultural property for trophies of war and reparations.

"Trophy" brigades were operating in the Soviet Zone with lists that were prepared by scholars under the direction of Professor Vladimir Bogdanov and that identified valuable objects in German museums and items that had even a remote connection to Russia. The painter, architect, and art historian Igor Grabar, a member of the Russian Academy of Sciences, had come up with the scheme to replenish destroyed Soviet museums with artworks from Germany. The lists were a map to future confiscations. In fact, Grabar's scheme evolved into a plan to create a huge, new museum in Moscow filled with art trophies.[22] This Linz-like plan eventually came to naught, though millions of artworks, books, archives, and other cultural objects were shipped to the Soviet Union by the Trophy brigades. On 30 July 1945, for example, six hundred paintings were selected from the Dresden Art Gallery and shipped by train to Russia.[23] Entire collections were removed from Berlin, including

[19] *Foreign Relations, 1946*, vol. 2, *Council of Foreign Ministers*, p. 515.

[20] Ibid.

[21] CORC/P(46)80 (revise), 28 June 1946, File "CORC/P(46)76-150," Allied Control Council Documents, 1945–9, RG 43, Records of the Allied Control Council, Germany, 1941–1950.

[22] Konstantin Akinsha and Grigorii Kozlov, *Beautiful Loot: The Soviet Plunder of Europe's Art Treasures* (New York: Random House, 1995), pp. xi, 19–20, 33.

[23] Ibid., p. 120.

those of the Ethnographic Museum, the Art Library, and the Museum for Pre- and Early History.[24] The Pushkin Museum, in particular, received many valuable items, including 52 crates with 146,258 coins and medals, the Dresden Historical Museum collection, and Western European paintings, sculptures, and miniatures. All in all, the museum received over five hundred crates of materials.[25] The brigades operated under orders approved by Stalin and made no distinction between looted Russian property, German-owned cultural items, or loot stolen by the Nazis from Russia's allies. The legality and propriety of Soviet actions were hotly debated at the time and came to the fore again in the post-communist era of the 1990s.

General Clay, with the active encouragement of Richard F. Howard, chief of the MFA&A section in OMGUS, ordered that a U.S. proposal be submitted to the CORC for consideration.[26] Howard's role is very important in this particular matter and in all subsequent cultural restitution decisions. By the summer of 1946, the Roberts Commission had ceased its work, and the MFA&A section in OMGUS was the only governmental unit focusing exclusively on cultural matters in Germany. By this point, the War Department's Civil Affairs Division and the State Department deferred to Clay on most matters relating to the occupation. Howard's immediate supervisor, Colonel John Allen, chief of the Restitution Branch, concentrated on noncultural economic matters and left MFA&A affairs to his subordinates.[27] Though the MFA&A staff was small – from mid-1946 onward, it never numbered more than a dozen – it was influential. Howard's views on the French restitution-in-kind are very clear. In a telephone interview with the author, the former MFA&A head complained that the French were "constant thieves" and claimed items that were not theirs.[28] With such an anti-French bias, it is hardly surprising that OMGUS took a negative position on restitution-in-kind.

An American counterproposal was designed to meet French demands for compliance with the ACC decision to issue a "special instruction" and at the same time limit the program as much as possible. General Harper presented the paper on 9 July to the CORC and plainly told his colleagues the United States would consider claims only for items of great rarity, which the Allied Control Authority would consider on a case-by-case basis.[29] Weighing each case individually meant that the ACC would not need to create elaborate machinery for a restitution-in-kind program. Yet by requiring that any claims be submitted to the DRDR as the appropriate quadripartite forum,

[24] Ibid., p. 84.

[25] Ibid., p. 130.

[26] Richard F. Howard to Michael J. Kurtz, telephone interview, 21 April 1981.

[27] Ibid.

[28] Ibid.

[29] Minutes of the Sixty-Third Meeting of the Coordinating Committee (CORC/M(46) 34, Appendix A), 9 July 1946, File "CORC/P(46)," Allied Control Council Documents, 1945–9, RG 43, Records of the Allied Control Council, Germany, 1941–50.

the American delegate made it clear that any claims were not to be handled unilaterally in each zone of occupation. Rather, they were to be processed under the auspices of the Allied Control Authority. This point was reinforced at the sixty-first meeting of the DRDR on 25 February 1947. Harper went on to propose five categories of items eligible for possible replacement: works of art by the masters of painting, engraving, and sculpture; important works of masters of applied art and outstanding examples of national art; historical relics; manuscripts and rare books; and objects of importance to the history of science.[30] This was a far cry from the French proposals. Because the Soviets and British supported the American paper, the French had to acquiesce if they hoped for any replacement. The CORC accepted the American proposal in principle and directed the DRDR to prepare implementing procedures.

In the DRDR, the French once again tried to gain what they had lost in the CORC. The French delegate argued for a more elaborate process for handling restitution-in-kind claims, with the American representative dissenting from the need for any procedure. The DRDR, representing the four Occupying Powers, agreed with the American position and stated that any zone commander could inform any restitution claimant that

after having been notified by all four zones of the failure of all research pertaining to a restitution claim, the claimant nation, if it considers that the object falls into at least one of the categories established by CORC/M(46)34 Appendix A will be able to submit to the RD&R Directorate a claim for a replacement or an equivalent basis, so that any action taken on each claim may be based on the evidence presented and the merits of each case.[31]

This meant that no nation, including any of the four Occupying Powers, had the authority to obtain restitution-in-kind other than by submitting a claim on a case-by-case basis to the DRDR for study and approval. No claims were ever received by the DRDR for review or decision. If the French believed their acquiescence to the American position would ensure at least cultural restitution-in-kind, they were greatly disappointed with the results. Soviet refusals to provide lists of German art objects prevented essential pooling of information, and American intransigence on machinery prevented the necessary organization. Richard Howard revealed in his final report the overall effectiveness of the restitution-in-kind program when he wrote:

This principle [replacement- or restitution-in-kind] was agreed upon in the European Advisory Commission in 1944 and was vaguely reiterated in the Allied Control Authority definition of restitution. Upon the theory, however, that two wrongs

---

[30] Ibid.

[31] Minutes of the Sixty-First Meeting of the Reparations, Deliveries, and Restitution Directorate, 25 February 1947, File "(DRDR/M(47)7) 1-15," Masterfile, 1945–8, Records of the U.S. Elements of Inter-Allied Organizations, Records of the U.S. Element, Allied Control Authority, Records of the Reparations, Deliveries, and Restitution Directorate, RG 260.

do not make a right, this Headquarters has consistently refused to take steps to implement this general agreement. Also it is believed that it would be impossible to do so without the pooling of information and of available valuable German works of art throughout the four zones. Here again the Soviets from their zone gravely affect even a consideration of the problem. It is believed the entire matter should be forgotten.[32]

## OMGUS Pushes Restitution

The conflict over restitution-in-kind did not mean that OMGUS wanted to slow down or hinder the general restitution program. Quite the contrary was true. As Howard observed, General Clay was not interested in restitution, but he wanted to get it over with as soon as possible.[33] This was partly so out of a desire to relieve OMGUS of as much responsibility as possible and to further certain American foreign policy interests. The American effort in the ACC during the spring and summer of 1946 to broaden the number of nations eligible to participate in the restitution program reveals the interaction between these two motivating factors.

In mid-March, the JCS directed General Clay to obtain quadripartite or tripartite agreement to include ex-enemy nations among those eligible to receive restitution from Germany. These nations – Bulgaria, Finland, Hungary, and Italy – were to receive works of art, industrial and agricultural machinery, and certain kinds of transportation equipment taken by the Germans after these nations turned on their former masters.[34] Clay was directed to implement the plan, even if the other Allies did not agree. It is not clear from the documentation who in Washington originated this idea. Given Clay's dominant role in formulating policy for Germany, it is quite possible that the idea originated in American military government. The JCS directive was similar to the interim policy followed by the United States prior to the quadripartite agreement on the definition of *restitution*. The directive permitted restitution for property taken by force by the Germans or by a puppet government controlled by the Germans.[35]

General Clay presented this idea to the CORC, where it received a less than enthusiastic reception. Further discussions in the DRDR meetings revealed detailed objections. The Soviet representative in the DRDR, General Valerian Zorin, said the governments of the four Occupying Powers had to agree on the principle of restitution to ex-enemy nations before the ACC could set

---

[32] Richard F. Howard, "Report upon Separation, 18 November 1948," File "Final Reports – Reparations and Restitution," Reports and Related Records Re: Restitution, 1945–50, Records of the Reparations and Restitution Branch, Records of the Property Division, RG 260.

[33] Richard Howard to Michael J. Kurtz, telephone interview, 21 April 1981.

[34] *Foreign Relations, 1946*, vol. 2, *Council of Foreign Ministers*, p. 526.

[35] Ibid.

FIGURE 7. Meeting of the Allied Control Council, 10 July 1946. *Credit:* Courtesy National Archives, photo no. 260-MGG-570.

procedures for such a program.[36] The British delegate, G. S. Whitham, urged a coordinated study with the Transport Directorate to see if the logistical infrastructure existed to expand the restitution program.[37] American motivations for this proposal were apparent in the negotiations surrounding the Paris Peace Conference. The conference met between 29 July and 15 October, 1946, to review drafts of peace treaties with the lesser ex-enemy nations prepared by the Council of Foreign Ministers.[38] Each of the five treaties contained clauses providing for reparations and restitution. It is interesting to note that the treaties did not distinguish between items obtained by force and those obtained through other means.[39] The assumption was that all items were obtained by the former enemies from Allied nationals through force. This contrasted with the ACC definition of restitution that acknowledged dispossession through nonforceful methods and made restitution contingent

[36] Minutes of the Thirty-Eighth DRDR Meeting, 16 July 1946, File "DRDR/M(46) 21-37," Masterfile, 1945–8, Records of the U.S. Elements of Inter-Allied Organizations, Records of U.S. Element, Allied Control Authority, Records of the Reparations, Deliveries, and Restitution Directorate, RG 260.

[37] Ibid.

[38] U.S. Department of State, *Foreign Relations of the United States: Diplomatic Papers,* 1946, vol. 3, *Paris Peace Conference: Proceedings* (Washington, D.C.: U.S. Government Printing Office, 1970), p. 258.

[39] Ibid., p. 5.

on the reparations program and German economic needs. This clearly limited the right to restitution. The five draft treaties made restitution for all objects an absolute right. These provisions treated the lesser enemy states more harshly than Nazi Germany. Nonetheless, these treaties did provide for restitution to the ex-enemies of items taken by the Germans. The U.S. proposal in the ACC was designed to expedite a process that the draft treaties presaged. In addition to this, there were other motivating factors.

The American government received a number of pointed comments from the ex-enemy states about the stringent reparations and restitution clauses in the draft treaties. The Italian ambassador to the United States complained that the Western Allies had assured Italy that its treaty would not contain a reparations clause.[40] But Soviet insistence on this point had forced the Allies to renege on their promise. The Hungarian minister in Washington, Aladár Szegedy-Maszák, prophetically warned that the harsh economic clauses in the treaties, along with the lack of effective guarantees to protect Western interests in Eastern Europe, would partition the continent into two blocs.[41] In the Hungarian minister's opinion, Soviet dominance of Eastern Europe was thus inevitable.

Secretary of State Byrnes, while attending the Paris Peace Conference during the summer of 1946, conferred with the anxious Hungarian Foreign Minister, János Gyöngyössi. Byrnes noted with alarm the possibility that the Hungarian economy would collapse during the coming winter. The secretary of State promised that the U.S. representative on the ACC in Germany would continue to seek quadripartite agreement for restitution to Hungary of industrial and transportation equipment looted by the Germans.[42] Apparently, the United States hoped to soften at least some of the harsh terms imposed on the former enemies by hastening a restitution effort in their favor. By this point, Allied wartime collaboration was mostly a thing of the past. The American government hoped to maintain some influence with the former German allies in Eastern Europe by returning urgently needed items. While cultural items did not come under the rubric of economic necessity, the former enemy states obviously desired the return of their precious works of art. This was part of an American effort to counter Soviet influence in Eastern Europe and Italy.

In an effort to secure the goodwill of liberated countries and ex-enemy nations as well, the American, British, and French governments issued a démarche to neutral states on 8 July, at the beginning of the peace conference. The Allies urged the neutral nations to seek out looted materials within their borders and to prevent their export or sale, pending resolution of restitution claims. The liberated countries, including the U.S.S.R., and the ex-enemy nations were urgently requested to submit lists of looted property to the neutrals as a critical first step in stopping the black market in gold, securities,

---

[40] Ibid., p. 21.
[41] Ibid., p. 12.
[42] Ibid., p. 258.

and art. Though the Allied declaration was mainly hortatory, it did recognize the flood of looted works loose in Europe and elsewhere, as well as the diplomatic pressure from all countries seeking the return of property.[43]

Despite repeated American efforts in the ACC to gain acceptance of restitution to ex-enemies, agreement was impossible. As usual, the Soviet Union was not interested in any restitution effort that benefited other states. They particularly resented returning property not directly taken by the Germans.[44] The French wanted to slow restitution efforts to Hungary in a move to accelerate Hungarian payments to France. In light of this opposition, the United States finally permitted restitution missions from the ex-enemy nations to operate in the American Zone only after the respective peace treaties came into effect late in 1947. Diplomatic circumstances, as well as heavy responsibilities in the American Zone, had forced the United States into another effort to expedite restitution.

In August, the United States submitted a proposal to the DRDR that set 31 December 1946 as the final date for filing restitution claims. Completion date for processing the claims was 30 June 1947.[45] Colonel John Allen, the American delegate, explained that countries not yet eligible for restitution (i.e., the ex-enemy nations) would have three months from the date of their becoming eligible for restitution to file claims. These countries would have three months beyond the filing deadline for processing.[46] This proposal was designed to eliminate American responsibility in the restitution field as soon as possible. As such, this was consistent with the earlier proposals for interim restitution and restitution to ex-enemy nations.

The Soviet and British delegates generally agreed with the American proposal, but the French vehemently rejected it. The French were against the very principle of a time limit.[47] They believed that every item subject to restitution required return, whenever found. Colonel Allen again brought up this matter in the DRDR in October. The French argued that a great deal more time was required to obtain declarations from the Germans on looted property, examine the archives of German organizations engaged in

43 Tripartite Declaration on Looted Cultural Property (Cable 3342), 8 July 1946, File "400c – Fine Arts," Classified, General Correspondence, 1945–9, 1946 (400b-500), Records of the U.S. Political Advisor for Germany, RG 84.

44 Minutes of the Sixty-Third Meeting of the Coordinating Committee (CORC/M(46) 34), 9 July 1946, File "CORC/P(46)," Allied Control Council Documents, 1945–9, RG 43, Records of the Allied Control Council, Germany, 1941–50.

45 Richard F. Howard, "Report upon Separation, 18 November 1948," File "Final Reports – Reparations and Restitution," Reports and Related Records Re: Restitution, 1945–50, Records of the Reparations and Restitution Branch, Records of the Property Division, RG 260.

46 Minutes of the Forty-Second DRDR Meeting, 27 August 1946, File "DRDR/M(46) 21-37," Masterfile, 1945–8, Records of the Reparations, Deliveries, and Restitution Directorate, Records of the U.S. Elements of Inter-Allied Organizations, Records of U.S. Element, Allied Control Authority, RG 260.

47 Ibid.

looting, and await the final decisions on the peace treaties for the ex-enemy states.[48] The Soviet delegate agreed with the U.S. proposal, but he argued the workload required putting the dates in the American proposal back six months. The British agreed with the Soviet point of view.[49]

French disturbance over the proposed termination dates for restitution was so great that they approached the State Department on the matter. The State Department sent a cablegram to General Clay cautioning him on the need to continue the restitution program until the return of all the loot.[50] Also noted in the cablegram were the facts that the British returns had not yet reached a peak and Soviet returns were minor.[51] From the State Department's point of view, it was not advisable to press for cutoff dates until the status of restitution was known in all four zones and it was determined when the countries entitled to restitution expected to submit their final claims.[52] Robert Murphy responded to the State Department cablegram by reporting that Clay did not advocate closing the restitution program, but only the date for submitting claims.[53] Murphy, somewhat contradictorily, argued that OMGUS believed that it was unnecessary to receive claims over an extended period at considerable expense, but was willing to carry on the restitution program as long as possible. Murphy overlooked the fact that the proposal submitted to the DRDR specifically set a date terminating the processing of claims. Because the United States continued to press its proposal in Germany, it is clear that State Department wishes in this matter did not carry a great deal of weight.

In early January of 1947, the DRDR again debated the proposed cutoff dates. The French delegate, Pierre Chauveau, emphatically stated that his country would not compromise on the unquestionable right of any nation to recover its property, irrespective of the time that had passed.[54] Hopelessly

---

48  Minutes of the Forty-Sixth DRDR Meeting, 7 October 1946, File "DRDR/M(46) 21-37," Masterfile, 1945–8, Records of the Reparations, Deliveries and Restitution Directorate, Records of the U.S. Elements of Inter-Allied Organizations, Records of U.S. Element, Allied Control Authority, RG 260.

49  Ibid.

50  War Department Cablegram (WX-87391), "Cut-Off Date for Restitution, 11 December 1946," File "Cables, Permanent, Outgoing, 1946, Unclassified," General Records, Cables Relating to Reparations and Restitution, Records of the Reparations and Restitution Branch, Records of the Property Division, RG 260.

51  Ibid.

52  Ibid.

53  Robert Murphy, Cablegram, 31 December 1946, File "Cables – General Clay," Personal Reading File of Cables, Personal Papers of General Lucius D. Clay, RG 200, Gift Collection Records, National Archives at College Park, Maryland.

54  Minutes of the Fifty-Fifth DRDR Meeting, 8 January 1947, File, "DRDR/M(47) 1-15," Masterfile, 1945–8, Records of the Reparations, Deliveries and Restitution Directorate, Records of the U.S. Elements of Inter-Allied Organizations, Records of U.S. Element, Allied Control Authority, RG 260.

deadlocked, the DRDR asked the CORC for a decision. The coordinating committee met on 5 February and soon reached the same impasse as the DRDR. They decided to postpone consideration of the proposal indefinitely.[55] Eventually, the United States was forced in 1948 to terminate unilaterally the filing of restitution claims.

American military government officials made a further attempt to relieve themselves of restitution responsibilities by vigorously advocating interzonal transfers of cultural material. The basic purpose was to provide for interzonal exchange of articles moved by the Germans for wartime security. As early as the fall of 1945, the Americans and British were exchanging German cultural objects that belonged to institutions in their respective zones. OMGUS estimated that 2 percent of the holdings in the U.S. zone were subject to interzonal exchange.[56]

By March 1946, the informal Anglo-American proposal had turned into an agreement. Religious, historical, and educational materials from museums, collections, archives, or libraries in one zone that belonged in the other zone were returned for comparable objects. Scientific equipment, private property, fragile items, and material removed from the Berlin Military District to the American Zone were exempted from the agreement.[57] The last item noted reflects the extremely delicate situation that existed in Berlin, where the Allies could not reach an agreement on the handling of German museum property. Similar agreements were not reached with the French or the Soviets at this point. After much debate, an agreement was reached with the French in November 1948, by which time the French were sure restitution of their property was complete. They did not want to take the risk that even a stray French item might find its way into another zone. The Soviets never agreed to interzonal exchanges. Because they viewed German cultural property as potential reparations assets, they had little to exchange. Once again, American efforts to reach quadripartite agreement on restitution policy were thwarted.

## Fractious Impasse

The fractious Allied efforts to reach agreements on restitution reflect, as previously noted, the overall tenor of diplomatic relations. By 1946, the ACC

---

55 "Brief Report of the Restitution Section for February, 12 March 1947," File "Monthly Restitution Reports – 1947," Monthly Restitution Reports, June 1946–October 1948, Records of the Restitution Section, Records of the Reparations and Restitution Branch, Records of the Property Division, RG 260.

56 USFET Cablegram (SC-6266), 13 November 1945, File "Cables, Outgoing, Closed," General Records, 1938–48, Records Concerning the Central Collecting Points, RG 260.

57 "Interzonal Exchange of Cultural Materials, 2 May 1946," File "Policies and Procedures – General," General Records, 1938–48, Records Concerning the Central Collecting Points, Records of OMGUS Headquarters Relating to the Central Collecting Points, RG 260.

was already stalemated. It was impossible for the United States and the Soviet Union or France to agree on the political or economic future of Germany. The United States wanted a federal state based on capitalist, democratic principles. The Soviets wanted a strong, centralized state, with authority exercised only by approved, "antifascist" elements. The French really wanted German partition. In the face of these conflicting interests and desires, a cohesive Allied restitution policy was impossible. Implementation of restitution at the ACC level basically ended by 1947. American efforts to get a united policy for restitution to ex-enemy nations were blocked by the Soviets, and the French would not agree to a proposal for setting a final date for filing restitution claims. The Soviets blocked American efforts to get quadripartite agreements on interzonal transfers of German cultural property and to recognize Jewish organizations as inheritors of heirless Jewish property.

The impasse was exemplified by the Soviet refusal to let restitution missions enter their zone, provide an account of their restitution program, or report on their management of German cultural property.[58] Though ACC directives had abolished the Nazi Party and confiscated its property, as well as all items that glorified Nazi and German militarism, these issuances did not sanction the use of German cultural heritage for reparations and restitutions purposes. These directives encompassed only the property of organizations or individuals directly linked to the Nazi regime.[59] Though the ACC restitution directives were broad and general, reflective of Allied dissent, they did envision a unified program. Looted property was to be returned to the country of origin, and German cultural property was not to be removed except on a case-by-case basis after review by the ACC. Soviet assertions at this time, and later, not withstanding, there was no Allied support or agreement

---

[58] Owen R. McJunkins to Major General L. I. Zorin, October 1948, File "Correspondence, October 1948," Correspondence and Related Records, 1946–9, Records of the Restitution Section, Records of the Reparations and Restitution Branch, RG 260; Major General L. I. Zorin to Colonel John Allen, 26 May 1947, File "May 1947," Records of the Restitution Section, Records of the Reparations and Restitution Branch, RG 260; Soviet Removals of Cultural Materials, 13 May 1947, File "WDSCA 000.4, 13 June 1946–31 May 1947," Security Classified General Correspondence, June 11, 1946–1947, Civil Affairs Division General Records, RG 165.

[59] Control Council Proclamation No. 2, Abolition of the Nazi Party, 20 September 1945; Control Council Law No. 2, Providing for the Termination and Liquidation of Nazi Organizations, 10 October 1945; Control Council Law No. 10, Punishment of Individuals Guilty of War Crimes and Crimes Against Peace and Against Humanity, 20 December 1945; Control Council Law No. 58, Addendum to Law No. 2 of the Control Council, 20 August 1947; Control Council Directive No. 30, Elimination of German Military and Nazi Monuments and Museums, 13 May 1946; Control Council Directive No. 38, Arrest and Punishment of War Criminals, 12 October 1946; File "Enactments and Approval Papers of the Control Council and Coordinating Committee, 1945–1948," Records of Unidentified Allied Control Authority Units, Records of the U.S. Elements of Interallied Organizations, Records of the U.S. Element of the Allied Control Authority, RG 260.

allowing the retention of looted property or the looting of German-owned cultural property.

With the failure of the ACC to develop an effective, quadripartite program, cultural restitution became essentially a zonal operation for those countries interested in the matter. For all practical purposes, restitution occurred in the zones of the three Western Allies. With the American Zone containing most of the recovered cultural loot, the focus turned to OMGUS and how it mastered its responsibilities.

PART THREE

AMERICA LEADS

# 7

## Cultural Restitution in the American Zone, 1946–1949

The bulk of U.S. cultural restitution work took place during the years of military occupation from spring 1945 through September 1949. The diplomatic gridlock that hindered a German-wide cultural restitution program continued after the first year of occupation, and the impact would affect restitution policies and programs. American hopes for a world based on collective security, open markets, and national self-determination were countered by Stalin's mixture of Marxist internationalist ideology and Tsarist imperial policies.[1] The United States and the other Western Allies were deeply alarmed by Soviet domination of Eastern Europe and the influence of communist parties in Western European coalition governments. The futile Moscow Council of Foreign Ministers' Conference in March and April of 1947 forced the Western leaders to acknowledge the need for a truncated German state as a balance to Soviet power.[2]

Stalin's prohibition of the Eastern European satellites from participating in the Marshall Plan for the economic reconstruction of Europe contributed to the hardening of political divisions in Europe. The communist coup in Czechoslovakia in February 1948 heightened Western fears. By this point, the French were deeply concerned about the communist threat and continuing economic trouble.[3] In June 1948, the three Western Allies, along with the Benelux countries, agreed to move toward unifying the three western zones in Germany. This was done ostensibly for economic reasons, but the outline of a new state was clearly in sight.[4] The blockade of Berlin in the winter

---

[1] John Lewis Gaddis, *We Now Know: Rethinking Cold War History* (Oxford: Clarendon Press, 1997), p. 13.
[2] Ibid., p. 117.
[3] Marc E. Trachtenberg, *A Constructed Peace: The Making of the European Settlement* (Princeton, N.J.: Princeton University Press, 1999), pp. 66–71; David Reynolds, *One World Divisible: Global History Since 1945* (New York and London: W. W. Norton, 2000), p. 30.
[4] Gaddis, *We Now Know*, p. 119.

of 1948–9 only strengthened Western determination. The establishment of the North Atlantic Treaty Organization (NATO) in April 1949 provided a framework for eventually integrating German military power into a collective framework, satisfying one of the deepest concerns of the victors of World War II.[5]

So, the stage was set for the establishment of the Federal Republic of Germany in May 1949. Though reunification remained an official Allied goal, security and economic needs took precedence.[6] By the fall of 1949, a balance of power existed between Russia and America, built around a divided Europe.[7] By this point, both nations had the atomic bomb, and within five years both would have the hydrogen bomb. Thus, a balance of power (or terror) existed.[8] In this tense international environment, effective quadripartite management of Germany never happened. Zonal autonomy was the reality in occupied Germany. This basic fact set the framework for organizing restitution in the U.S. Zone of Occupation. These controversies, as we will see, definitely affected the implementation and spirit of the cultural restitution program in the American Zone. Although not directly related to reparations or industrial restitution, cultural matters were adversely affected by the increasing acrimony in Allied relations. Before we explore the intricacies of cultural restitution during the occupation, let us briefly look at OMGUS restitution policy and organization as it developed during the occupation.

## Organizing Restitution

General Eisenhower's reorganization of October 1945 placed the responsibility for negotiating Allied policy agreements on restitution in the Restitution Branch of the Economics Division. The MFA&A section of this branch (located in Berlin) was specifically entrusted with formulating policy on cultural restitution and for conducting discussions with representatives of claimant governments.[9] The organizational complexity of American military government in Germany is clearly evident from the fact that operational control of cultural restitution was not assigned to the MFA&A section but was in another section, the Restitution Control Branch. This section was located in Frankfurt (also the site of USFET headquarters) and coordinated field investigations, the activities of foreign restitution missions, and the physical return of looted property.[10] Thus, two sections of the same branch were

5 Trachtenberg, *A Constructed Peace*, p. 86.
6 Gaddis, *We Now Know*, pp. 122–3.
7 Reynolds, *One World Divisible*, p. 36.
8 Ibid.
9 "Organization Plan, December 5, 1945," File "Plans – OMGUS," General Records, 1938–48, Records Concerning the Central Collecting Points, RG 260.
10 Ibid.

involved in restitution activity, which, in addition, often required coordination with military operations controlled by USFET.

The first of several reorganizations affecting restitution and property control in general occurred in March 1948. The Restitution Control Branch, with the MFA&A section, was transferred to the newly created Property Division.[11] This was part of an OMGUS effort to centralize responsibility for property control in one organization. More important, the reorganization was part of General Clay's efforts to complete the remaining tasks of military government and transfer responsibility to a still to be created West German government, a goal that Clay ardently pushed.[12] This reorganization coincided with the first international steps leading toward the creation of the Federal Republic of Germany.

With the Western Allies, albeit with French reluctance, moving toward the termination of military occupation, completion of cultural and noncultural restitution, always viewed as an Allied responsibility, was imperative. To hasten this process, a further reorganization in June 1948 combined the Reparations and Restitution Branches of the Property Division into one branch.[13] This reflected the desire to complete both programs as soon as possible. When the cultural restitution program ended in December 1948, the remaining MFA&A functions were transferred to the Cultural Affairs Branch of the Education and Cultural Relations Division, where they remained until the end of OMGUS in September 1949.[14]

Military interest in ending its role in civil government is also evident in military government regulations concerning cultural property. In the spring of 1946, OMGUS issued its key internal directive on this matter: Title 18, "Monuments, Fine Arts and Archives." In this, responsibility for the preservation of cultural structures and for the activation of appropriate German civilian agencies was left to the German *Länder*, established in October 1945. American MFA&A officers were responsible only for overall supervision.[15] But complete responsibility for cultural restitution and the disposition of

---

[11] "Summary of the Restitution Program in the U.S. Occupied Zone of Germany," File, "Final Reports – Reparations and Restitution," Reports and Related Records Re: Restitution, 1945–50, Records of the Reparations and Restitution Branch, Records of the Property Division, RG 260.

[12] Edward N. Peterson, *The American Occupation of Germany: Retreat to Victory* (Detroit: Wayne State University Press, 1978), p. 75.

[13] "Summary of the Restitution Program in the U.S. Occupied Zone of Germany," File, "Final Reports – Reparations and Restitution," Reports and Related Records Re: Restitution, 1945–50, Records of the Reparations and Restitution Branch, Records of the Property Division, RG 260.

[14] Richard F. Howard, "Report Upon Separation, 18 November 1948," File, "Final Reports – Reparations and Restitution," Records of the Reparations and Restitution Branch, Reports and Related Records Re: Restitution, 1945–50, RG 260.

[15] "MGR 18," File "Policy and Procedure – General," General Records, 1938–48, Records Concerning the Central Collecting Points, RG 260.

unidentifiable cultural materials remained with OMGUS.[16] It was obviously inappropriate for Germans to have a major role in returning items they had stolen. This would only cause the victims to doubt the impartiality and thoroughness of the restitution effort. Carrying out this responsibility was more time consuming and laborious than OMGUS officials originally expected. The subsequent delay was in spite of OMGUS reorganizations, quadripartite agreement on general procedures for cultural restitution, and the thrust of Title 18, which implied German responsibility for most cultural structures, materials, and activities in the U.S. Zone of Occupation.

## Obstacles

Throughout OMGUS, there was an overriding desire to complete the restitution effort as soon as possible. In May 1946, the Economics Division submitted to General Clay a plan for terminating MFA&A activities. Proposed deadlines were set for restitution of readily identifiable cultural objects (30 September 1946) and for the completion of interzonal exchanges with the British (30 September 1946).[17] This required the inspection within four months of all fourteen hundred repositories in the American Zone, the transfer of all items presumed looted to central collecting points for screening and inventorying, and the return of bona fide looted items to the country of origin. This was a Herculean task. The impetus for this came from the top of military government. Deputy Military Governor Clay, at a conference in November 1946, stressed his interest in rapid completion of cultural restitution.[18] This was part of Clay's determined effort to reduce the burdens of military government and thus lighten the expenses carried by the American taxpayer. That the process of cultural restitution took until 1949 to complete is testimony to the complex logistical and policy problems that hindered the whole process.

With emphasis on redeployment of American personnel and assumption of responsibility by German agencies, the number of MFA&A officers was inadequate to achieve Clay's goal of rapid restitution. There were only about twelve MFA&A specialists for the entire American Zone, which included *Länder* of Greater Hesse, Bavaria, Württemberg-Baden, and the Bremen enclave, as well as MFA&A headquarters in Berlin.[19] Matters were

---

[16] Ibid.

[17] Gen. William Draper, "MFA&A Personnel Requirements, 13 May 1946," File "Policy and Procedure – General," General Records, 1938–48, Records Concerning the Central Collecting Points, RG 260.

[18] Charles Fleischner, "Conference with General Clay, 7 November 1946," File "Policy and Procedure – General," General Records, 1938–48, Records Concerning the Central Collecting Points, RG 260.

[19] Gen. William Draper, "MFA&A Personnel Requirements, 13 May 1946," File "Policy and Procedure – General," General Records, 1938–48, Records Concerning the Central Collecting Points, RG 260.

particularly serious for archival materials. By July 1946, there were only two archivists active outside headquarters.[20] One was the archives officer for *Land* Greater Hesse, and the other was director of the Offenbach Archival Depot. The archivists, overwhelmed by the volume of work, restricted their activities to inventorying uncovered, looted archival collections and processing restitution claims. As archivist and Offenbach Archival Depot Director, Captain Seymour J. Pomrenze noted that military officials wanted to reduce the number of American personnel and were not interested in aiding German archives.[21] MFA&A officers were thus unable to give their German colleagues much assistance in reviving German archives. In Württemberg–Baden, the loss of an MFA&A slot in the Table of Organization meant there was no cultural restitution for the entire *Land* after 1946.[22] Between October 1945 and the end of 1946, the number of MFA&A personnel declined from eighty-six to twelve! When General Clay decided in the spring of 1948 that restitution must end, the whole personnel problem came to a head.

When Clay ordered restitution expedited and finished, he also stated that at least one MFA&A officer in each *Land* should work on cultural restitution.[23] This raised the question of what to do about *Land* Württemberg–Baden. On top of that, the chief of military government in *Land* Greater Hesse planned in the spring of 1948 to eliminate the director's position at the Offenbach Archival Depot and thus terminate restitution functions. Underlying this conflict was the belief of the *Land* military governments that restitution and reparations activities should be an OMGUS not a *Land* function. Colonel John Allen, the chief of the Restitution Branch in the Property Division of OMGUS, noted a hesitancy to tell a *Land* director to use adequate personnel to carry out OMGUS functions assigned to his *Land*. Because the MFA&A section could not issue orders directly to the *Land* military governments, a complex series of negotiations occurred.[24]

Colonel John Allen, accompanied by his assistants for cultural and industrial restitution, met with top officials in the military government of Greater

---

[20] Leslie Poste, "The Development of U.S. Protection of Libraries and Archives in Europe During World War II," 2 vols. (Ph.D. dissertation, University of Chicago, 1958), vol. 2, ch. 6, p. 10.

[21] Seymour J. Pomrenze to Oliver W. Holmes, 13 March 1946, File "Case 145-E5: Preservation of European Archives," Extra-Federal Archival Affairs Cases, Records of the National Archives, RG 64, National Archives at College Park, Maryland.

[22] Col. John Allen, "MFA&A Functions in the U.S. Zone, 12 March 1948," File "Correspondence, March 1948," Correspondence and Related Records, 1946–9, Records of the Reparations and Restitution Branch, Records of the Restitution Section, RG 260.

[23] Charles Fleischner, "Conference with General Clay, 7 November 1946," File "Policy and Procedure – General," General Records, 1938–48, Records Concerning the Central Collecting Points, RG 260.

[24] Col. John Allen, "MFA&A Functions in the U.S. Zone, 12 March 1948," File "Correspondence, March 1948," Correspondence and Related Records, 1946–9, Records of the Reparations and Restitution Branch, Records of the Restitution Section, RG 260.

Hesse. This meeting, which took place in May 1948, typifies how problems were solved in the complex structure of American military government. Allen made it clear that Berlin headquarters wondered how Clay's order on cultural restitution could be implemented without bodies. When Allen stressed how important this was to OMGUS, *Land* officials agreed to reinstate the director's position for the Offenbach Archival Depot and assign three other slots to restitution activities.[25] Thus, MFA&A headquarters obtained results through persuasion, not command.

In addition to inadequate personnel and local military governments not overly interested in restitution activity, there were other logistical problems. USFET issued a letter order on 27 November 1946, titled "Coal for U.S. Army." This order formally established what heretofore was an informal policy and listed the priority for each Army unit or function in using the precious supply of coal available for the winter. Collecting points, though a military government responsibility, were not permitted to use coal for heat.[26] This was a problem during the winters of 1945–6, 1946–7, and 1947–8 and jeopardized hundreds of millions of dollars of fragile works of art. The shortage of coal forced the closure of the Offenbach Archival Depot from October 1945 through March 1946. This certainly slowed restitution activity. MFA&A officers in Bavaria were able to secure barely sufficient amounts of coal from German sources for protection of the contents of the Munich Central Collecting Point.[27] By January 1948, the officer in charge of the Wiesbaden Central Collecting Point had scraped together some coal for his facility and averted disaster.[28] The archival depot at Offenbach and the various repositories scattered throughout the zone continued to suffer from lack of fuel, which in turn led to some difficult preservation problems. MFA&A officers were not notably successful in convincing their superiors in military government of the danger posed to America's relationships with its allies if restitutable property were damaged through neglect. Harried OMGUS officials only knew that there was not enough coal for German homes and essential industry.

Compounding all the other problems was the perennial one of transportation, which hearkened back to the war period. MFA&A personnel could

---

[25] Col. John Allen, Cablegram on *Land* Hesse, File "Correspondence, May 1948," Correspondence and Related Records, 1946–9, Records of the Reparations and Restitution Branch, Records of the Restitution Section, RG 260.

[26] Ibid.

[27] Col. John Allen, "Brief Report of the Restitution Branch for November 1947, 4 December 1947," File "Monthly Restitution Reports – 1947," Monthly Restitution Reports, June 1946–October 1948, Records of the Reparations and Restitution Branch, Records of the Restitution Section, RG 260.

[28] Lester K. Born, "Final Report, Monuments, Fine Arts and Archives Section, 30 December 1948," File "Final Reports – Reparations and Restitution," Records of the Reparations and Restitution Branch, Reports and Related Records Re: Restitution, 1945–50, RG 260.

rarely rely on a truck being regularly available for their inspection work or for bringing materials to the collecting points. For example, in Greater Hesse the last two trucks assigned to the MFA&A section were scheduled for withdrawal when a large repository was evacuated in October 1946.[29] The problems with personnel, fuel, and transportation impeded the speed of the restitution effort, regardless of General Clay's wishes.

## Masterpieces and Politics

Despite the significant obstacles, MFA&A officers restituted millions of items during the OMGUS era. Never far from the surface, though, were the political and diplomatic factors that complicated the effort. When General Clay changed his position in the late summer of 1945 on no restitution until an overall Allied agreement was reached, a plethora of pressures descended on the MFA&A staff. The most pressing came from Allied governments that demanded the return of their most precious national treasures. Fortunately, MFA&A Chief L. Bancel La Farge was ready. Credited by fellow MFA&A Officer Edith Standen with "brilliant and simple planning," La Farge worked out the details for rapid location and return of national treasures.[30] Among the most insistent was the Belgian government, which pressed for the immediate return of the famous Van Eyck altarpiece *The Adoration of the Mystic Lamb*. The altarpiece, a symbol of Nazi revanchist art policy, was at the top of the Category A artworks requiring immediate restitution. In mid-August 1945, Donald Heath, director of the U.S. political advisor's office in Berlin, informed the RDR Division at OMGUS that the American ambassador in Brussels urged a speedy return of the altarpiece.[31] Ambassador Sawyer explained:

I was asked yesterday in Ghent if we could not effect the return to Ghent of the Van Eyck triptych (Agneau Mystic), which they understand to be reposing, perhaps deteriorating, in a salt mine in south Germany after its theft by the Germans. It is my assumption that famous art treasures of this sort, stolen from countries like Belgium, will be returned to them eventually. Could we not take the initiative in this without waiting for demands from respective governments for such action to which they are obviously entitled?

[29] Col. John Allen, "Weekly Progress Report, 1 October 1946," File "Monthly and Weekly Restitution Reports – 1946," Meritorious Restitution Claims, 1948–9, Records of the Reparations and Restitution Branch, Records of the Restitution Liaison Office, RG 260.

[30] Edith A. Standen Papers, "Art Among the Ruins: May 1945–July 1947 (undated manuscript)," p. 5, Collection of Donated Papers, Monuments, Fine Arts, and Archives Officers, RG 28, Gallery Archives, National Gallery of Art, Washington, D.C.

[31] Donald R. Heath, "Return to Belgium of the Van Eyck Triptych," File "400C – Restitution Fine Arts, January–September 1945," Classified General Correspondence, 1945–9, Records of the Office of the U.S. Political Advisor for Germany, RG 84.

It would be an event of major importance in maintaining the good relations between the U.S. and Belgium if we could announce with proper publicity that on a given date art treasures of Belgium would be returned to her and particularly this famous painting to Ghent.[32]

Belgium had been liberated almost a year earlier, yet no cultural treasures had returned. Though the altarpiece was safe in the collecting point in Munich, politically and diplomatically the situation was untenable. This reality, in addition to Clay's determination to unilaterally begin restitution, meant the Belgians were the first to receive a cultural icon rescued by the Americans. In less than a week after Ambassador Sawyer's request, the altarpiece was flown from Munich to Brussels, with a formal restitution ceremony set for 3 September, the first anniversary of the liberation of Brussels from German occupation. The profound significance of the return is clear from the solemn ceremony of restitution. It began at 11:00 in the morning at the Royal Palace in Brussels.[33] All seventeen panels of the altarpiece were mounted in a large hall with Charles, Prince Regent of Belgium, presiding over the event. American diplomats and military officers joined the Belgian cabinet, high church officials, and other leaders for the emotional event. The Prince Regent, Ambassador Sawyer, and Belgian Minister of Education made presentations, and the MFA&A officer in attendance, Mason Hammond, noted that "the quality of the speeches was unusually high for such an occasion and the Belgians clearly felt deeply moved by the return of so important a national treasure."[34]

Hammond in his report to the RDR division director echoed Ambassador Sawyer's comment that this was the "first and most important step in the restitution of art."[35] From Hammond's perspective, the restitution was appropriate, reflected well on OMGUS, and "marked an auspicious beginning of the program of restitution. If followed shortly by restitution to other countries, there should be no feeling that Belgium was unduly favored."[36] The return of the Ghent altarpiece brought to the fore the political and diplomatic tensions prevalent in the immediate aftermath of the war. The Belgian government did not invite any French participation in the ceremony, though the French had accepted custody of the altarpiece in 1940 on behalf of Belgium. The Belgians bitterly resented the fact that the Vichy government had turned over the altarpiece to the Germans. Though the United States

---

[32] Ibid.
[33] Lt. Col. Mason Hammond, "Report on Temporary Duty to Brussels by Lt. Col. Hammond and Capt. Hathaway of the MFA&A Branch, 5 September 1945," File "400C – Restitution Fine Arts, January–September 1945," Classified General Correspondence, 1945–9, Records of the Office of the U.S. Political Advisor for Germany, RG 84.
[34] Ibid.
[35] Ibid.
[36] Ibid.

FIGURE 8. Van Eyck's *The Adoration of the Mystic Lamb* altarpiece displayed after return to the Royal Palace, Brussels. *Credit:* Charles Parkhurst Papers, National Gallery of Art, Gallery Archives.

pressed the French position, that honor required their participation, diplomatic tensions made it "impolitic to include French representatives in the ceremony."[37]

The State Department, keenly aware of such tensions and anxious to prevent complaints from other countries, urged that other nations be treated in a fashion similar to the Belgians. They were particularly concerned about the French, who insisted on the immediate return of seventy-four cases of stained glass taken from the cathedral at Strasbourg, as well as five cases containing treasures from the cathedral at Metz.[38] The French were disturbed about the conditions in the salt mine in Heilbronn in *Land* Württemberg, Germany. Captured in April 1945, the machinery in the mine pumping out water had collapsed, causing damage to the collections stored in the repository. Though the machinery was repaired and the walls were reinforced, the French insisted on the return of the stained glass, which the Germans had stored in the Heilbronn mine.[39] The return of *The Adoration of the*

---

[37] Ibid.

[38] Robert Murphy, Cablegram A-268, 30 October 1945, File "400C – Restitution Fine Arts, October–December 1945," Classified General Correspondence, 1945–9, Records of the Office of the U.S. Political Advisor for Germany, RG 84.

[39] Ibid.

*Mystic Lamb* meant that the Strasbourg glass had to soon follow. On the heels of the Belgian return, OMGUS arranged for the return of the glass and the objects from the Metz Cathedral treasury. MFA&A Officer Lieutenant Charles Parkhurst arranged for the turnover of the glass to the French on 17 September 1945, with the Metz items, which had been removed from a copper mine at Siegen and stored at a collecting point in Marburg, turned back to the French a few days later.[40]

The next request received by the United States indicated how far back and complicated were cultural restitution issues. In September, the Danish foreign minister, J. Christmas Moller, asked the U.S. minister in Copenhagen for assistance in gaining the return of a statue stolen by the Prussians in 1864![41] The *Lion of Isted* was a statue erected by the Danes in 1850 to commemorate soldiers killed in an insurrection backed by the Prussians. At the conclusion of the Austro-Prussian War with Denmark in 1864, the Prussians removed the statue from the cemetery at Flensburg and took it to Berlin. As Foreign Minister Moller put it, "The removal of this sepulchral monument, which in this country is considered as a national sanctuary, and its erection in a German military academy, caused a resentment which till this very day is very much alive in wide circles of the Danish people."[42]

A Danish correspondent had approached the American commanding officer in Berlin, Major General Floyd Parks, inquiring about the statue and its possible return. Parks, with General Eisenhower's blessing, indicated the U.S. military would gladly return the lion.[43] Though this request was outside the purview of the restitution program, American Minister Monnet B. Davis urged its acceptance to General Eisenhower's political advisor, Robert Murphy. With State Department approval, the statue was returned in an impressive ceremony on 20 October 1945, presided over by King Christian X. The King and the Danes appreciated the effort Army engineers took in breaking down the five-thousand-pound bronze statue into ten separate pieces and then carefully packing the lion, and safely returning it to Copenhagen.[44] An eighty-year-old wound to Danish national pride was healed!

A far more volatile and complex situation revolved around the return of the famed Veit Stoss altar to Cracow in Poland. The return of the altar, a national symbol of Poland's cultural patrimony, was initiated by Polish

---

[40] Ibid.
[41] Monnet B. Davis to Robert Murphy, 21 September 1945, File "400C – Restitution Fine Arts, January–September 1945," Classified General Correspondence, 1945–9, Records of the Office of the U.S. Political Advisor for Germany, RG 84.
[42] Ibid.
[43] Ibid.
[44] Donald R. Heath, "Return of the Isted Lion to Denmark, 26 October 1945," File "400C – Restitution Fine Arts, October–December 1945," Classified General Correspondence, 1945–9, Records of the Office of the U.S. Political Advisor for Germany, RG 84.

FIGURE 9. Lion of Isted prior to return to Denmark. *Credit:* Courtesy National Archives, Photo no. 11-SC-226033.

art historian and restitution liaison Professor Karol Estreicher. The twenty-seven-car train began its journey in Nuremburg and arrived in Cracow to an emotional and joyful welcome on 30 April 1946. City officials decorated the platform in Polish and American flags, with MFA&A Captain E. Parker Lesley, Jr., and the American military contingent receiving lavish praise for the return of the altar and other Polish cultural treasures.[45] Despite this auspicious start, there were problems lurking just beneath the surface. For whatever reasons, not all twenty-five members of the American party had received orders to travel to Poland. Further, the official ceremony of return was set for 5 May, immediately following the 1 May workers' day celebrations and the 3 May Polish independence day. Tensions were high in Cracow between communist supporters and their opponents. On 3 May, Polish militia and army units, joined by Russian soldiers, broke up an anticommunist demonstration, inflicting thirty casualties and arresting some eight hundred students at the University of Cracow.[46]

The day of the ceremonial return, 5 May, was marred by accusations from the Polish militia that an enlisted man in the American detail had shot and wounded two Polish militiamen. The American guard detail was put under detention on the U.S. train, and a tense standoff ensued as the Americans prepared to leave on the afternoon of 6 May. The Polish militia identified one of the Americans, Private Curtis Dagley, as the culprit, though after some hesitancy another enlisted man, Private First Class Calvin Vivian, told his superiors he had left the hotel and shot his pistol, apparently wounding one militiaman. U.S. military attache Colonel Walter Dashley decided to say nothing, leave the falsely charged soldier behind because he believed there were witnesses to prove he never left the hotel and return the guilty man without Polish knowledge to Germany for a U.S. military trial. Leaving the innocent enlisted man behind, the train finally left Cracow on 7 May.[47] The shooting marred the return of the altar and allowed the Polish militia, already under communist influence, to use what was a minor incident of misconduct to attempt to create anti-American sentiment. Cold War tensions were already marring and interfering with the restitution program.

## The Collecting Points at Work

Even though the return of high-profile art treasures continued, OMGUS and its MFA&A contingent continued their hard work of cleaning out the German repositories and transporting millions of items to the central collecting points at Munich (looted art), Wiesbaden (German collections, internal loot), and Offenbach (books, archives, Jewish cultural property). During the

[45] Lt. Juliana Bunbar, "Informal Report Covering Return of Veit Stoss Altar and Cultural Objects to Poland, 24 May 1946," File "400C – Fine Arts," Classified General Correspondence, 1945–9, Records of the Office of the U.S. Political Advisor for Germany, RG 84.

[46] Ibid.

[47] Ibid.; E. Parker Lesley Papers, "Statement on Cracow Shooting," Personal Materials, Collection of Donated Papers, Monuments, Fine Arts, and Archives Officers, RG 28, Gallery Archives, National Gallery of Art, Washington, D.C.

FIGURE 10. Veit Stoss altarpiece, Church of Our Lady, Cracow. *Credit:* Courtesy National Archives, photo no. 260-MCCP-Folder 4.

summer and fall of 1945, MFA&A officers, fighting to overcome immense logistical hurdles, created and secured facilities to protect the recovered cultural property. In Munich, Lieutenant Craig Hugh Smyth assumed the awesome task of rebuilding the heavily damaged office complex of the Nazi Party and turning it into a facility suitable for storing priceless art treasures. Smyth, a 1941 graduate of Princeton's fine arts program and curator at the

FIGURE 11. Karol Estreicher holding Leonardo's *Cecilia Gallerani. Credit:* Courtesy National Archives, photo no. 111-SC-238878.

National Gallery of Art, eagerly took up the challenge. As was the case with most of the MFA&A officers, Roberts Commission member Paul Sachs had recommended Smyth for service in the MFA&A.[48]

Selected by his superiors and aided by colleagues James Rorimer, Robert Posey, and Lincoln Kirstein, Smyth began his Herculean labors. Within just a few months, he had organized German artisans and laborers to repair the bomb-damaged buildings, construct proper storage areas for the art coming from the repositories, and restore the vitally needed heating system. Smyth forced a balky Third Army command to provide essential security and, even more amazingly, organized a corps of German art experts to inventory and catalogue the incoming art. Smyth did all this during his brief tour of command between June 1945 and April 1946![49] By the end of July, Smyth had received more than six thousand items, many of which were cases containing multiple works of art. Fabulous treasures included the Czernin Vermeer,

[48] Lynn Nicholas, *Rape of Europa: The Fate of Europe's Treasures in the Third Reich and the Second World War* (New York: Alfred A. Knopf, 1994), p. 358.
[49] Ibid., pp. 358–9.

FIGURE 12. Main entrance to the Munich Central Collecting Point, Koenigsplatz. *Credit:* Courtesy National Archives, photo no. 260-MCCP-36.

Göring's personal collection, and pictures from Monte Cassino, among many other works of art.[50]

With the flow of materials coming in, clearly other collecting points were needed. A second central collecting point was set up in Wiesbaden, in the Landesmuseum. Captain Walter Farmer, an engineer in civilian life and a volunteer for MFA&A work, had the daunting task of turning the heavily damaged German museum into a facility that could store displaced German art collections, including those from the Berlin State museum, as well as loot seized by the Nazis within Germany.[51] Ready for operation by 20 August, the collecting point received fifty-two truckloads of material in its first week of business.[52] More would come.

At war's end, the U.S. Army found a huge cache of looted Jewish, Masonic, Soviet, and even Nazi books, archives, and ceremonial objects at Hungen near Frankfurt. Almost a million items were located. Clearly, yet another collecting point was needed. Slowly, the items were moved to nearby Offenbach.

[50] Ibid., p. 374.
[51] Ibid., pp. 376–7.
[52] Ibid.

FIGURE 13. Storage room for paintings at the Munich Collecting Point. *Credit*: Craig Hugh Smyth Papers, National Gallery of Art, Gallery Archives.

FIGURE 14. Chaplain Samuel Blinder studying looted Torah scrolls in the cellar of the Race Institute in Frankfurt, Germany, 6 July 1945. *Credit:* Courtesy National Archives, photo no. 1100 (*War and Conflict*).

Work proceeded at an uneven pace until the Office of Military Government for Greater Hesse redesignated the collecting point as the Offenbach Archival Depot on 2 March 1946 and appointed the energetic Captain Seymour J. Pomrenze as director. Pomrenze, in civilian life an archivist with the National Archives in Washington, knew German, Hebrew, and Yiddish and had served as an MFA&A officer in *Land* Württemberg–Baden. He expanded the German personnel from 6 to 176 by the end of April.[53] Through his efforts, trucks were located to bring materials to the depot, and restitution shipments began. Pomrenze created several branches to speed the work of the depot. The Administrative Branch handled transportation and security; the Operations Branch was responsible for care and preservation, sorting, boxing and crating, and shipping; and the Liaison Branch served the Allied restitution officers assigned to Offenbach.[54]

[53] Ibid., p. 8.
[54] Ibid., p. 13.

With State Department concurrence, OMGUS had permitted restitution missions from the Allied nations to operate in the American Zone since September 1945, at the point when Clay's interim restitution program began. The Netherlands, for example, sent three restitution officers: Dr. Dirk Graswinkel, head of the Netherlands State Archives; Captain Johannes Georg Schoenau; and Captain Hans Jaffe. These officers used lists of titles provided by the staff of the Bibliotheca Rosenthaliana, one of the most significant Jewish library collections looted by the Nazis and carefully worked with the depot staff to identify and mark items for restitution. By the end of March 1946, crates of items belonging to the Bibliotheca Rosenthaliana and other Dutch institutions were returned to the Netherlands. By early June, almost 900,000 volumes were returned to countries of origin.[55] This episode, among many others, demonstrates the fact that the dynamism of MFA&A officers was largely responsible for overcoming numerous obstacles and pushing restitution forward. Unlike the Ghent altarpiece and the Veit Stoss altar, the Bibliotheca's holdings were not always easy to identify, and the great volume created difficulties that were typical of the vast majority of cultural restitution shipments.

Another key element in successful restitution was the dedication of the foreign restitution officers. Pomrenze remembered that Graswinkel worked "like an itinerant preacher" roving throughout Hesse and Bavaria looking for Dutch property. Such a partnership inspired Pomrenze and the other Americans to double their efforts. Graswinkel's discoveries in Bavaria led to Offenbach's redesignation as a zonal depot for all Jewish property, books, and archives located in the U.S. Zone.[56] Captain Isaac Bencowitz, an officer knowledgeable in various Eastern European languages, succeeded Pomrenze and contributed to the MFA&A program by creating finding aids to assist crews sorting through and identifying thousands of books and manuscripts. Bencowitz's organizational skills, and those of his successors, were sorely tested by great increases in the workload.[57]

A tremendous boost in the holdings of the collecting points at Munich and Wiesbaden and the Offenbach Archival Depot occurred in April 1946, when OMGUS implemented Military Government Law No. 52 by requiring declarations of looted property from German citizens. The regulations required each German to report on property obtained in other countries during the war through unlawful dispossession. Although penalties were provided for lack of compliance, OMGUS followed an informal amnesty policy for those

---

[55] Ibid., p. 6.
[56] Seymour J. Pomrenze, "Offenbach Reminiscences," *The Spoils of War International Newsletter* no. 2 (15 July 1996); Robert G. Waite, "Returning Jewish Cultural Property: The Handling of Books Looted by the Nazis in the American Zone of Occupation, 1945 to 1952," *Libraries and Culture* 37 (Summer 2002): 215.
[57] Poste, "U.S. Protection of Libraries," vol. 2, ch. 9, p. 21.

who filed reports. Eventually, 24,000 declarations were filed, and thousands of cultural items were turned over to military authorities.[58] Foreign restitution missions stationed in the American Zone pored over these declarations, as well as documentation from their own countries and, by the end of the occupation period, filed slightly more than four thousand claims for cultural restitution. By OMGUS accounting, this resulted in the return of 1,625,258 items of value to owner nations from the collecting points.[59] Numerous items, however, were shipped by the U.S. Army directly from German repositories to owner nations. For example, between 25 October and 2 December, 1945, thirty-five freight cars filled with six thousand artworks were shipped from Ludwig II's castle at Neuschwanstein to France. A major repository for the ERR, the castle contained treasures from the Rothschild, David-Weill, and other private collections. In similar fashion, the Soviets received twenty-five freight cars of archival materials and museum objects, taken mostly from Riga and Kiev.[60]

## The Push for Closure

As noted earlier, by the summer of 1948, the international climate made it clear that the end was in sight for military government. As a result, General Clay ordered the acceleration of the restitution program.[61] In August, the heads of the foreign restitution missions accredited to OMGUS were told that the last date for submitting claims for cultural restitution was 15 September, with processing completed by 31 December.[62] Only claims that could not be submitted before 15 September were treated as an exception. The foreign restitution missions responded with a flood of 2,500 claims, in addition to the 750 active ones already on the books of the MFA&A. By 1 November, this load was reduced to six claims, four of them relating to one involved case. Working under strict deadlines, the MFA&A staff rejected

[58] "Military Government Information Bulletin No. 82, 3 March 1947," Records of the Reparations and Restitution Branch, Records of the Restitution Section, RG 260.

[59] Lester K. Born, "Final Report, Monuments, Fine Arts and Archives Section, 30 December 1948," File "Final Reports – Reparations and Restitution," Reports and Related Records Re: Restitution, 1945–50, Records of the Reparations and Restitution Branch, RG 260.

[60] Edward E. Adams, "Looted Art Treasures Go Back to France," *Quartermaster Review* (September–October 1946): 19; Patricia Kennedy Grimsted, "Displaced Archives on the Eastern Front: Restitution Problems from World War II and Its Aftermath," *Janus* 2 (1996): 47.

[61] "Statement by Mr. DeKeyserlingk to Foreign Restitution Missions, 18 June 1948," File "Correspondence, June 1948," Correspondence and Related Records, 1946–9, Records of the Reparations and Restitution Branch, Records of the Restitution Section, RG 260.

[62] "Statement by Mr. McJunkins to the Chiefs of Foreign Restitution Missions in Karlsruhe, 9 August 1948," File "Correspondence, August 1948," Correspondence and Related Records, 1946–9, Records of the Reparations and Restitution Branch, Records of the Restitution Section, RG 260.

almost half of the recently submitted claims on the grounds of insufficient value or lack of conclusive proof that the items were in the American Zone.[63] This led to resentment among many of the foreign restitution missions, but OMGUS could state that cultural restitution to other governments was basically completed. There was little else that could be done because adequate personnel were never allocated to restitution work from 1946 through 1948. By January 1949, there were only five MFA&A officials left in the American Zone.[64]

Even though 1,600,000 cultural items were located and returned to owner nations in a rather routine fashion, almost 2,000,000 more items involved OMGUS in complicated legal and international problems. The three problems of disposition of German-owned cultural property, internal restitution, and the disposition of heirless Jewish property delayed cultural restitution as much as the logistical problems that beset OMGUS. The question of how to dispose of German-owned cultural property was a knotty one and caused complications in several areas. The strict property controls in Military Government Law No. 52 meant OMGUS had responsibility for millions of items found in repositories, as well as in the collecting points. Much of this was certain to be of German ownership and thus of little direct interest to the American military government. But procedures were needed to ensure that items subject to external restitution were not left in German hands. In addition, what was to be done with property belonging to the former *Reich* and *Land* governments? Another difficult issue was the disposition of German private property for which there were no heirs.

General Clay established a Property Disposition Board in February 1946 to recommend a long-range program for the ultimate disposition of all categories of property in Germany under the responsibility of military government. The board, in an interim report on 26 March, recommended that by 30 June 1946 only the Central Collecting Point in Munich contain restitutable cultural property. The contents of the other central collecting points should be turned over to the German *Land* governments by 30 June. The *Länderrat* (Council of Länd Ministers–President in the American Zone) had the responsibility for drawing up a plan to release objects to agencies, institutions, or persons within the U.S. Zone.[65]

While the timing of the Property Disposition Board's recommendations was unrealistic, General Clay agreed with the main thrust. This sentiment

---

[63] "Recent Reorganization and New Personnel, 28 January 1949," General Records, 1944–9, Records of the Reparations and Restitution Branch, Records of the Museum, Fine Arts and Archives Section, RG 260.

[64] Ibid.

[65] Charles Fahy, "Interim Report of Property Disposition Board, 26 March 1946," File "Property Disposition Board," Administrative Records, 1944–51, Records Concerning the Central Collecting Points, Records of the Wiesbaden Central Collecting Point, RG 260.

was not shared throughout military government. James R. Newman, Director of the Länd Greater Hesse Office of Military Government, objected to turning over control to German authorities of the property contained in the Wiesbaden Central Collecting Point. Newman opposed the divisions of responsibility between the Germans and Americans as harmful to the contents and the building, and he emphatically stated that restitution could not be delegated to the Germans.[66] Newman disputed the premise that property control was too onerous for military government.[67] In response to Newman, Clay's adjutant general, Lieutenant Colonel G. H. Garde, presented the basic philosophy that became OMGUS policy. Garde pointed out that it was the responsibility of military government to turn over to the Germans control of their cultural property as soon as possible. This was in line with paragraph 1186 of SHAEF's *Handbook Governing Policy and Procedures for the Military Occupation in Germany*, which stated that it was the policy of the supreme commander to maintain or reactivate civilian agencies charged with the care of monuments and fine arts in Germany.[68] Garde declared a workable plan had to be drawn up that completed restitution and gave Germans control of the central collecting points under the general supervision of the military government.[69]

General Clay's attitude was perfectly clear in a directive issued by OMGUS on 3 April 1947, entitled, "Return to German Agencies of Cultural Material." This order transferred to German agencies with proper facilities works of art and cultural material under the custody of military government.[70] Clay's directive exempted material that was restitutable to foreign countries, but did allow the ministers-president to designate special agencies as custodians for items looted within Germany.[71] This caused immediate dissent by Jewish organizations and hastened the OMGUS resolution of the problem of internal loot and heirless property. The hopes of the Property Disposition Board and General Clay for an early transfer of German-owned cultural property were thwarted by a variety of factors. MFA&A officers felt the need to thoroughly screen repositories and collecting points for items subject

[66] James T. Newman, "Administration of Wiesbaden CCP, 23 September 1946," File "Wiesbaden Central Collecting Point, 1945–1950," General Records, 1945–52, General Reports, Special Reports, and Investigation Files, 1945–51, Records Concerning the Central Collecting Points, Records of the Wiesbaden Central Collecting Point, RG 260.

[67] Ibid.

[68] Lt. Col. G. H. Garde, "Administration of Wiesbaden CCP, October 1946," General Records, 1938–48, Records Concerning the Central Collecting Points, RG 260.

[69] Ibid.

[70] Gen. Lucius Clay, "Return to German Agencies of Cultural Material, 3 April 1947," File "Policy, 205-3," Administrative Records, 1946–9, Policy and Procedures, 1946–8, Records Concerning the Central Collecting Points, Records of the Offenbach Archival Depot, RG 260.

[71] Ibid.

to restitution. This had to occur before Germans could assume custody of cultural property. With the lack of MFA&A personnel and the tremendous amount of material turned in through the declarations of looted property, the screening process was lengthy. In addition, German facilities required extensive repairs before they could receive property.

The first major turnover took place 23 December 1947, when a paper transaction transferred control of the Wiesbaden Neuss Museum from military government to German authorities, even though the contents remained temporarily at the Wiesbaden Central Collecting Point.[72] Resolving the internal restitution and heirless-property problems delayed further the turning over of German-owned cultural property at the Munich Central Collecting Point and the Offenbach Archival Depot until 31 August 1948.[73] A further complicating factor was the disposition of property belonging to the former Prussian state museums. Because these museums were located in Berlin, final control rested with the four-power Berlin Kommandatura. Allied agreement proved impossible, so American authorities decided to turn over custody of Prussian state museum materials stored at the Wiesbaden Central Collecting Point to the minister-president of *Länd* Greater Hesse.[74]

The most diplomatically delicate issue involving German-owned cultural property was the 202 German paintings taken to the United States for preservation in 1945. In February 1948, General Clay recommended the return of the paintings as soon as possible. Conditions were now suitable, and Clay noted the excellent public relations value of prompt restoration in the face of unbridled looting of art treasures by the Soviets.[75] The return of the paintings would also undercut Soviet propaganda, which sought to exploit German feelings on the subject. Clay wanted to thwart communist efforts at dominance in Germany and to keep the reputation of the U.S. Army spotless. Undersecretary of the Army William Draper urged an exhibition for the paintings in the United States before they were returned, as was originally planned in 1945. Clay cabled Draper that it was a little late now to exhibit the paintings and urged their prompt return. By 26 February, concurrence

---

[72] Lester K. Born, "Final Report, Monuments, Fine Arts and Archives Section, 30 December 1948," File "Final Reports – Reparations and Restitution," Reports and Related Records Re: Restitution, 1945–50, Records of the Reparations and Restitution Branch, RG 260.

[73] K. S. DeKeyserlingk, "Brief Report of the Restitution Branch for August 1948, 4 September 1948," File "Monthly Restitution Reports," Monthly Restitution Reports, June 1946–October 1948, Records of the Reparations and Restitution Branch, Records of the Restitution Section, RG 260.

[74] K. S. DeKeyserlingk, "Brief Report of the Restitution Branch for July 1948, 6 August 1948," File "Monthly Restitution Reports," Monthly Restitution Reports, June 1946–October 1948, Records of the Reparations and Restitution Branch, Records of the Restitution Section, RG 260.

[75] Secretary of the Army Kenneth Royall to Sen. Chan Gurney, 9 April 1943, Executive Office Decimal File, 1948, Records of the Civil Affairs Division, RG 165.

from the Departments of the Army and of State, as well as the president, ratified Clay's position.[76]

Unexpected problems occurred in the Senate, where Senator J. William Fulbright proposed a bill to keep the paintings in the United States until a German national government was formed. Clay immediately objected. He felt a hesitancy to return the items would signal American doubts about security in Germany and play into the hands of the Soviets.[77] Eventually, a compromise was worked out with the Senate Armed Services Committee that returned immediately fifty of the most delicate paintings, allowed the others to tour the United States before they were returned, and allocated the proceeds of the tour to a German children's relief fund.[78] This averted a potential propaganda debacle and further ill-will among the Germans.

Another player in the art world also resisted the idea of an American tour for the German masterpieces. John Walker, chief curator at the National Gallery, worried about possible damage to the art during an extensive tour and urged their prompt return. Though he lost this battle, Walker had no doubts about the propriety of the original transfer to the National Gallery, dismissing the reaction of MFA&A officers and others in the museum world in 1945 to "plain, everyday jealousy." The opinionated and caustic Walker summed up the whole controversy with the observation, "We had them and we showed them. We weren't going to send them around the country. I was against that. But eventually we agreed to send them around to other museums. Then the hostility to their coming died out very quickly."[79] The return of the 202 paintings, though, did not immediately end problems for the American government. Throughout 1948, the German press speculated that American art and official circles were interested in selling German art, both public and private, to finance relief and rehabilitation efforts. This was another version of the art for reparations issue, and German art and museum officials reacted with bitter denunciations.[80] By this point, the American government had no interest in such ideas, and gradually the speculation and dissent subsided.

Early in the occupation period, OMGUS began to wrestle with the question of restitution for acts of dispossession that occurred in Germany during the Nazi regime. Charles Fahy, legal advisor to General Clay, recommended in February 1946 a comprehensive act covering claims for the restitution of property or for damages or injuries suffered as a result of Nazi persecution

[76] Ibid.

[77] Ibid.

[78] Under Secretary of the Army William Draper to William S. Hathaway, 7 June 1948, Executive Office Decimal File, 1948, Records of the Civil Affairs Division, RG 165.

[79] Interview with John Walker conducted by Annie G. Ritchie, 23 October 1990, Gallery Archives, National Gallery of Art, Washington, D.C.

[80] Ardelia Hall, "Proposed Sale of Public German Art Collections, 30 March 1948," 1945–9 Decimal File (862.4031/3-3048), RG 59.

FIGURE 15. Richard F. Howard (r) inspecting 202 paintings on return to Germany. *Credit:* Courtesy National Archives, photo no. 111-SC-308745.

in Germany between 1933 and 1945.[81] Individuals could file these claims, and German citizenship was not a condition for filing a claim. This would benefit non-German citizens who had lived in Germany and German Jews who might have changed their citizenship. Primary liability was placed on the German governments or individuals, if named. Fahy urged the creation of an international mixed commission to handle the claims.[82] Fahy's recommendations, as well as those of various Jewish groups, other refugee organizations, and concerned Allied governments, formed the basis for internal restitution in the American Zone.

By early May 1946, the *Länderrat* had a committee working on legislation for the U.S. Zone providing for what was known as internal restitution. In the spring of 1947, the ministers-president reported to OMGUS that they believed internal restitution was proper and necessary, but they

---

[81] Charles Fahy, "Brief of Staff Study: Subject: Claims for the Restitution of Property or for Damages or Injury Suffered as a Result of Nazi Persecution or Discriminatory Acts in Germany, 1 February 1946," File "Correspondence, February 1946," Correspondence and Related Records, 1946–9, Records of the Reparations and Restitution Branch, RG 260.
[82] Ibid.

objected to certain American proposals. Their greatest objection was that equity demanded a uniform law in all four zones. If this was not obtained, they felt it was unfair to have an internal restitution law for only one zone.[83] They also objected to the proposed deadline for filing claims (31 December 1948) as too long and that there was no leeway in dealing with individual cases.[84] In response to German objections, OMGUS unsuccessfully attempted to reach quadripartite agreement. In spite of the failure to reach Allied agreement, Clay wanted to end military government responsibilities in this area and sought a *Länderrat*-promulgated German law for the American Zone. The ministers-president met on 7 October 1947 and could not agree on a restitution law, mainly because of doubts about a law at the zonal level. They referred the matter to a parliamentary advisory council.[85] This council urged a German-wide law, an easing of liability for German restitutors, and a weakening of successor organizations, which were to inherit heirless property. This point was to preclude excessive concentration of economic power by a single organization. When OMGUS rejected the proposed modifications, the *Länderrat* refused to promulgate a law.[86]

General Clay, understanding the reluctance of the *Länderrat* to enact a restitution law limited to the American Zone, issued Military Government Law No. 59 on 10 November 1947.[87] This was designed to provide for restitution of identifiable property confiscated by the Nazis within Germany between 1933 and 1945. German and non-German citizens could submit claims to the Central Filing Agency at Bad Neuheim no later than 31 December 1948. Germans who had wrongfully taken possessions from their fellow citizens or foreigners living in Germany were required to file reports with the Central Filing Agency no later than 14 May 1948. This

---

[83] Gen. Lucius Clay, Cablegram (CC-8351) on German reaction to the proposed Restitution Law, 12 March 1947, File "Cables, January–September 1947," General Records, Cables Relating to Reparations and Restitution, 1945–8, Records of the Reparations and Restitution Branch, Records of the Branch Headquarters, RG 260.

[84] Ibid.

[85] Cablegram (CO 154) from the Regional Government Coordinator's Office to the Legal Division on the proposed Restitution Law, 11 October 1947, File "Cables, January–September 1947," General Records, Cables Relating to Reparations and Restitution, 1945–8, Records of the Reparations and Restitution Branch, Records of Branch Headquarters, RG 260.

[86] Cablegram (CO 216) from the Regional Government Coordinator's Office to OMGUS on the proposed Restitution Law, 12 December 1947, File "Incoming Cables, June–December 1947," General Records, Cables Relating to Reparations and Restitution, 1945–8, Records of the Reparations and Restitution Branch, Records of Branch Headquarters, RG 260.

[87] Gen. Lucius Clay, Cablegram (CC-2120) on the Restitution Law, 29 October 1947, File "Outgoing Cables, June–December 1947," General Records, Cables Relating to Reparations and Restitution, 1945–8, Records of the Reparations and Restitution Branch, Records of Branch Headquarters, RG 260.

deadline was later extended to 14 August 1948.[88] The Central Filing Agency matched claims and reports and referred them to the appropriate restitution agency for amicable settlement, if possible. If an amicable settlement was not reached by the restitution agency, which was a part of the German *Länd* government, then the case was referred to the Restitution Chamber of the local German court. German law and procedures were followed in these cases, with direct military government involvement limited to a U.S. Court of Restitution Appeal.[89] A similar apparatus was set up by the French on 10 November 1947; the British did not follow until 12 May 1949. The Russians did not establish internal restitution machinery.

By the end of October 1948, the Central Filing Agency had received 11,335 petitions, with petitions for heirless Jewish property yet to arrive. Slowly, the petitions were processed and, if accepted, forwarded to the restitution agencies for, hopefully, an amicable settlement. Clearly, years of work and litigation lay ahead.[90] Military Government Law No. 59 was supposed to complement the external restitution effort to foreign governments and thus end military government responsibility for property control. Even though a completely accurate figure is not available, reports indicate that more than 1,730,000 cultural objects were returned to German owners through either the program to reactivate museums, archives, and libraries or Military Government Law No. 59.[91] The major problem with the internal restitution law was Jewish reaction to its procedures and the ultimate disposition of heirless Jewish property. This difficult question reflected the agony of the Jewish experience under the Nazis.

[88] Louis E. Pease, "After the Holocaust: West Germany and Material Reparations to the Jews – From the Allied Occupation to the Luxembourg Agreements," (Ph.D. dissertation, Florida State University, 1976), p. 155.

[89] Lt. Col. G. H. Garde, "Restitution of Identifiable Property, 2 August 1948," File "Board of Review – Law Reg. to Law 59-Art. 69," Records of the Property Control and External Assets Branch, Records of the Section Chief, 1945–8, RG 260.

[90] "Report on Restitution Program under Military Government Law No. 59, 2 December 1948," File "Law 59 – Progress Report, November 1948," General Records, 1944–50, Records of the Property Division, Records of the Office of the Director, Records of the . Secretarial Section, RG 260.

[91] Lester K. Born, "Final Report, Monuments, Fine Arts and Archives Section, 30 December 1948," File "Final Reports – Reparations and Restitution," Reports and Related Records Re: Restitution, 1945–50, Records of the Reparations and Restitution Branch, RG 260.

# 8

## A Special Concern

### *The Jewish Inheritance*

No doubt the most difficult problems in the American restitution effort related to the disposition of looted Jewish property, much of which was heirless. The aftereffects of the Jewish agony created political, diplomatic, and administrative difficulties that have yet to be completely resolved. The struggles to resolve this matter involved not only the Occupying Powers but also the remnants of Jewish communities in Europe and Jews around the world, particularly in the United States and Palestine. To a very great extent, the divisions that arose after the war reflected earlier, differing reactions to the Nazis and to the Holocaust.

### The Jewish Reaction

The coming of the Nazi regime exposed fissures in German Jewry and elsewhere. Two conflicting stances toward the Nazis emerged from 1933 onward. Many German Jews who were assimilated into the broader German society sought to ensure the community's existence in Germany. The leaders of the Jewish community fought to maintain economic rights and the community's viability. Those outside Germany, Jews and non-Jews alike, who supported this position sought to pressure the Nazis and modify their behavior through economic and political boycotts.[1]

Other Jews, particularly the Zionists, saw the future of the Jewish people in a new homeland in Palestine. The Zionists urged emigration to Palestine as the answer to the dilemma in Germany. The Zionists negotiated with Nazi leaders to permit emigration and set up two organizations to further the cause, Youth Aliyah and the Central Office of the Jewish Agency for the Settlement of the Jews in Germany in Palestine.[2] Though the number of

---

[1] Leni Yahil, *The Holocaust: The Fate of European Jewry* (New York and Oxford: Oxford University Press, 1990), pp. 75–6, 91, 99.
[2] Ibid.

emigrants grew as the situation deteriorated in the late 1930s, no effective unified German Jewish response to the Nazis emerged. Historian Leni Yahil found similar disarray among the Jews outside Germany: "Having almost no practical or even spiritual common ground or unified leadership, the Jewish people reacted with limited, often haphazard and counterproductive measures."[3]

By the time the Jews of occupied Europe realized in 1941 the fate that awaited them, it was too late to take effective action. Flight was now impossible; the limited resistance that took place did nothing to derail the Holocaust; and cooperation with the authorities was equally futile. The Jews in the United States were horrified by Hitler and his regime but were not able to forge a consistent and independent position as a community. American Jewish leaders, according to Holocaust historian Raoul Hilberg, were paralyzed by the reality of the Holocaust.[4] Efforts to prod the Roosevelt administration into taking effective action against the machinery of the Holocaust were unavailing. American Jews accepted War Department policy, stated in February 1944, that "It is not contemplated that units of the armed forces will be employed for the purpose of rescuing victims of enemy oppression unless such rescues are the direct results of military operations conducted with the objective of defeating the armed forces of the enemy."[5] There would be no air attacks on the killing centers or the rail lines that carried the victims.[6] At the root of it all was a fundamental divide over the "Jewish Question": For the Allies, it was a humanitarian issue, involving a scattered people with no formal international standing, and for the Nazis, it was a political and strategic issue requiring the extreme solution of annihilation.[7]

## A New Vision

American Jews were concerned in the early 1930s with events at home as well as in Germany. Among the many expressions of concern, one in particular eventually bore fruit in the reconstruction of the Jewish cultural heritage. Shortly after Hitler came to power in early 1933, a small group of Jewish intellectuals in New York began to meet to discuss how the Nazi lies about the Jews could be countered. Led by Morris Raphael Cohen, a philosophy professor at City College, and Salo W. Baron, professor of Jewish history, literature, and institutions at Columbia University, the ten to twelve intellectuals met often over a two- or three-year period to decide on a course of

---

[3] Ibid., p. 80.
[4] Raoul Hilberg, *The Destruction of the European Jews* (Chicago: Quadrangle Books, 1967), p. 719.
[5] Yahil, *The Fate of European Jewry*, p. 639.
[6] Hilberg, *The Destruction of the European Jews*, p. 723.
[7] Yahil, *The Fate of European Jewry*, p. 548.

action.[8] One result of the discussions was the establishment of the Conference on Jewish Relations (CJR) in 1936. Albert Einstein presided over the founding dinner, and Cohen was elected president.[9] At Baron's behest, the conference supported the issuance of a journal, which first appeared in January 1939. As Baron, the journal's first editor recalled, "We needed a journal badly . . . to study the position of the Jews in the modern world . . . [and] establish the real history and the real demography of the Jews."[10] Alarmed by rising American anti-Semitism, Morris Cohen noted that "With the growing complexity and urgency of these problems in the United States as well as in the world at large, accurate and verifiable information in this field has become a matter of vital necessity."[11]

As the war drew nearer, Salo Baron came increasingly to public attention as a speaker and lecturer. Forty-five years old in 1940, Baron was near the peak of his intellectual powers. Born in Austrian Galicia (now Poland), Baron had a brilliant mind and, by the mid-1920s, had earned three doctoral degrees. He emigrated in the late 1920s, among the first in what would be a stream of Jewish scholars who emigrated to the United States and Palestine.[12] A stout man who enjoyed both his meals and strenuous walking, Baron was a confident and somewhat dominating individual. A well-known workaholic, Baron had published his most well-known scholarly work in 1937, *A Social and Religious History of the Jews*.[13] During the war and for decades afterward, Baron devoted himself to the cause of recovering the Jewish cultural and intellectual heritage. Like many others, he focused his hopes on the new Jewish homeland in Palestine and on the Jewish diaspora, particularly in the United States. Again, like many others, Baron was late in realizing the dimensions of the Holocaust. He feared for the family he left behind in Europe, and far into the war he thought the Nazi war effort would distract them from persecuting the Jews.[14]

Early in the war, before the United States entered the conflict, Baron and other leaders recognized the great dislocation and disruption European Jewish communities faced. In 1940, in the *Jewish Forum* and in the *Contemporary Jewish Record*, Baron argued for the need to reconstruct Jewish communities in Europe after the war. He also argued for the necessity to use

---

[8] Grace Cohen Grossman, oral history interview with Salo W. Baron, 3 July 1988, Skirball Cultural Center, Los Angeles, California.

[9] Ibid. According to Baron, several meetings of intellectuals were held between 1933 and 1936 to discuss creating a Jewish journal. Baron noted that the meeting, which Einstein presided over, occurred in 1936.

[10] Ibid.

[11] Robert Liberles, *Salo Wittmayer Baron: Architect of Jewish History* (New York and London: New York University Press, 1995), p. 225.

[12] Ibid., pp. 25, 52.

[13] Ibid., pp. 5–6, 186–8.

[14] Ibid., p. 279.

some property from destroyed communities to sustain developing Jewish settlements in Palestine. As the war went on, the depth and extent of destruction became ever more apparent. Restitution and reconstruction for Jewish victims of the Nazis were an urgent matter for Jewish leaders. In November 1944, for example, the Board of Deputies for British Jews called for a Jewish Trusteeship for each country freed from Nazi or Axis control. The trustees would represent all interests in restitution or compensation of Jews in cases where the owners or their heirs could not be found or the Jewish communities or other bodies could not be restored.[15]

In this concept, the trustees would be recognized as the "heirs and successors of the Jews who left no other heirs and would be authorized to use the property of exterminated or vanished Jewish families for general Jewish needs, or for Jewish reconstruction and settlement."[16] Jewish leaders among the United Nations argued that heirless property should not revert to the local government, as was customary under international law, because many of these governments had committed crimes against the Jews. The Jewish situation was unique. As victims of mass murder, heirless property should not fall to the State, but to the Jewish people as a whole, who must be recognized as the surviving inheritors. Representatives of the Jewish people should then distribute all the transferred property. The question of who should represent the Jewish people elicited much discussion, but the concept drew strong support from Jews in the United States, Great Britain, and Palestine. Cecil Roth, a prominent leader in the British Jewish community and a noted historian, urged during the war that all heirless cultural property be placed in the custody of the Hebrew University in Jerusalem.[17] Others, particularly in the United States, backed the idea of creating a successor organization comprising representatives from major Jewish groups and interests. In the summer of 1944, the Conference on Jewish Relations established the Commission on European Jewish Cultural Reconstruction, under the leadership of Salo Baron, to join with similar groups in other countries, with the common aim of assisting in dispersing heirless Jewish cultural property recovered from the Nazis.

As the war in Europe was drawing to a close, Baron and other members of the commission realized the need to document Nazi plundering as a first step to restitution and reconstruction. After a Herculean eight-month effort, the commission's research staff, headed by a brilliant young émigré scholar, Hannah Arendt, published in 1946 a "Tentative List of Jewish Cultural

---

[15] "Jewish Trusteeship over Property of Exterminated Jews Demanded by the Board of Deputies, 8 November 1944," *JTA News*, File "Folder 320-Restitution of Property," Abraham G. Duker/Irving Dwork Papers, Office of Strategic Services, Research and Analysis Branch – Jewish Desk, RG 200.

[16] Ibid.

[17] Cecil Roth, "The Restoration of Jewish Libraries, Archives and Museums," *Contemporary Jewish Record* 8 (June 1944): 253.

Treasures in Axis-Occupied Countries" as a supplement to *Jewish Social Studies*.[18]

Salo Baron had obtained the position of research director for Arendt, another brilliant intellectual émigré. A German Jew with a doctorate in philosophy, Arendt had fled Germany in 1933, working with the Zionist Youth Aliyah organization in Paris to aid Jewish youth emigrating to Palestine. Arendt wanted "to do practical work, exclusively and only Jewish work."[19] This she was able to do after coming to New York and beginning work with Baron and the Commission for European Jewish Cultural Reconstruction. An intense woman with eyes her friend Mary McCarthy later described as "deep, dark, remote pools of inwardness,"[20] Arendt's research efforts on the "Tentative List" provided her first insights into the nature of the Nazi regime. This helped lead to her path-breaking work, *The Origins of Totalitarianism*.[21]

Arendt and her staff used the resources of the New York libraries, as well as the questionnaires filled out by hundreds of scholars who had fled the Nazis, to document the Jewish cultural treasures that had existed before the war. The staff realized that

In view of the wholesale destruction of Jewish life and property by the Nazis reconstruction of Jewish cultural institutions cannot possibly mean mechanical restoration in their original form or, in all cases, to their previous locations. The Commission intends, in collaboration with other agencies of good will, to devise if necessary some new forms better accommodated to the emergent patterns of postwar Europe. Ultimately it may also seek to help redistribute the Jewish cultural treasures in accordance with the new needs created by the new situation of world Jewry.[22]

Thus, Salo Baron and his colleagues began the arduous task of confronting and resolving the painful and complex issues involving heirless Jewish cultural property.

## Negotiating a Settlement

As the war in Europe drew to a close, Salo Baron and his colleagues, particularly Columbia Law School professor Jerome Michael, began a series of

---

[18] "Tentative List of Jewish Cultural Treasures in Axis-Occupied Countries," *Supplement to Jewish Social Studies* 8 (1946): 6. Published subsequently were "Tentative List of Jewish Periodicals in Axis-Occupied Countries," *Supplement to Jewish Social Studies* 9 (1947), and "Addenda and Corrigenda to Tentative List of Jewish Cultural Treasures in Axis-Occupied Countries," *Supplement to Jewish Social Studies* 10 (1948).

[19] Derwent May, "Hannah Arendt," in *Lives of Modern Women*, edited by Emma Tennant (Hammondsworth, England: Penguin Books, 1986), pp. 38–42.

[20] Ibid., p. 17.

[21] Elizabeth Young-Buehl, *Hannah Arendt: For Love of the World* (New Haven, Conn.: Yale University Press, 1982), pp. 187–8.

[22] Ibid.

intense negotiations with the State Department over the fate of Jewish cultural property. Michael, a member of the New York bar, a former city attorney in Athens, Georgia, and special assistant to the U.S. attorney general,
provided invaluable assistance during the negotiations.[23] The three-way discussions between the Jewish organizations represented on the CJR, the State
and War departments, and OMGUS would last until February 1949, almost
the end of U.S. military occupation.

During 1945 and 1946, Baron and Michael frequently traveled from New
York to Washington at their own expense to prod the government into focusing on the urgent Jewish situation.[24] Michael summarized the Jewish position
in two lengthy memoranda he sent to Assistant Secretary of State General
John H. Hilldring in the summer of 1946 (a similar version was also sent to
Luther Evans, the Librarian of Congress). In the first, dated 5 June, Michael
presented a "plan for the preservation and ultimate disposition of the Jewish
religious and cultural treasures which are still to be found in Germany and
Austria."[25] On behalf of the CJR, Michael expressed concern for the huge
caches of materials found by the American Army at the end of the war and
stored at Offenbach. But the greater concern involved their ultimate disposition.[26] Michael argued that they must be disposed of so "they can never
again be misused to make war upon the Jews, by processes of distortion and
falsification, and thus to disturb the tranquility of the world."[27] Michael
clearly stated: "This implies that to the extent that they exceed the religious
and cultural needs of the Jews who may continue to reside in the countries
of their origin, they must be removed therefrom."[28] In passionate, almost
tender terms, Michael urged: "These objects must, in the second place, be
so disposed of that they can be used, as the Jews who created them and the
Jews who throughout the centuries lovingly collected and cared for them
intended that they should be used, to serve the spiritual and religious needs
of European Jews, of the Jewish people as a whole, and of all mankind."[29]

To Baron, Michael, and their colleagues on the CJR, the ravages of the
Holocaust left no doubt that the future centers of Jewish cultural and spiritual
life would be in Palestine and the United States. Hence, they argued for
restitution to individual owners, or heirs, and surviving communities only in
proportion "to the prospective religious and cultural needs of the community

---

[23] Edward M. M. Warburg to the Secretary of State, 13 November 1947, 1945–9 Decimal File
(740.00119EW/11-1347), RG 59.
[24] Baron oral history interview, 3 July 1988.
[25] Ephraim Fischoff to Dr. John Slawson, 20 August 1946, Records Concerning Restitution,
Records of the American Jewish Committee, New York, NY. Included are a copy of the
5 June letter from Jerome Michael to John Hilldring and a draft of a subsequent letter to be
sent by Michael.
[26] Ibid.
[27] Ibid.
[28] Ibid.
[29] Ibid.

and its capacity to retain, to care for, and to use them for the religious and cultural purposes for which they were intended."[30] Heirless property or property in excess of capacity to preserve and use should be distributed among Jewish communities in Europe, Palestine, America, and elsewhere.[31]

To further these goals, Michael sought Hilldring's support in designating the United States as the official trustee in its zone of all Jewish cultural treasures for their former owners and for the Jewish people. He also raised the possibility of the Occupying Powers turning over this responsibility to a Jewish trustee agency. In any event, Michael argued for the creation of an advisory board to assist OMGUS authorities in the execution of the trustee function. Consisting of nominees from the CJR, the Hebrew University, and the Synagogue Council of America, the board could provide specialized expertise about the objects themselves and the religious and cultural needs of the Jewish people.[32] In closing, Michael protested against an OMGUS announcement of 27 April 1946, proposed to return the control of "property which was the subject of . . . wrongful acts of confiscation, dispossession, or spoiliation" to the German *Land* governments for restitution responsibility.[33] As Michael put it, "We protest as emphatically as we can against the inclusion of Jewish religious and cultural objects in this program. To entrust the disposition of these objects to the German Länder governments or other German agencies is to desecrate them and gratuitously to offend deeply the Jewish people."[34]

This letter began a series of intense discussions among American officials in the State and War departments and OMGUS and between Michael, Baron, and members of Hilldring's staff. Though sympathetic from the beginning, American officials had several concerns. The State Department was not inclined to a board of advisors but rather turning the whole trusteeship responsibility over to a Jewish agency. However, American officials, particularly General Clay, were concerned that the interests of Jews remaining in Europe, particularly in Central Europe, be represented in any Jewish trusteeship body. Further, Clay and others doubted that a private organization had the standing under international law and Allied Control Authority agreements to determine restitution to sovereign governments.[35]

[30] Ibid.
[31] Ibid.
[32] Ibid.
[33] Ibid.
[34] Ibid.
[35] War Department Cablegram (WX94368) on disposition of Jewish religious and cultural treasures found in Germany and Austria, 15 July 1946, File "400c-Fine Arts," Classified General Correspondence, 1945–9, 1946 (400c–500), RG 84; see also Memorandum of Conversation, "Jewish Cultural Treasures in Germany and Austria: Comments on One Phase of the Proposal for an International Jewish Trustee Corporation Submitted by the Commission on European Jewish Cultural Reconstruction, 24 September 1946," File "Proposed International Jewish Trustee Corporation," Records Maintained by the Fine Arts and Monuments

After a series of meetings in Washington, Michael submitted a revised proposal on 26 August, that proposed that a Jewish corporation, which included European Jewish interests, assume the trusteeship function. This, in part, met U.S. concerns. However, from the American perspective the need to get Allied and international acceptance of the scheme remained, though Michael acknowledged that the United States would have to honor existing international arrangements requiring restitution. A new factor introduced by Michael was the demand that the proposed new trusteeship organization should "[a]scertain what Hebraica and Judaica and what other Jewish religious or cultural objects are owned by or in possession of German and Austrian state, municipal and other publicly owned or maintained libraries, archives, museums and similar institutions in the American Zone of Occupation, whenever and however they were acquired by such institutions."[36] As an earlier draft of this letter revealed, Michael and his colleagues had in mind that lost Jewish cultural treasures should be replaced by "comparable objects of like value" from German and Austrian collections.[37] Adamantly opposed to restitution-in-kind when proposed by the French or the Soviets, American authorities were no less opposed when it came from the Jewish community. In fact, as Salo Baron later explained, the Jewish demand really included monetary reparations for those objects for which comparable items did not exist. This was even more unacceptable to the United States.[38] Clay and his colleagues feared what they felt could become legalized looting of German cultural property acquired prior to the Nazi accession to power. This would cause the United States grave problems in Germany and before the court of world opinion.[39]

Advisor, 1945–61, RG 59; Memorandum of Conversation, "Restitution of Jewish Cultural Treasures from and to the Various Countries of Europe, and the Role of the Proposed International Jewish Trustee Corporation, 14 November 1946, File "Proposed International Jewish Trustee Corporation," Records Maintained by the Fine Arts and Monuments Advisor, 1945–61 RG 59; "Plan for Preservation and Ultimate Disposition of Jewish Treasures in Germany – Summary Sheet (000.4), 25 September 1946, File "000.4, 13 June 1946–31 May 1947," RG165, Records of the Civil Affairs Division, General Records, Classified General Correspondence, 1943–July 1949, 11 June 1946–7 segment, National Archives at College Park, Maryland; Lucius D. Clay, Cablegram (CC-6925) on restitution of heirless Jewish property, 15 June 1946, File "Offenbach Archival Depot, Secret," Records of the Property Division, Central Collecting Points, General Records of the Wiesbaden Central Collecting Point, 1945–52, RG 260.

36 Ephraim Fischoff to Dr. John Slawson, 20 August 1946, Records Concerning Restitution, Records of the American Jewish Committee; Jerome Michael to John H. Hilldring, 26 August 1946, 1945–9 Decimal File (740.00119EW/8-2646), RG 59.

37 Ibid.

38 Salo Baron to Nahum Goldman, 21 March 1952, File "JCR, 1951–June 1954," Papers of Salo W. Baron (M580), Department of Special Collections, Stanford University, Palo Alto, California.

39 Michael J. Kurtz, *Nazi Contraband: American Policy on the Return of European Cultural Treasures, 1945–1955* (New York and London: Garland, 1985), pp. 203–6.

As a signal of General Clay's interest in the Jewish restitution issue and his desire to wrap up the entire restitution effort, Baron, Michael, and other colleagues met with Clay and his legal advisor on Jewish affairs, Max Lowenthal, in New York City on 1 December 1946. In a lengthy and cordial session, participants explored the shape of the restitution law that Clay was drafting for consideration by the German *Länderrat* in the U.S. Zone and hopefully by the Allied Control Council for all Germany. Clay recognized that some form of reporting requirement was needed for looted property still in German hands, though he feared an extensive campaign to uncover loot would alienate the Germans and flood OMGUS with another wave of cultural property to manage. All parties understood the need for representation of European Jews in any successor organization. The needs, and often competing interests, of surviving Jewish communities were frankly explored. Clay and other American officials, although supportive of turning over heirless or unclaimed Jewish cultural property to a successor organization, were reluctant to turn over all cultural property to the successor organization for its determination of what the surviving communities needed and could use. Even though Clay clearly understood the rationale advanced by Michael and Baron, he also realized that this aspect of the proposal was fraught with emotion and potential for conflict.[40] Clay also stressed that, while he understood the unique Jewish situation, moving outside government-to-government restitution machinery required Allied consent. Even though the Jewish participants understood the government view, they insisted that the communities in Germany and in countries such as Poland, with much reduced Jewish populations and strongly anti-Semitic, should receive only what was needed.[41] The remainder should be distributed to places where the Jewish heritage thrived.

Much of 1947 was spent with Clay trying to obtain German and Allied cooperation in promulgating a restitution law that would settle the issue of internal loot and heirless property. Success eluded him. The Germans insisted that German courts and agencies administer the law, a position unacceptable to Jews and other Nazi victims. Also, the Germans fought against any widespread, intrusive efforts to locate loot still in private hands.[42] Their insistence that any law must apply to all German territory meant Clay could not even get agreement in the U.S. Zone for a law. His efforts with the Allies were similarly unavailing. The British and French were inclined to turn all

[40] Jerome Michael to Lucius D. Clay, 17 October 1947, File "Jewish Cultural Reconstruction, Inc. and Restitution Committee," Papers of Salo W. Baron (M580); John H. Hilldring to Jerome Michael, undated, File "Jewish Cultural Reconstruction, Inc. and Restitution Committee," Papers of Salo W. Baron (M580).

[41] Ibid.

[42] Gen. Lucius D. Clay, Cablegram (CC-7532) on proposed restitution law, 2 January 1947, File "Cables – Permanent Outgoing, 1947," Records of the Reparations and Restitution Branch, Cables Relating to Reparations and Restitution, 1945–8, RG 260.

restitution matters over to the Germans, and the Soviets had no interest in the issue at all. No foreign restitution missions were admitted to the Soviet Zone, and no returns took place for internal loot or German-owned property. To the Soviets, all cultural property in their zone was the legitimate target of the Trophy Commission.[43]

Faced with diplomatic stalemate and the need to conclude the restitution program, Clay issued on his authority Military Government Law No. 59 in November 1947. The law contained several key compromises. First, though the Germans were required to report property falling under the terms of the law, items did not have to be turned in unless held by a suspected war criminal.[44] Jews and other victims were hardly mollified by the last provision, and in the final analysis little was reported. But OMGUS avoided alienating Germans or receiving a new flood of cultural property to manage. Though the law established German restitution agencies, they were under OMGUS supervision, another compromise that eased Jewish concerns to some extent.[45] Though Military Government Law No. 59 recognized successors in interest to heirless property, there was no specific successor recognized for heirless Jewish property. An internal U.S. government debate broke out when the Department of the Army (formerly the War Department) turned from its earlier stance supporting a Jewish trustee corporation to advocating a successor organization recognized by the German legal system.[46]

General Clay realized that he and the State Department had made a commitment to the Jewish successor organization concept, and with a 31 December 1948 deadline for filing claims under Law No. 59 looming ahead, the issue of heirless Jewish property had to be settled. After all, the reality was that 95 percent of heirless property was Jewish![47] After getting the Army Department's acquiescence, Clay issued Regulation 3 to Law No. 59 on 23 June 1948, establishing application procedures for charitable or nonprofit organizations desiring appointment as a successor organization.[48] Specifically, the regulation recognized the Jewish Restitution Successor

---

43 Brigadier C. F. C. Spedding to Col. John Allen, 20 May 1948, File "Correspondence – May 1948," Records of the Reparations and Restitution Branch, Records of the Restitution Section, Correspondence and Related Records, 1946–9, RG 260.

44 Col. John Allen, "Brief Report of the Restitution Branch for March 1948, 8 April 1948," Records of the Reparations and Restitution Branch, Records of the Restitution Section, Monthly Restitution Reports, June 1946–October 1948, RG 260.

45 Ibid.

46 Gen. Daniel Noce, Cablegram (WX-95426) on successor organizations, 31 January 1948, Personal Papers of Gen. Lucius Clay, RG 200.

47 Gen. Lucius Clay, Cablegram (CC-3127) on successor organizations, 6 February 1948, Personal Papers of Gen. Lucius Clay, RG 200.

48 Lt. Col. G. H. Garde, "Appointment of a Successor Organization, 23 June 1948," File "Implementing Regulation No. 3 Successor Organizations," Records of the Property Division, Property Control and External Assets Branch, Financial Records, RG 260; *Encyclopedia Judaica*, 1971 ed., s.v. "Jewish Restitution Successor Organization."

Organization (JRSO) as the successor body for heirless Jewish property covered by Law No. 59.[49] Incorporated in 1947 in New York State as the Jewish Restitution Commission, the JRSO could file claims for all heirless Jewish property, cultural and noncultural. Because it contained representation from Jewish communities in the United States, Palestine, and Europe, including the Central Committee of Liberated Jews in Germany, Clay's fears on this account were eased.[50]

Salo Baron, Jerome Michael, and the CJR had also created a corporation under New York laws in 1947 in preparation for the issuance of the restitution law. Jewish Cultural Reconstruction, Inc., formed in April 1947, became a member organization of the JRSO and eventually its cultural agent. The JRSO and its leaders, such as Saul Kagan and Benjamin Ferencz, provided the critical financial and logistical support that the JCR would need.[51] With Baron as president and Michael chairman of the board of directors, JCR membership initially included the American Jewish Committee, the American Jewish Conference, the American Jewish Joint Distribution Committee, the Board of Deputies of British Jews, the CJR, the Council for Protection of Rights and Interests of Jews from Germany, the Hebrew University, the Jewish Agency for Palestine, the Synagogue Council of America, and the World Jewish Congress. Soon representatives of French and German Jewry were included.

Hailed, at least initially, by some German Jewish leaders, the JRSO and the JCR were poised for action.[52] Yet, even though the JRSO began its work in June 1948 with noncultural property, the sensitive area of cultural treasures required final resolution. Baron and his colleagues recognized that succeeding as trustee to all Jewish cultural property was not acceptable to the American government. The agreement finally reached in February 1949 provided for the transfer to JCR of "unidentifiable" cultural properties held by OMGUS, which included Jewish books, archives, documents, Jewish religious and ritual objects, Jewish paintings and furnishings, and any other Jewish cultural properties that JCR and OMGUS would agree to transfer.[53]

In receiving these objects, the JCR was to act as "trustee . . . for the Jewish people and in distributing it to such public or quasi-public religious, cultural, or educational institutions as it sees fit to be used in the interest of perpetuating Jewish art and culture."[54] Excluded from this agreement were

---

[49] Ibid.

[50] Ibid.

[51] *Encyclopedia Judaica*, 1971 ed., s.v. "Jewish Cultural Restitution."

[52] Louis E. Levinthal to the Department of State, 29 November 1947, 1945–9 Decimal File (740.00119EW/11-2947), RG 59.

[53] Owen R. McJunkins, Memorandum of Agreement, "Jewish Cultural Property, 15 February 1949," File "Restitution Monthly Reports," Records of the Reparations and Restitution Branch, Reports and Related Records Re: Restitution, 1945–50, RG 260.

[54] Ibid.

the properties of surviving individuals and communities. The JCR would have to deal on a case-by-case basis with the survivors on any potential redistribution of treasures. Neither JRSO nor JCR had international standing as Law No. 59 was purely an OMGUS issuance. Hence, there could be no direct dealing with the Soviet Union, Poland, or other countries. Eastern European countries would particularly object to the work of the successor organizations, though the United States would counter this by defending the unique Jewish position and noting that the Paris Conference on Reparations had called for compensation for nonrepatriable victims of German actions.[55]

The February 1949 agreement held JCR responsible for keeping collections intact until any claims were settled and to meet a stiff 30 May 1949 deadline for cleaning out the Depot at Offenbach. As already noted, Jewish positions on restitution-in-kind, further looting investigations, and German exclusion from restitution administration were either rejected or met with compromise. The end of the occupation, the imperatives of the Cold War, and the need to keep German goodwill all mitigated against Jewish positions. Yet the recognition of JRSO and JCR were significant events. Only the United States recognized a vibrant successor organization and supported it. OMGUS did retain final responsibility for restitution and worked in close harmony with the JRSO and JCR. The British and French efforts lagged further behind and were limited at best. The Soviets, of course, did nothing. Law No. 59 meant that the unclaimed Jewish holdings at Offenbach and the other collecting points would remain in Jewish hands. The heroic efforts that ensued greatly contributed to the mission of preserving Jewish cultural heritage.

## JCR at Work

With an agreement finally in hand, the JCR Board of Directors moved to create a small staff of experts to work in Germany under the guidance of Executive Secretary Joshua Starr and his successor, Hannah Arendt. For the critical position of field director in Europe, the JCR Board selected Dr. Bernard Heller, a distinguished rabbi, educator, and author.[56] Assisting Heller with the mammoth task of sorting through some 250,000 heirless, unclaimed books and manuscripts at the Offenbach Depot was Schlomo Shunami, representative of the Hebrew University in Jerusalem, and Dr. Ernest Lowenthal, a founding member of the Anglo-Jewish Committee on Restoration

---

55  Louis E. Pease, "After the Holocaust West Germany and Material Reparations to the Jews –
    From the Allied Occupation to the Luxembourg Agreements" (Ph.D. dissertation, Florida
    State University, 1976), p. 131.
56  Minutes of Special Meeting of JCR Board of Directors, 11 January 1949, File "923a – Jewish
    Cultural Reconstruction," Records of the Jewish Restitution Successor Organization, Central
    Archives for the History of the Jewish People, Jerusalem, Israel.

of Continental Jewish Museums, Libraries, and Archives.[57] Dr. Mordechai Narkiss from the Bezalel Museum in Jerusalem focused on the textile materials and silver ceremonial objects stored at the Wiesbaden Collecting Point, as well as on helping with the classification and sorting of the Offenbach books. While the JCR staff in Germany prepared to begin work, the JCR Board – aided by an advisory committee with experts such as Dr. Alexander Marx of the Jewish Theological Seminary in New York, Dr. Guido Schoenberger, and Rabbi I. Edward Kiev – wrestled with the difficult but key issue of where to distribute the books.

After difficult discussions, the board and its advisory committee agreed on a set of priorities for distribution and the formula for allocation. First priority was assigned to the Jewish National and University Library in Israel, which was entitled to single copies of titles that it currently lacked. Second priority went to surviving Jewish communities in western Germany. These communities were to receive allocations sufficient for their current use. This decision, as we will find, caused serious conflicts with Jewish survivors in Europe. As a third priority, wherever possible, European institutions outside Germany subsidized by the American Jewish Joint Distribution Committee were to receive "proper consideration."[58] Finally, allocations to any other institutions would be determined by the JCR Board after analyzing the returns from questionnaires distributed by the organization.[59]

The board also adopted four restitution procedures designed to ensure that the beneficiary institutions were held accountable for the handling of the restituted books: (1) Each receiving institution was to agree in advance to place any duplicate titles at the disposal of the JCR; (2) JCR approval was required prior to the sale or disposal of any material received; (3) within six months of receipt, each institution had to furnish the JCR with an itemized receipt listing authors and short titles; and, (4) finally, for a period of two years after receipt, institutions had to return books for which claims were received from owners or heirs.[60] After intense discussion, the JCR board also decided on the formula for allocations. Forty percent of books was to go to Israel, with the National and University Library receiving the bulk; another 40 percent was sent to Jewish seminaries and schools in the United States; and the remainder went to Great Britain, South Africa, and other countries. Advisory groups in Israel and the United States ironed out contending claims from various institutions.[61] The allocation formula clearly showed that the constituent groups of the JCR put first priority to transferring heirless and

---

[57] Oscar Rabinowicz to Salo Baron, 14 October 1949, File "Jewish Cultural Reconstruction Inc., and Restitution Committee," Papers of Salo W. Baron (M580).

[58] Minutes of Special Meeting of JCR Board of Directors, 11 January 1949, File "923a – Jewish Cultural Reconstruction," Records of the Jewish Restitution Successor Organization.

[59] Ibid.

[60] Ibid.

[61] Hannah Arendt to Eli Rock, 1 September 1950, File "923c – Jewish Cultural Reconstruction," Records of the Jewish Restitution Successor Organization.

unclaimed property to the new Jewish homeland in Israel and to the site of the greatest Jewish presence: the United States. This formula was definitely in keeping with international Jewish sentiment that developed during the war. Although often resented in Europe, the formula did ensure that the most flourishing areas of Jewish life were sustained by the cultural remnants of the Holocaust.

With the allocation policy for books set, Heller and his colleagues rushed to complete the processing at Offenbach. They were finished in the unbelievable time of three months. By 31 May, all the books were on the way to their assigned destinations.[62] On the afternoon of 31 May at a small party arranged for all the workers, Jewish and non-Jewish, who had labored on the project, Bernard Heller expressed his feelings about the meaning of what had been accomplished, particularly the contribution of the German workers:

In the work which you have been engaged I see a deeper meaning. I do not merely wish to congratulate you for a task well performed. In your difficult and cooperative efforts to help the AMG return the looted books and Torah scrolls I perceive a desire on your part to undo – as far as was in your power – a great wrong. You have collaborated in the work of making *some* restitution to the bereaved Jewish people.[63]

Heller was surprised by the favorable reaction to his comments from both the former displaced persons aiding the project, and the German workers. This was despite the fact the two groups had kept away from each other during the hour-long ceremony.[64] Despite this incredible feat, there was still much more to do. Institutional collections, silver ceremonial objects, textile materials, and Torah scrolls required classification, allocation, and shipment by 31 August, the date the Wiesbaden Central Collecting Point was scheduled to close. Heller, Shunami, Lowenthal, and Narkiss feared that anything left after that date would be turned over to the Germans.[65] With this anxiety motivating them, the men worked frantically throughout the summer. Dr. Narkiss, for example, had to sift through the textile ritual objects item by item to decipher the writing and separate the valuable from the useless. More than ten thousand silver ceremonial objects were inventoried and placed into two categories: museum objects and ordinary items for synagogue use. To accomplish such a Herculean task, Narkiss worked seven days a week, ten to fourteen hours per day. By mid-July, the textile materials and the silver ceremonial objects were packed and ready for shipment.[66]

[62] Bernard Heller, "Field Report No. 8, 25 July 1949," File "923b – Jewish Cultural Reconstruction," Records of the Jewish Restitution Successor Organization.
[63] Ibid.
[64] Ibid.
[65] Ibid.
[66] Ibid.

The allocation formula for these items was somewhat similar to that used for the 250,000 books. Two hundred twelve cases were shipped, with eighty-seven cases of museum and synagogue material going to Israel and eighty-three cases of both categories shipped to the United States. Three cases of synagogue material went to Great Britain, three to South Africa, and eleven to the American Jewish Joint Distribution Committee in Paris for allocation to needy Jewish communities in Europe. Also, twenty-three cases of unusable silver fragments were sent to Britain for smelting.[67] These decisions aroused controversy. Oscar Rabinowicz wrote an irate protest to Salo Baron on behalf of the Committee on Restoration of Continental Jewish Museums, Libraries, and Archives.[68] The British committee registered an emphatic protest about not being informed in advance of the smelting of the "unusable" silver fragments.[69] This, in the opinion of the British committee, put them in a difficult position. Many people assumed that, because the smelting was done in Sheffield, the British committee must have authorized it. Further, and more important, some believed that in fact some of the items could have been repaired and used once more for their original purpose.[70]

Rabinowicz also complained about another task undertaken by the JCR staff in Germany: the allocation of unclaimed or heirless Jewish-owned art stored at the Munich Collecting Point.[71] Mordechai Narkiss worked on the project, as well as his Offenbach labors, during the pressured summer of 1949. He identified 125 paintings, 150 drawings and prints, 200 miniatures, and a number of wood-carved angels. The JCR Board and Advisory Committee agreed on an allocation formula similar to that used for the Offenbach books and the ceremonial objects: 40 percent for Israel, 40 percent for the United States, and 5 to 7 percent each for Britain, South Africa, Canada, and Argentina.[72] From the British perspective, this was an unjust formula. For of the countries receiving the art, "only we in Britain have suffered great damage and destruction at the hands of the enemy, and that accordingly our museums in this country have a claim for a higher share of the total of

---

[67] Mordechai Narkiss, "Two Reports on Ceremonial Objects, 19 June 1949, 10 July 1950," File "923b – Jewish Cultural Reconstruction," Records of the Jewish Restitution Successor Organization; Bernard Heller, "Field Report No. 8, 25 July 1949," Records of the Jewish Restitution Successor Organization.

[68] Oscar Rabinowicz to Salo Baron, 14 October 1949, File "Jewish Cultural Reconstruction Inc., and Restitution Committee," Papers of Salo W. Baron (M580).

[69] Ibid.

[70] Ibid.

[71] Ibid.

[72] Memorandum, "Paintings and Other Art Objects Turned Over to JRSO by Military Government, 14 March 1950," File "296a – Jewish Cultural Reconstruction," Records of the Jewish Restitution Successor Organization; Minutes of Advisory Committee Meeting, 19 September 1949, Skirball Cultural Center.

the museum objects to be distributed."[73] Though the JCR and the British committee agreed to exchange representatives to serve on their respective boards, the working relationship remained uneasy.

The collecting point at Wiesbaden still contained the so-called Baltic Collection, books from former German-Jewish institutions, and approximately twelve hundred rare volumes. With the approaching closure of the collecting points and OMGUS soon to be replaced by a high commissioner with oversight responsibility for the new Federal Republic that was emerging from the three western zones of occupation, clearly the American restitution effort would soon end. The JCR once again faced a deadline and what it perceived as the threat of German control over restitution. The Baltic Collection consisted of books and manuscripts looted, for the most part, from Jewish institutions and individuals during the Nazi occupation of Estonia, Latvia, and Lithuania. Few Jews remained in the area, and the situation was complicated by the fact that the United States refused to recognize the Soviet annexation of the Baltic republics. Given the pressure to terminate American occupation responsibilities, the State Department agreed to transfer the Baltic Collection to the JCR, with several provisos. The material had to be out of Wiesbaden by 31 August, and, because there were many identifiable items, the JCR had to maintain the collection intact for two years pending receipt and resolution of claims from heirs and owners.[74] The JCR shipped 12,418 items to Israel with the Mapu Library from Kovno given to the Hebrew University for trusteeship for two years, and the libraries of Kohel, Kovno, and the Slobodka Yeshiva were restituted to their former owners, who had relocated to Israel. The JCR sent 16,346 items to Paris, where they were stored by the American Jewish Joint Distribution Committee for the two-year waiting period.[75]

The American decision on the Baltic Collection stirred Soviet ire. Yet, the fact was that the Soviets and the communist regimes in Czechoslovakia and Poland were not turning over what Jewish property they located to the few survivors of the Holocaust. In Czechoslovakia, Jews had to prove "national trustworthiness," and in Poland those seeking restitution incurred considerable expenses for court fees, taxes, and lawyers' fees.[76] American action was influenced by the emerging Cold War stand-off and the unique Jewish situation. The sensitivity of the issue comes across with Gershom Scholem's complaint to Hannah Arendt about Bernard Heller's press interview noting

---

[73] Oscar Rabinowicz to Salo Baron, 14 October 1949, File "Jewish Cultural Reconstruction Inc., and Restitution Committee," Papers of Salo W. Baron (M580).

[74] Eli Rock to Moses A. Leavitt, "Conference with JCR, 27 July 1949," File "923b – Jewish Cultural Reconstruction," Records of the Jewish Restitution Successor Organization.

[75] Bernard Heller, "Field Report No. 9, September 1949," Records of the Jewish Restitution Successor Organization.

[76] Nehemiah Robinson, "Restitution of Jewish Property," *Congress Weekly* 10 (12 March 1948): 11–12.

the transfer of Baltic books to Israel. To Scholem, this could alert the Soviets and lead to claims for restitution that, because the Israeli diplomatic position was different from the American diplomatic stance on the Baltic States, would put Israel in an awkward position.[77]

To counter any criticism about its handling of the collection, the JCR board decided to publish in Jewish centers of learning throughout the world the names (approximately sixteen thousand) of owners identified in the collection.[78] Thus, owners or heirs could file claims within the stipulated two-year period. At the conclusion of the waiting period, the unclaimed items in the Baltic Collection were distributed along the lines previously followed. Israel received 40 percent, the Western Hemisphere received 40 percent, and the remaining 20 percent went to all other countries.[79] The board vote on this allocation was twelve in favor, five against, and one abstention. A departure from the usual consensus approach, the vote reflected tension between those who felt Israel should receive the entire collection, an idea originally favored by the board, and those who felt that library needs in Europe and America required a broader distribution.[80] Jewish communal needs far outstripped what had been saved from the devastation of the Holocaust.

Though work on the Baltic Collection was completed by 31 August, the overworked JCR team could not complete processing of the German-Jewish institutional collections and unclaimed or heirless privately owned books of Jewish origin by the deadline. In fact, the Wiesbaden Collecting Point would remain open until December 1950. The JCR, through the JRSO, received title to these collections and again faced the task of sorting, classifying, and shipping. The most important German-Jewish institutional library collections included the Hermann Cohen collection, formerly the property of the Jewish community in Frankfurt, the Jewish Theological Seminary at Breslau, and the Berlin Gemeinden. In view of the fact that the Cohen Collection consisted primarily of books with non-Jewish content – philosophy and Christian theology for the most part – the JCR board and its advisory committee decided to assign the collection to the Hebrew University in Jerusalem.[81] This followed board policy that books or collections of non-Jewish content should be allocated only to Jewish libraries. Non-Jewish libraries would only receive offers of Judaica. The other institutional collections – as well as those

---

[77] Gershom Scholem to Hannah Arendt, 30 April 1950, File "Jewish Cultural Reconstruction [JCR] – Correspondence and Memoranda 1950–51," Papers of Salo W. Baron (M580).

[78] Minutes of Special Meeting of JCR Board of Directors, 19 December 1949, File "923b – Jewish Cultural Reconstruction," Records of the Jewish Successor Restitution Organization.

[79] Memorandum, "Mail Vote on the Baltic Collection and the Frankfurt Ceremonial Objects, 11 July 1951," File "Jewish Cultural Reconstruction to December 1951," Papers of Salo W. Baron (M580).

[80] Memorandum, "Disposition of the Baltic Collection, 12 June 1951," Papers of Salo W. Baron (M580).

[81] Minutes of Advisory Board Meeting, 19 September 1949, Skirball Cultural Center.

privately owned books of Jewish origins determined to have no claimants or identifiable heirs, and the so-called twelve hundred rare books – were also allocated in accordance with the board's policy.

Determining that the privately owned books had no owners or heirs caused a particular headache for the JCR. In the rush to clean up its occupation duties, U.S. military government officials insisted that the JCR take title to items that potentially had owners. Reluctantly, the JCR agreed. As with the Baltic Collection, the JCR board knew that steps must be taken to protect the organization against future criticism or claims. So, the JCR made strenuous efforts to publicize the names of owners who had six or more books in JCR custody.[82] Only after a waiting period similar to that made for the Baltic Collection could distribution along the usual lines take place.

Though the JCR experienced some conflict with its British counterpart, and at times with OMGUS, the most serious problems arose in connection with the surviving German-Jewish communities. Hannah Arendt, who became JCR executive secretary after Joshua Starr resigned in 1949, made several trips to Europe in an attempt to forge a positive relationship. She found that the surviving communities, debilitated and with few members or resources, could not preserve or use cultural treasures that were deteriorating at an alarming rate. She also found that in such chaotic and impoverished conditions, communal property could become private property. Even more disturbing, German municipal authorities would turn over any Jewish property they found, no matter what its nature or former owner, to local Jewish community leaders, thus leaving the JCR no option other than tedious and difficult negotiations on a community-by-community basis.[83]

For example, the conflict between JRSO/JCR and the Frankfurt community over 450 ceremonial objects from the former Jewish Museum in Frankfurt clearly revealed the dilemma. At first, the Frankfurt community had promised not to contest the claim brought by JRSO/JCR to the items. Then it gained access to some items and turned over others to the municipality of Frankfurt. After much negotiating, the JCR did obtain the collection, though controversy was not at an end.[84] Considering that this was a problem in the American Zone, which had the only robust successor apparatus in place, the situation must have been even more problematic in the other zones.

Many members of the JCR board and the advisory committee believed that the Bezalel Museum had received more than its fair share when the ceremonial objects at Wiesbaden were distributed. Members thought that "the

82 Minutes of Special Meeting of the JCR Board of Directors, 21 December 1950, File "Jewish Cultural Reconstruction – Minutes, Field Reports," Papers of Salo W. Baron (M580).
83 Hannah Arendt, "Report of My Mission to Germany, 12 April 1950," File "Jewish Cultural Reconstruction, Field Reports, 1949–50," Papers of Salo W. Baron (M580).
84 Minutes of Special Meeting of the JCR Board of Directors, 21 December 1950, Skirball Cultural Center.

diaspora countries are as much interested in these objects as is Israel, and that they should therefore be chiefly distributed among the museums outside of Palestine."[85] Those advocating a different procedure in this case argued that the number of visitors to the Jewish Museum in New York, for example, strengthened the justification for not sending the first choice to Israel. Further, the Bezalel was considered to have "at least ten times the number of really old Jewish ceremonial objects (i.e., dating back to the early eighteenth century or older) than the six American institutions together."[86] Mordechai Narkiss indignantly protested against the attitudes expressed by the JCR board and advisory committee members. He thought that the number of museum visitors should not be a determining factor in allocation, though, he tartly noted, the Bezalel had a larger number of visitors than the New York Museum. He disputed that his museum had a greater share of treasures than the American museums and, more to the point, that the Bezalel was the "central museum" of the Jewish people.[87] To Mordechai Narkiss, the JCR policy that Israel and Jerusalem should have priority ought to remain in place.

A divided JCR Board did finally decide to give American museums the first choice in the selection of museum objects from the Frankfurt Collection, with a total of 40 percent to the United States, 40 percent to Israel, and 20 percent to other countries, with special consideration given to Great Britain because of its wartime losses. Synagogue pieces not claimed by the Frankfurt Jewish community would go to Israeli congregations.[88] This decision came in the face of concerns from the Committee on Restoration of Continental Jewish Museums, Libraries, and Archives that the Frankfurt Collection ought to be retained as a unit and, they proposed, sent to the Tel Aviv Museum of Art.[89]

Other conflicts occurred where some German officials actively hindered Jewish restitution efforts. Few archives or manuscript material had been found at Offenbach or Wiesbaden. Much remained in state, municipal, and private hands. The situation in Bavaria proved particularly difficult. Dr. Philip Auerbach, the *Land* restitution chief, proved difficult and obstructive. After an initial period when he seemed favorable to the Jewish situation, Auerbach used the local Jewish community to dispute and block JCR claims, placed through the JRSO, for the Bavarian Jewish Community Archives. Using similar tactics, Auerbach blocked efforts to recover Jewish books

---

[85] Ibid.

[86] Memorandum, "Disposition of 18 Cases Containing About 450 Ceremonial Objects from Frankfurt, undated," File "Jewish Cultural Reconstruction to Dec. 1951," Papers of Salo W. Baron (M580).

[87] Mordechai Narkiss to Elishu Dobbin and Berl Locker, 22 August 1951, Papers of Salo W. Baron (M580).

[88] Memorandum, "Mail Vote on the Baltic Collection and the Frankfurt Ceremonial Objects, 11 July 1951," Papers of Salo W. Baron (M580).

[89] Oscar Rabinowicz to Hannah Arendt, 23 January 1951, Papers of Salo W. Baron (M580).

in the Munich Municipal Library and ceremonial objects from Augsburg. According to Meir Ben-Horin, on special assignment for the JCR in Europe, Auerbach "takes an offensive position vis-à-vis the 'international' Jewish organizations and prevents German authorities from cooperating with the Jewish organizations. He is also said to boast of being persona non grata with the American occupation forces."[90]

Similar problems occurred in other zones. The old archives of the Jewish community of Worms, in the French Zone, was discovered in the wall of the local cathedral. Municipal authorities refused to release the valuable materials, which included a thirteenth-century parchment prayer book used for festivals and eighteen charters from the sixteenth to the eighteenth centuries bearing the seals of German emperors. Only after years of negotiation and the intervention of Federal Chancellor Konrad Adenauer were the old archives transferred to Jerusalem, with copies of the archival materials made for Worms.[91]

In Hamburg, in the British Zone, another dispute over valuable archives dragged on for years. In this case, the local Jewish community had agreed to transfer the archives to Jerusalem, but German authorities resisted. The city regarded the records, which went back at least three hundred years, as public property because the city had thwarted the Gestapo from seizing the collection. Also, German officials claimed that the records dealt mainly with the relationship of the Jews with the city of Hamburg.[92] After years of argument, a compromise was reached in 1959. Records describing the inner life of the Jewish community were transferred to Israel, with copies made for Hamburg. The remaining records, mostly pertaining to Jewish relations with city authorities, remained in Hamburg, with copies sent to Israel.[93] All this indicated that Jewish restitution efforts faced an uncertain future in the Federal Republic.

In the fall of 1950, a restitution problem came to the fore; it illustrated the complex intersection of military government, German authorities, and Jewish claimants. As the Offenbach Archival Depot prepared to close in May 1949, 100,000 unclaimed "non-Jewish" books were transferred to the custody of German authorities in *Land* Hesse. JCR staff soon ascertained that not only did many of these "unclaimed" books have claimants, but many of the items were Jewish in origin. Gershom Scholem of Hebrew University found Judaica from the seventeenth and eighteenth centuries, valuable pamphlet collections, and literature about the

[90]  Meir Ben-Horin, "Field Report No. 21, September 1950," File "Jewish Cultural Reconstruction, Field Reports, 1949–50," Papers of Salo W. Baron (M580).
[91]  Historical Society of Israel, *The Jewish Historical General Archives* (Jerusalem: Historical Society of Israel, 1961), pp. 3–5.
[92]  Ibid.
[93]  Ibid.

1800 emancipation of the Jews in Germany. Non-Jewish material included valuable material in philosophy, history, and socialism.[94] Fortunately for the JCR, the attitudes of authorities in Hesse differed from those in Bavaria. Hannah Arendt was able to negotiate a satisfactory settlement. The Hesse authorities, with Professor Hanns Wilhelm Eppelsheimer leading the effort, agreed to restitute items when owners or heirs filed valid claims and to divide the remainder between JCR and German libraries on a 50/50 basis.[95] The JCR board decided that all of the Judaica and two-thirds of the non-Jewish material it received should go to Jerusalem, with the balance shipped to the United States for use by Brandeis University and Yeshiva College.[96] JCR's British counterpart argued that, given the British Museum's wartime losses, it should receive first choice of all non-Jewish books not sent to Israel. After some discussion, the JCR board again rejected the British position, noting its policy that non-Jewish institutions, such as the British Museum, could only receive Judaica.[97]

All these protracted negotiations, which faced different situations zone to zone and community to community, highlighted the urgency of a nation-wide approach for further restitution of Jewish cultural treasures. The closing of the Wiesbaden Collecting Point on 31 December 1950, which signaled the end for all practical purposes of the American restitution program, only added to the sense of urgency. Hannah Arendt based her efforts during a trip to Germany on "the assumption that Nazi-confiscated Jewish cultural property must have found its way into German libraries, museums and archives and that it could be discovered only through active cooperation of the German personnel in charge of such institutions."[98] Arendt worked assiduously to gain the cooperation of German officials, particularly in light of the fact that the reporting requirement for looted Jewish cultural property (Article 73) in Military Government Law No. 59 remained basically a dead letter. Arendt met with German library officials and persuaded the president of the German Library Association, Dr. Gustav Hofmann, to issue an appeal to all libraries to search their collections for confiscated Jewish material and report it to the JCR.[99] Arendt did not mention restitution because the law differed in each of the western zones, with no effort possible in the Soviet Zone. To Arendt, the "centralization of information is a first and

[94] Gershom Scholem, "Special Report by Prof. G. Scholem on the Non-Jewish Books in Frankfurt, 14 September 1950," File "923c – Jewish Cultural Reconstruction," Records of the Jewish Restitution Successor Organization.

[95] Ibid.

[96] Minutes of Special Meeting of the JCR Board of Directors, 21 December 1950, Skirball Cultural Center.

[97] Ibid.

[98] Hannah Arendt, "Report of My Mission to Germany, 12 April 1950," File "Jewish Cultural Reconstruction, Field Reports, 1949–50," Papers of Salo W. Baron (M580).

[99] Ibid.

the most important step."[100] Unfortunately, no reports came in partly because of German reluctance to comply and partly because many collections were still crated from wartime storage. To further the prospects for reporting and centralizing information, Arendt sought to get the Permanent Länder Conference of Ministers of Culture to issue a decree providing a legal basis for voluntary reporting.[101] No decree was issued.

In view of the difficult prospects for Jewish cultural restitution, Salo Baron and the JCR Board sought other avenues to advance their cause. Baron wrote Nahum Goldman of the Conference on Material Claims Against Germany, an umbrella organization seeking to expand German responsibility to compensate Jewish victims, requesting assistance. Baron resurrected the old CJR proposal to seek reparations-in-kind for lost Jewish cultural treasures. With the conference serving as an intermediary between Israel and the Federal Republic over matters of compensation and restitution, Baron argued that lost manuscripts, incunabula, rare books, and works of art could not be replaced by money. Though he recognized that reparations were not within the scope of the negotiations, Baron felt that with few persons left in Germany interested in Jewish history, the Germans would feel little or no loss if part of the rich Jewish collections in state and municipal institutions were voluntarily turned over to the Jewish people.[102]

The Hague Agreement of September 1952 gave stateless persons, refugees, and expellees the right of direct petition for restitution or compensation; cultural reparations were not addressed. JCR efforts to get a uniform federal restitution law were also unavailing, leaving in place the three disparate restitution laws and machinery left over from the occupation period. With the material formerly in the hands of the American military government safely distributed, the JCR closed its European operation by mid-1951, leaving the JRSO to handle any restitution matters that might arise.

It was highly unlikely that the JRSO could handle restitution matters in any significant fashion. German politicians and bureaucrats had no intention of disturbing their cultural institutions and citizens, and the Allies sought to integrate the Federal Republic into the first line of defense against the communist bloc. The Hague Agreement, with its emphasis on monetary compensation, reflected the reality of what could be accomplished.

## JCR: A Success?

In the final analysis, the JCR could only be as successful as the American restitution program. OMGUS restituted much Jewish cultural property and

---

[100] Ibid.
[101] Ibid.
[102] Salo Baron to Nahum Goldman, 21 March 1952, File "JCR, 1951–June 1954," Papers of Salo W. Baron (M580).

had turned over heirless or unclaimed Jewish cultural treasures to the JCR. But the American effort was only partly successful. Though the materials hidden in repositories were placed in the central collecting points and returned, much internal loot, a great deal of it Jewish, remained in German institutional or private hands. Military Government Law No. 59, with its requirement to report but not turn in looted property, was a compromise that reflected new geopolitical realities. After the collecting points received the bulk of their holdings during the first year of occupation, little else came in.

The Monuments, Fine Arts, and Archives officers, few in number, efficiently managed the collecting points and ensured that millions of items were restituted. The JCR staff, also few in number, made a similarly prodigious effort to restitute the over half-million cultural items – books, Torahs, art, religious objects – given into its custody. As did the MFA&A, the JCR did a superlative job of managing the contents of the collecting points. Despite several disputes, JCR allocation and distribution policies were widely accepted as credible and fair. Given the fact that most of the heirless and unclaimed Jewish cultural property was found in the U.S. Zone, this was a noteworthy accomplishment.

Yet, in the final analysis the JCR was only partially successful. Relations with the German-Jewish communities remained prickly at best, with cooperation difficult to obtain. The OMGUS policy of turning over ever-greater responsibility to the Germans meant that the JCR was basically at the mercy of German officials for materials not already in the hands of the military government. Even though some German officials sought to work with the JCR, such as the authorities in *Land* Hesse, overall little else was accomplished. The issue went even deeper than German reluctance to search thoroughly their collections and restitute Jewish property. In truth, only a fragment of the Jewish heritage had survived. Much of it disappeared, as had European Jewry itself, and reconstruction could only be partial at best.

PART FOUR

# COLD WAR AND BEYOND

# 9

## Conflict and Cooperation

*The Politics of Restitution in the Cold War*

The massive American restitution effort reflected the varying quality of our diplomatic relations with the different European states. As was the case in other areas, the most serious difficulties in restitution arose in policy conflicts with the Soviet Union and the Eastern European states, although relations with the French were also testy. During the Cold War period, particularly during the 1940s and 1950s, suspicion and mistrust often characterized the politics of restitution. America's need to contain communism and build a cohesive Western alliance also affected restitution policies and decisions. The best place to begin is with the former ally with which the United States had the greatest conflicts, the Soviet Union.

### Russia and Restitution

Cultural restitution issues involving Russia and the Eastern European countries reflected the general political and economic stalemate in Germany. With Russia, the disputed issues revolved around tardy Soviet cooperation with the American restitution effort, Soviet removal of cultural items from its Zone of Occupation, and restitution to the Baltic states and Polish territory, formerly independent, but now occupied by the Soviet Union. Soviet reluctance to cooperate in the economic sphere is clearly shown by the fact that OMGUS had to make repeated approaches to the Soviet military command to procure a permanent restitution mission. The Americans were anxious to do this to relieve themselves of a burdensome responsibility for protecting valuable Russian works of art. The Russians, for reasons not entirely clear, were the slowest nation to respond to the October 1945 OMGUS invitation to send a restitution mission. They may have been reluctant because they did not wish to reciprocate with a similar invitation. It was not until June 1946 that the Russians agreed to send a permanent mission.[1] Even so, the constant replacement of Russian personnel caused the Americans to protest that this immeasurably slowed the restitution process.[2]

Despite their own tardiness, the Russians complained that all their property was not being returned. This forced OMGUS to prepare a series of reports in response. In October 1946, they were able to report the return of 100,000 books, with 133 crates of pictures, icons, and scientific collections.[3] By June 1947, OMGUS noted that, though three Russian missions had worked in the American Zone, there remained at least 15,000 volumes from a Kiev research institution, with 1,000 pieces of scientific equipment, 9,269 books, and 1 fountain from Leningrad.[4] In all, OMGUS restituted almost half a million items to the Soviets stored in the collecting points. This does not include the museum objects, archives, and libraries directly returned to the Soviets by the Allies from Nazi repositories in Austria, Czechoslovakia, and Germany.[5] A further point of friction with the Soviets was the OMGUS effort to require all restitution missions to file all their claims on a standard form. This was a further effort to expedite the claims process. All the restitution missions, except for that of the Soviets, agreed. The Russian Reparations Administrator, Major General L. I. Zorin, bitterly protested. Zorin claimed that the current Soviet form contained all the information required by quadripartite agreements.[6] Furthermore, any change would necessitate a reorganization of the work of the Russian Restitution Section.[7] In light of this reaction, MFA&A dropped the idea.

The Soviets had the same attitude concerning German cultural property as they exhibited in reparations toward industrial equipment. It was clear that

---

[1] Memorandum, "Russian Mission for Restitution to the USSR, 19 June 1946," File "June 1946," Correspondence and Related Records, 1946–9, Records of the Reparations and Restitution Branch, Records of the Restitution Section, RG 260.

[2] Orren R. McJunkins to Maj. Gen. L. I. Zorin, October 1948, File "Correspondence – October 1948," Correspondence and Related Records, 1946–9, Records of the Reparations and Restitution Branch, Records of the Restitution Section, RG 260.

[3] Memorandum, "Progress Report on Restitution in the Soviet Zone, 25 October 1946," File "Correspondence – October 1946," Correspondence and Related Records, 1946–9, Records of the Reparations and Restitution Branch, Records of the Restitution Section, RG 260.

[4] OMGUS Cablegram (CC-9423) to the War Department on restitution to the Soviet Union, 4 June 1947, File "Cables, Outgoing, Classified and Unclassified, June–December 1947," Cables Relating to Reparations and Restitution, 1945–8, General Records, Records of the Reparations and Restitution Branch, RG 260.

[5] Patricia Kennedy Grimsted, "'Trophy' Archives and Non-Restitution: Russia's Cultural 'Cold War' with the European Community," *Problems of Post-Communism* 45 (May/June 1998): 12–13.

[6] Maj. Gen. L. I. Zorin to Col. John Allen, 26 May 1847, File "Correspondence – May 1947," Correspondence and Related Records, 1946–9, Records of the Reparations and Restitution Branch, Records of the Restitution Section, RG 260.

[7] Ibid.

the Soviets were not slow in removing cultural materials from their zone. Published reports in the press and secret American government investigations revealed what was, in effect, widespread looting in the Soviet Zone. Between mid-December 1945 and April 1946, the Russians emptied the cellars and storerooms of museums in Berlin's Soviet Sector.[8] Museums looted included Pre-History and Early History, East-Asiatic art, ethnology, and the State Art Library. Events such as these occurred throughout the Soviet Zone for the next several years.[9] An estimated 900,000 works of art, along with extensive library and archival materials, were carried off to Russia. These included such notable items as the Pergamum Altar, Greek and Roman sculpture, and thousands of old masterpieces. Much of this treasure either was German or belonged to countries other than Russia. Reporters speculated that more than $170 million worth of art was taken from Germany.[10]

Why did the Russians pursue a course so different from that of the Western Allies? Nazi depredations naturally fueled Russian hate. After helping to bring the Germans to their knees, the Soviets were in no mood to show mercy. The All-Russian Trophy Commission removed thousands of works of art and other items to rebuild devastated museums in the homeland. Yet the picture of complete Nazi responsibility for all cultural destruction was not accurate. With the collapse of the Soviet Union and the opening of archives in the early 1990s, it is now clear that much of Russia's losses, particularly of archival material, were due to the Soviets intentional destruction of archives and other cultural items, which could not be removed prior to the arrival of the Nazi invaders. For example, in July 1941 commanders in Dnepropetrovsk were told, "If it is impossible to bring out the materials designated for evacuation, they are to be burned unconditionally."[11] In the Ukraine, archives that were not evacuated or destroyed were left completely disorganized to eliminate their usefulness to the Germans. Though the Germans were blamed for the dynamiting of the Uspens'kyi Cathedral in Kiev, recently opened records reveal that the Soviets had laid the dynamite, which the Germans were unable to defuse.[12] Yet, in the final analysis, it was the German invasion that started the cultural conflagration in the Soviet Union.

The Russians, in any event, believed they had suffered far more than other nations and had made the greatest contribution to the defeat of Germany. They felt no need to discover and return property that belonged to foreign

[8] "Soviet Removals of Cultural Materials (000.4), 13 May 1947," Executive Office Decimal File, 11 June 1946–7, Records of the Civil Affairs Division, RG 165.

[9] "War Chronicle of the Museums of Berlin, May 1946," File "Inter-Zonal Exchange," Records Maintained by the Fine Arts and Monuments Advisor, 1945–61, RG 59.

[10] "Soviets' Dresden Booty was $170,000,000," *New York Times*, 30 January 1948.

[11] Patricia Kennedy Grimsted, "Displaced Archives on the Eastern Front: Restitution Problems from World War II and Its Aftermath," *Janus* 2 (1996): 44–5.

[12] Ibid.

nationals. Another factor, which was noted by American art journals, was that the cash-starved Soviets could sell the looted art on the world market and bring in much-needed currency. But there was a deeper motivation for retaining foreign cultural items, particularly archives, than replenishing war losses or profitable sales. As Soviet forces rolled over Eastern Europe and into Germany, material previously looted by the Germans, such as extensive intelligence records collected from European governments, records of various socialist organizations, and, perhaps of greatest interest to the Soviets, documents of émigré groups fell into Russian hands.[13] The taking of these foreign-captured records, never admitted during the long years of the Cold War, provided unique operational advantages for the Soviet intelligence services. Captain A. A. Iur'ev of the secret police, the NKVD (People's Commissariat for State Security), argued for the policy eventually pursued by the government:

Use [of that archives], in my opinion, should have an exclusively specific, limited character, namely utilization only with the meaning of operational aims of the NKVD, VD, MO [Defense], and ID [Foreign Affairs]. No scholarly research whatsoever can be carried out on the basis of that archive, and to be sure, no access whatsoever can be permitted to that archive for representatives of any scholarly institutions.... There is no need for compiling full inventories nor is there need for arranging the files [according to archival principles]. The only immediate need is to use the documents there for operational arms support.[14]

When it came to the satellite nations, the Soviets eventually adopted a somewhat different stance. Anticommunist riots and revolts in East Germany, Poland, and Hungary convinced the Soviets that positive action was needed to retain the cooperation and friendship needed to maintain their dominance in Eastern Europe. Cultural restitution provided a ready tool. The papers of Admiral Horthy were returned to Hungary in 1959, twelve thousand paintings and museum objects to the Poles, with the German Democratic Republic (GDR) obtaining the most because of its strategic position confronting the Western NATO alliance. Between the mid-1950s and late 1980s, almost two million items were returned to the GDR and, more than twelve hundred objects were returned to the Picture Gallery in Dresden, along with two hundred tons of German archival materials.[15]

A joint USSR-GDR declaration in January 1957 explained that both parties were committed "to examine all questions arising in the context

---

[13] Ibid., pp. 54–6.
[14] Ibid., p. 56.
[15] Petra Kuhn, "Comments on the Soviet Returns of Cultural Treasures Moved Because of the War to the GDR," *Spoils of War International Newsletter*, 4 (August 1997): pp. 45–6; Jan P. Prussynish, "Poland: The War Losses, Cultural Heritage, and Cultural Legitimacy," *Spoils of War International Newsletter*, 4 (August 1997): p. 52.

of mutual returns of cultural treasures (art objects, archival material, etc.) in order to bring to an end the resolution – initiated by the government of the Soviet Union – of the specific problems deriving from war times."[16] In the 1960s, some additional transfers took place, with the 1980s witnessing a decided increase in restitution because of the critical political situation in the GDR. Some forty tons of archival materials, mostly of the medieval records of the Hanseatic League cities of Bremen, Lübeck, and Hamburg, were returned.[17] Clearly Soviet restitution gained only transitory goodwill, if any at all, and played no role in aiding the Soviets in maintaining dominance in Eastern Europe. In fact, the post–Cold War era would see heightened tensions over cultural restitution.

## Estrangement

By their actions in the removal of cultural property, the Russians clearly considered cultural property as eligible for reparations, the same as industrial plants or machinery. Clay's decision to halt reparations payments to Russia in May 1946 was also an indication of frustration over the restitution program. The Russians refused to file detailed reports on restitution activity in their zone, as required by the ACC. Clay and other Americans believed that the Russians were failing to fulfill their commitments in both the reparations and restitution spheres. In addition to conflicts over reparations and restitution, the United States was disturbed over other Soviet policies and actions in their zone that affected the German cultural heritage. Hundreds of castles and manor houses that survived the war were confiscated under a 1945 land reform act. More than two hundred of these buildings, many filled with priceless art, sculpture, and libraries, were burned or torn down. This wanton destructiveness strained American sympathy for or understanding of the Soviets.[18]

As noted previously, the spring of 1947 clearly demonstrated Russian control over Eastern Europe. The monarchy was overthrown in Rumania, the ruling Small Holders Party was subverted in Hungary, and any pretense of a coalition government ceased in Poland. These developments caused numerous difficulties for the United States. American economic interests in the Eastern bloc were expropriated, political and religious persecutions created great concern among ethnic groups in the United States, and effective Russian power was projected into the heart of Europe. Related restitution

---

[16] Kuhn, "Comments on the Soviet Returns," pp. 45–6.
[17] Grimsted, "Displaced Archives," p. 58.
[18] "Translation from *Die Zeit*: Destroyed, Wasted, Squandered . . . Castles and Manor Houses under the Pickaxe: The Fate of the Saxonian Museums and Collections, 10 November 1949," File "USSR," Records Maintained by the Fine Arts and Monuments Advisor, 1945–61, RG 59.

problems involved the disposition of property of foreign nations currently occupied by the Soviet Union and the return of property belonging to Eastern European refugees. The American response to Russian claims filed for cultural property looted from Baltic and Polish territory it then occupied reflected general American diplomatic policy. The United States consistently refused to recognize the Soviet Union's incorporation of Latvia, Estonia, and Lithuania. Consequently, the United States would accept information from the Soviet Restitution Mission but made no commitment on the disposition of claims.[19] In the final analysis, the United States never processed these claims.

The response regarding Polish territory incorporated into the Soviet Union was different and more conciliatory. The United States understood the extreme Soviet sensitivity regarding a secure Polish frontier. The Americans were also realistic enough to realize that the Polish expansion to the Oder-Neisse River, and the consequent expulsion of the Germans, was a long-term phenomenon at the very least. Therefore, the War Department informed OMGUS that the Soviet Union was the proper claimant regarding restitution to areas transferred from Poland.[20]

The question of how to treat the property of refugees fleeing the Soviet Union or its satellite states, on the contrary, was a very difficult one. From the earliest period of Allied planning regarding restitution, it was clear that the return of property was through owner-nations, who were obligated to return items to private owners, where appropriate. In the glow of Allied cooperation, this was a feasible stance. The takeover of Eastern Europe by the communists and the coming of the Cold War made a change inevitable.

Early in the postwar period, it was clear that most areas in Eastern Europe remained inhospitable for Jews. One problem was what to do with the property of those who refused to return to or stay in their native countries or who were victims of the Nazi Holocaust and had left no heirs. The Soviet Union, Poland, and the other Eastern European states submitted claims demanding the return of property under accepted quadripartite procedures. By early 1947, the American government was faced with a large number of these cases. Equity, domestic political pressures, and foreign policy interests all dictated a change. The State, War, and Navy Coordinating Committee (SWNCC) decided that the property of a refugee who fled for religious or

[19] General Keating to Col. General F. A. Kurochkin, 15 March 1947, File "Correspondence – March 1947," Correspondence and Related Records, 1946–9, Records of the Reparations and Restitution Branch, Records of the Restitution Section, RG 260.
[20] War Department Cablegram (WX-87846) to OMGUS on Soviet claims, 18 December 1946, File, "Restitution," General Records, 1945–52, Records Concerning the Central Collecting Points, Records of the Wiesbaden Central Collecting Point, RG 260.

racial reasons should be returned to the individual, not to the country of origin.[21]

This was a momentous change. First of all, this was a new development in international law. Previously, only nations had legal international standing. Now, the rights of certain categories of individuals took precedence over the claims of governments. As we will see, this conceptual change in international law was later expanded. Second, this decision was a clear indication that the United States had changed its attitude toward the Soviet Union. This was part of the change in American foreign policy thinking that produced the Truman Doctrine and the Marshall Plan. OMGUS attitudes on this question are clearly revealed in the actions of Seymour J. Pomrenze. During his tenure as director of the Offenbach Archival Depot, Pomrenze was against returning any materials to countries that were "Judenrein." He attributed his attitude to the anti-Semitic history of some of the Eastern European and former Baltic nations. Pomrenze asserted that he accomplished this legally with the assistance of Army and State Department officials.[22] Little documentation on how this policy was implemented has surfaced.

By 1948, the tide of refugees had turned into a flood. This prompted a further change in policy. General Clay reported to his superiors in Washington on the manifold problems created by the influx of refugees. Many of these refugees were not Jewish, and thus their property claims did not fall under the 1947 SWNCC decision regarding religious or racial refugees. Many of these individuals were middle- or upper-class Poles, whose property was originally taken by the Germans. Now, OMGUS faced conflicting claims from the refugees and the Polish government. The State Department introduced a draft directive on this issue in the State, Army, Navy, and Air Force Coordinating Committee (SANACC), successor of the SWNCC. The directive, subsequently adopted, dealt with various aspects of external restitution. Specifically, OMGUS was instructed to avoid restitution of property claimed by a nonnational or a refugee national of the claimant country.[23] This was clearly aimed at Eastern European communist governments and created a great deal of bitterness with the Polish and Hungarian governments. As was the case with the SWNCC decision, I discovered little documentation on the implementation of this policy. Richard F. Howard stated that he could

---

[21] SWNCC Memorandum, "Restitution from Germany of Works of Art Removed from Hungary to Germany (204.46), 27 January 1947," General Records, 1938–48, Records Concerning the Central Collecting Points, RG 260.

[22] Seymour J. Pomrenze to Michael J. Kurtz, letter, 10 May 1981.

[23] War Department Cablegram to OMGUS (WX-8362), "External Restitution from Germany, 28 August 1948," File "Correspondence – August 1948," Correspondence and Related Records, 1946–9, Records of the Reparations and Restitution Branch, Records of the Restitution Section, RG 260.

remember only one case that fell within these guidelines.[24] But this case had implications that would last for decades.

An intriguing example of the complexities involved in this policy shift is the case of the so-called Lubomirski Dürers. In April 1947, Prince George Lubomirski, a Polish aristocrat who had fled Poland at the end of the war and settled in Switzerland, filed a claim for the return of twenty-seven Dürer drawings. The drawings had a complicated history. Prince George's grandfather, Prince Henry K. Lubomirski, had given his collection of books, medals, paintings, drawings, and antiquities in 1823 to Count Jósef Maksymillian Ossolinski for an institute dedicated to Poland's cultural heritage. This agreement, and an 1866 foundation charter for the Ossolinski Institute incorporated the Lubomirski Collections and an entailed estate into the institute.[25] Other conditions of the charter provided for reversion of the Lubomirski collections and estate to the family if the institute was abolished or used for purposes outside the scope of the foundation charter, indicated successor status to other families if the Lubomirski and Ossolinski families became extinct, and provided for the resumption of a relationship if the family lines specified in the charter still existed and if no more than fifty years had elapsed since the break in the Lubomirski-Ossolinski relationship.[26] All in all, it was a complex arrangement.

Adding to the complexity was that the institute was established in Lemberg, then part of the Austro-Hungarian Empire. After 1918, Lemberg became part of Poland (Lwów), so the institute and its component unit, the Lubomirski Museum, operated under Polish laws. As a result of the Hitler-Stalin Pact of August 1939, the Red Army invaded eastern Poland, which was incorporated into the Soviet Republic of Ukraine. The Ossolinski Institute and the Lubomirski Museum were closed, and the contents became part of the V. Stefanyk Library of the Academy of Sciences of Ukraine. When the Germans attacked the Soviet Union and occupied Lviv (the former Lwów, Lvuv, Lemberg) in June 1941, Kajetan Mühlmann made a beeline for the institute and museum. Sent to the museum by Göring, who knew Hitler's passion for any works of Dürer, Mühlmann seized the drawings and sent them to Berlin. They included such outstanding works as *Self-Portrait at the Age of Twenty-two*, *Male Nude*, and *Nude Woman with a Staff*. Hitler was so thrilled with the drawings that he kept them with him at his Eastern front headquarters until the exigencies of war forced their storage in the salt mine at Alt Aussee.[27] After the war, the drawings were stored at the Munich Central Collecting Point. In the postwar period, the Polish government

---

[24] Richard F. Howard to Michael J. Kurtz, letter, April 1981.
[25] Konstantin Akinsha and Sylvia Hochfield, "Who Owns the Lubomirsky Dürers?" *ARTnews* (October 2001): pp. 158–63.
[26] Ibid.
[27] Ibid.

reestablished the Institute in Wroclow, which laid the basis for future claims.

When Prince George first came on the scene, Munich Central Collecting Point director Herbert S. Leonard interrogated Kajetan Mühlmann about the provenance of the drawings and the history of the Ossolinski Institute and the Lubomirski Museum.[28] Based on what he learned and the standard practice of restituting only to governments, Leonard turned the prince down. Prince George was not one to give up. He filed a formal claim in July 1948 and pledged to donate the drawings to the National Gallery of Art in Washington, D.C. Richard F. Howard at first supported the prince's claim because of the new policy on returning property to refugees. Soon after telling Leonard to return the drawings "without publicity," Howard had a change of heart. He now wondered if the drawings and other parts of the original donation were actually national property and not family property at all.[29] OMGUS lawyer James Heath had doubts about the validity of the claim that Prince George's father, Prince Andrew, had really ceded his rights to his son, and varying translations of the original statute caused further concerns. There was also the distinct possibility that both the Soviet Union and Poland might file claims.[30] At the recommendation of the State Department, a decision on the case was postponed. Conflicts with the Soviets over Berlin and other Cold War issues did not make this an opportune moment to change Allied restitution policy.

But by 1950, Prince George's persistence paid off. The central collecting points were closing, and the State Department decided that the drawings did indeed belong to Prince George as the Lubomirski family heir. Despite protests from the family, Prince George received the drawings in May 1950. After the National Gallery of Art declined to buy them (for $315,000), Prince George had dealers in London and New York sell them. Though other family members received not a dime, Prince George lived comfortably, dying in the south of France in 1978 at the ripe old age of 91. After the end of the Cold War, this case would surface again with tremendous legal and political complications.[31]

One indication that the SANACC guidelines were mostly symbolic was that OMGUS failed, despite the Lubomirski case, to develop general procedures for handling claims from individuals for external restitution before the end of the occupation.[32] Jewish property, of course, was turned over to

---

[28] Lynn Nicholas, *The Rape of Europa: The Fate of Europe's Treasures in the Third Reich and the Second World War* (New York: Alfred A. Knopf, 1994), pp. 429–31.

[29] Akinsha and Hochfield, "Who Owns the Lubomirsky Dürers?," pp. 158–63.

[30] Ibid.

[31] Ibid.

[32] Richard F. Howard, "Report Upon Separation, 18 November 1948," File "Final Report – Reparations and Restitution," Reports and Related Records Re: Restitution, 1945–52, Records of the Reparations and Restitution Branch, RG 260.

successor organizations such as the Jewish Cultural Restitution Agency, which handled property of Baltic Jewish origin. Any non-Jewish property cases were left for settlement between the owners and heirs and the German government. Obviously, long before the end of the occupation, American-Soviet relations over restitution were in ruins. This reflected the steadily deteriorating situation between the two superpowers. The Russians believed that they were cheated of what was rightfully theirs, while the United States resented Russia's lack of cooperation, charges of ill will, and ceaseless propagandizing over so-called American exploitation of the German cultural heritage. The hostile environment affected American relations regarding cultural restitution with the Eastern European satellite nations by 1948. This occurred despite an earlier American desire to woo these countries away from the Soviets as much as possible.

One interesting case – which had an ideological, rather than racial or religious, basis – did develop. This involved the museum of the Kuban Cossacks. They had fled Russia in 1920 and taken their relics with them, eventually storing them in Belgrade. The Germans seized the relics, but the Cossacks regained them after the war and placed them in American care. General Naumenko, the ataman or chief, requested their return to him. Despite sensitivity to possible Russian reaction, OMGUS returned the relics to the general, who planned on eventually settling in the United States.[33]

## Conflicts with the Satellites

Any remaining American hopes of sustaining some influence in Eastern Europe were shattered by the events of 1948. The Prague Coup in February convinced the Western Allies that they had to resolve the German question in order to contain what they viewed as relentless Soviet expansion and subversion. The six-power talks in London, with the aim of creating a state in western Germany, were logical steps flowing from the establishment of bizonia and the complete collapse of the wartime Grand Alliance. The Russians retaliated by walking out of the Control Council in Germany in March 1948 and blockading the western sectors of Berlin. In this kind of atmosphere, American foreign policy makers wanted to fortify their allies in Europe and thwart their foes. Cultural restitution disputes, with Poland and Yugoslavia for example, were handled in this context. Restitution disputes with the Poles and Yugoslavs revolved primarily around ownership and control of property. The problems with cultural restitution reflected the steady deterioration of bilateral relations, as well as the development of the iron curtain and two armed camps in Europe.

[33] Col. John Allen, "Kuban Cossacks Relics, 10 April 1948," File "Correspondence – April 1948," Correspondence and Related Records, 1946–9, Records of the Reparations and Restitution Branch, Records of the Restitution Section, RG 260.

Poland, as a result of boundary changes approved at the Berlin Conference, swiftly moved into eastern Prussia and forced the German inhabitants to leave their homes. The Poles also annexed the former free city of Danzig (Gdańsk), administered by the League of Nations during the interwar period. The Polish government claimed sovereignty and requested that the United States return any cultural materials, works of art, or industrial machinery located in the American Zone and taken from Danzig by the Germans.[34] The United States did not accept Poland's claim to Danzig and wanted all such matters deferred to a general peace settlement. The Americans continually, though with little success, attempted to prevent the status quo in Eastern Europe from freezing into permanence. In the face of steady Polish requests, the American government partly acceded to the demands, though with significant qualifications. Cultural materials and works of art were returned, but the Polish government had to pledge that the items would be returned to Danzig museums and churches because they were the lawful owners.[35] This reflected widespread complaints from Polish religious groups that the communist government was not returning church property to the rightful owners. In addition, the United States kept all other Danzig property, pending determination of the future status of the city.[36] The grudging American response did little to enhance relations with Poland.

A similar situation occurred with Yugoslavia. The Yugoslavs filed claims for restitution of property removed from Postumia in Venetia Giulia, former Italian territory occupied by Yugoslavia. The United States procrastinated in this case also, pleading the need to await a treaty of peace.[37] In reality, American hesitations had more to do with the desire to strengthen American influence in Italy. Despite Tito's break with Stalin, the United States continued to believe that it was important to keep communist influence from spreading beyond Yugoslavia. Also, the American government wanted to avoid alienating Italian popular opinion, a crucial factor in preventing communist control of the Italian government.

Even more serious problems developed late in the occupation period, when the Poles attempted to appoint a curator to care for the German interests of Polish citizens residing abroad. Most of these Polish citizens were refugees, Jewish and non-Jewish, who could not return to the communist

---

34 War Department Cablegram (WX-86460) to OMGUS on restitution to Danzig, 17 September 1947, File "Cables, Outgoing, Classified and Unclassified, June–December 1947," Cables Relating to Reparations and Restitution, 1945–8, General Records, Records of the Reparations and Restitution Branch, RG 260.

35 Ibid.

36 Ibid.

37 OMGUS Cablegram (CC-7131) to the War Department on restitution to Venetia Giulia, 27 November 1946, File "Correspondence – November 1946," Correspondence and Related Records, 1946–9, Records of the Reparations and Restitution Branch, Records of the Restitution Section, RG 260.

state. Many of these refugees were from the aristocracy, and much of their property in Germany was cultural and of significant monetary value. In January 1949, as OMGUS was completing the restitution program, the Polish government ignited new dispute when it requested recognition of a Dr. Gelb as the curator in absentia for former Polish nationals whose whereabouts were unknown.[38] The request initially caused a flurry of disagreement in OMGUS. The Property Division thought the Polish move was improper and doubted the validity of Gelb's appointment.[39] The Legal Division, on the other hand, thought that Polish courts could appoint curators and that this was congruent with German law and Articles 53 and 54 of Military Government Law No. 59.[40] These articles permitted restitution agencies to appoint a trustee despite the fact that the claimant was of non-German nationality and lived abroad. Also, the restitution law permitted someone resident in Germany to act legally on behalf of a claimant.[41]

Reaction from OMGUS property control and external assets officials was very negative. They pointed out that British and French authorities thought that German courts would not recognize the appointment of Dr. Gelb.[42] This was based on the fact that there were no reciprocal treaties between Germany and Poland and that the German courts had to have control of any curators to ensure proper protection and administration of the properties involved.[43] Other arguments advanced against recognizing the Polish curator were that many of the Poles covered by the law had sanctions placed against them in their country and that it was not at all clear that these people had participated in the proceedings appointing the curator.[44] Property control officials feared that the contested property would pass to the Polish government, rather than to the rightful owners or heirs. The Legal Division responded to these arguments by reversing its position. The reversal was based on the lack of notice to the claimants and the fact that the curator was to advance the interest of the Polish government rather than the claimants.[45] This effectively killed the possibility of any large-scale turnover of property to the Polish government.

---

[38] Fred Hartzsch, "Recognition by German Courts of a Curator in Absentium Appointed by Polish Courts, 11 January 1949," File "Polish Military Mission and Polish Property," General Records, 1947–9, Claims Section, RG 260.

[39] Ibid.

[40] James E. Heath, "Recognition by German Courts of a Curator in Absentium Appointed by Polish Courts, 15 February 1949," File "Polish Military Mission and Polish Property," General Records, 1947–9, Claims Section, RG 260.

[41] Ibid.

[42] Fred Hartzsch, "Recognition by German Courts of a Curator in Absentium Appointed by Polish Courts, 2 March 1949," File "Polish Military Mission and Polish Property," General Records, 1947–9, Claims Section, RG 260.

[43] Ibid.

[44] Ibid.

[45] James E. Heath, "Recognition by German Courts of a Curator in Absentium Appointed by Polish Courts, 5 July 1949."

As the satellite states, which included former enemies and allies, slipped further from Western influence, the United States attempted to use cultural restitution to maintain a foothold in at least one country: Hungary. The United States granted privileges to Hungary, even before a peace treaty or quadripartite agreements were concluded. These included return of all gold looted from the Hungarian treasury, certain transportation equipment, and all identifiable cultural objects.[46] The only exception to the last category was the politically sensitive Crown of Saint Stephen. The crown was viewed as the symbol of the Hungarian people. In 1944, the regent, Admiral Miklós Horthy, entrusted the precious symbol to Colonel Ernest Pajtas, Commandant of the Royal Crown Guards, who took it from Budapest to a monastery at Köszeg in western Hungary. In the spring of 1945, as the Russians poured across Hungary, Pajtas fled west with the crown and voluntarily turned it over to the Americans.[47] For a time, the crown was stored in the Wiesbaden Central Collecting Point.

Initially, Hungarian authorities did not press for return of the crown, given the growing confrontation between the state and the Catholic Church. However, József, Cardinal Mindszenty, primate of Hungary, encouraged the Vatican to obtain the crown for safekeeping. When the Holy See sought custody of it, the American government decided to send the highly symbolic crown to Fort Knox for storage until the conflict over ownership could be resolved.[48] In fact, the Hungarian national symbol was not returned until 1977 by the Carter administration. Despite American goodwill, manifested by Secretary of State Byrnes during the negotiations for the Hungarian Peace Treaty, growing communist influence in Budapest led to bitter clashes. In the restitution area, this showed itself in Hungarian complaints about the amount of material returned, as well as American complaints that the Hungarian restitution mission refused to follow procedures and was obstructionist. Ultimately, this led to the expulsion of the Hungarian restitution mission from the American Zone in April 1948.[49] This ended restitution to Hungary. By the spring of 1948, a bitter impasse separated the United States from the Eastern European governments.

---

[46] OMGUS Cablegram (CC-9674) to the War Department on restitution to ex-enemies, 26 June 1947, File "Cables, Outgoing, Classified and Unclassified, June–December 1947," Cables Relating to Reparations and Restitution, 1945–8, General Records, Records of the Reparations and Restitution Branch, RG 260.

[47] Linda Charlton, "Hungary's Ancient Symbol: A Long Strange Journey," *New York Times*, 6 January 1948.

[48] Col. John Allen, Crown of St. Stephen, 23 February 1946, File "400c – Fine Arts," Classified General Correspondence, 1945–9, Records of the Office of the U.S. Political Advisor for Germany, Berlin, RG 84.

[49] James Gantenbein, Memorandum on the expulsion of the Hungarian Restitution Mission, 26 April 1948, File "Correspondence – April 1948," Correspondence and Related Records, 1946–9, Records of the Reparations and Restitution Branch, Records of the Restitution Section, RG 260.

Throughout the occupation, no matter how bitter relations became with the Soviet Union and Eastern Europe, the United States continued to restitute all identifiable public property and much of the private property claimed through government-to-government procedures. The change in the international climate was clearly reflected though in the handling of cultural restitution not covered by quadripartite agreements. The United States gradually moved from a spirit of cooperation to one of confrontation. By the end of the occupation, the Americans refused to return property looted from areas whose sovereignty was in dispute. Also, the United States came to the point where it turned over unclaimed Jewish property to successor organizations and retained property where refugees independently filed a claim. The general breakdown of Allied negotiations regarding Germany meant that these problems were never explored in extensive diplomatic discussions.

## Working with Allies

The diplomatic atmosphere regarding cultural restitution in the Western-oriented nations of Europe was markedly different. Though there were several sharp policy differences, an overall spirit of cooperation prevailed. There were several reasons for this attitude. Close cultural and economic ties bound the United States and Western Europe. Also, the American government, after two world wars, accepted the fact that American security was inextricably tied to events in Europe. The Truman administration was determined to prevent the spread of Soviet power beyond Eastern Europe. American security needs were basic motivating factors in aid to Greece and Turkey, the Marshall Plan, the creation of the German Federal Republic, and the establishment of a defensive Atlantic alliance. Western Europeans needed American economic assistance and protection. This mutuality of interests and needs provided the backdrop for the cultural restitution relationship between the United States and her allies in Western Europe.

An important goal of American foreign policy was the establishment of a stable pro-Western democratic government in Italy. This is evident from, among other things, the handling of restitution for Italian state art objects taken before the end of the fascist regime in Rome in September 1943. These were returned regardless of the applicable dates for restitution set in War Department instructions or by the peace treaty with Italy.[50] This favorable attitude toward Italy did create conflict within OMGUS and later diplomatic difficulties between Italy and the Federal Republic of Germany. The issue

---

[50] OMGUS Cablegram (CC-9674) to the War Department on restitution to ex-enemies, 26 June 1947, File "Cables, Outgoing, Classified and Unclassified, June–December 1947," Cables Relating to Reparations and Restitution, 1945–8, General Records, Records of the Reparations and Restitution Branch, RG 260.

arose over the return of certain cultural items presented by Mussolini's regime to such prominent Nazis as Hitler, Göring, and von Ribbentrop. These items, which included the Vipiteno Altarpiece, Leonardo's *Leda and the Swan,* and the famed sculptural work, *Discobolus,* were protected by Italian law as national treasures. The fascist government had granted exceptions to the law and permitted exports to Germany. The Italian government requested the return of these masterpieces from OMGUS. The Vipiteno Altarpiece, for example, was principally the work of the outstanding fifteenth-century German sculptor and painter, Hans Multscher. The altarpiece, with the centerpiece formed of wood sculptures with painted wings on each side, had stirred the acquisitive lust of Hermann Göring. Mussolini had satisfied the Reichsmarshall by presenting this treasure to him as a birthday present in December 1942. The Italian press commented critically on the restitution of Hungarian artworks while their masterpieces remained in Germany.[51] The Italians presented two claims: one for thirty-nine works of art and the other for fifty works, which they claimed had been exported in contravention of Italian law. A mission led by Rodolfo Siviero, the head of the special office for the return of Italian art treasures, appeared in Munich to press the Italian position.[52]

Military government officials were unsure how to proceed because disposal of these items was not included in the quadripartite definition of restitution, the peace treaty, or other instructions.[53] Top OMGUS officials were anxious to rid themselves of the responsibility for these treasures. MFA&A officials, though, hesitated to recommend restitution. They feared a negative German reaction on returning objects that seemed a part of a legal transaction.[54] MFA&A was always concerned that German public opinion view the restitution effort as fair and impartial. They feared the reaction that might occur if restitution actions appeared to be based on political considerations.

Political considerations were definitely on the minds of policy makers in the United States. In the spring of 1948, they were concerned over the results of the upcoming Italian national elections, scheduled for 19 April. State Department officials feared that the critical Italian press commentary on the masterpieces still in Germany might lead to an anti-American backlash. The

[51] War Department Cablegram (WX-97041) to OMGUS on restitution to Italy, 24 April 1947, File "Phase IV Cables, January–September 1947," Cables Relating to Reparations and Restitution, 1945–8, General Records, Records of the Reparations and Restitution Branch, RG 260.

[52] Rodolfo Siviero, *Second National Exhibition of the Works of Art Recovered in Germany* (Florence: Sansoni, 1950), p. 20.

[53] OMGUS Cablegram (CC-1838) to the War Department on restitution to Italy, 3 October 1947, File "Cables, Outgoing, Classified and Unclassified, June–December 1947," Cables Relating to Reparations and Restitution, 1945–8, General Records, Records of the Reparations and Restitution Branch, RG 260.

[54] Ibid.

triumph of the pro-Western Christian Democrats was essential to prevent communist participation in the government. The State Department requested that the Department of the Army issue instructions returning the Vipiteno Altarpiece. The Civil Affairs Division demurred because this did not constitute an overall policy instruction. Besides, such a policy instruction would have to go through the JCS.[55] In light of the urgent political situation in Italy, the Department of the Army relented and agreed to work out a State-Army position and transmit instructions to OMGUS.

The slow bureaucratic process resulted in a new policy only two days before the Italian election. The cablegram sent to OMGUS reiterated that the policy of the United States was to protect the cultural heritage of all nations. Where equitable, claimant nations were to receive cultural objects acquired by the Nazis in violation of laws of claimant nations.[56] These violations included granting unusual permits, licenses, or exemptions made because of close personal relationships between officials of the claimant country and the Nazis, political reasons, or improper pressure and corruption.[57] The Vipiteno Altarpiece was noted as the outstanding example for this category of restitution.[58]

OMGUS was instructed to announce this policy before the Italian elections if it concurred. Implementation was not immediately forthcoming. Clay and his top assistants had no problems with this policy, though some MFA&A officials did object. The fact that the State-Army directive was limited to Italian objects and not to others, such as the Hungarian Crown of Saint Stephen, meant there was a policy of favoritism that, they believed, would reflect poorly on the entire restitution effort. When Clay gave his concurrence, the chief of the Munich Central Collecting Point, Herbert S. Leonard, resigned in protest.[59] In Richard Howard's view, Leonard's resignation was less the result of his disagreement with the return of the Italian art objects than the latest manifestation of Leonard's personal and emotional problems.[60] It was not until June that OMGUS began the actual restitution. Despite American fears that the controversy would adversely affect the Italian elections, this did not occur.

[55] Maj. Gen. Daniel Noce to Assistant Secretary of State Charles E. Saltzman (000.4), 6 April 1948, Executive Office Decimal File, 1948, Records of the Civil Affairs Division, RG 165.

[56] War Department Cablegram (WX-99722) to OMGUS on Italian restitution, 15 April 1948, File "Correspondence – April 1948," Correspondence and Related Records, 1946–9, Records of the Reparations and Restitution Branch, Records of the Restitution Section, RG 260.

[57] Ibid.

[58] Ibid.

[59] Memorandum, "Return of Art Objects to Italy (000.4), 22 December 1948," Executive Office Decimal File, 1948, Records of the Civil Affairs Division, RG 165.

[60] Richard F. Howard to Michael J. Kurtz, letter, April 1981.

Twelve works of art were returned before OMGUS ceased operations in 1949, with negotiations over the remaining items taking place between Italy and the Federal Republic of Germany in the early 1950s. These negotiations were based on the 1952 Settlement Convention between the Federal Republic and the three Western Occupying Powers, which, among other things, left final handling of restitution claims with the Federal Republic. For all practical purposes, direct American and Allied involvement with restitution was at an end.

Though German reaction in 1948 to the OMGUS action involving the disputed Italian art was muted, an incident in the mid-1950s indicates how sensitive were German feelings. The Italians, at the instigation of Rodolfo Siviero, wanted to present a copy of the *Discobolus* to the United States.[61] The Germans were greatly offended. They believed the *Discobolus* and the twelve other works OMGUS had restituted in 1948, were really German property. They noted that the purchase of these items occurred before the war and that the Reich had paid a fair price and all the requisite Italian taxes. The Germans strongly believed that restitution was inappropriate for these items, particularly because no compensation was made for the monies originally expended for the purchases. Furthermore, the Germans believed that, in subsequent negotiations with the Italians over this class of claims, they had made numerous and generous concessions far beyond what was required by the Settlement Convention of 1952.[62]

The State Department was greatly disturbed at being in the middle of the recriminations. Both Italy and the Federal Republic were important partners in the quest to contain communism. The Department's Fine Arts Officer, Ardelia Hall, strongly believed that Richard Howard, the MFA&A officer in 1948, was most responsible for the original mishandling of this dispute. She agreed with the German position that the restitution actions in 1948 were an error. In her view, the policy directive of that time related only to inalienable national treasures, such as the Vipiteno Altarpiece. Hall charged that Howard had never informed Clay that a number of the items that the Italians wanted returned were acquired before the war or the German occupation of Italy and that adequate compensation had been paid for them. In Hall's opinion, Howard was responsible for restituting as many as eighteen works of art without adequate investigation and on dubious grounds. In effect, Hall was belatedly taking the side of Herbert S. Leonard, former head of

---

[61] "Proposed Gift of the Discobolus Copy to the United States Government (A-295), 21 October 1953," File "Ownership – Italian," Records Maintained by the Fine Arts and Monuments Adviser, 1945–61, RG 59.

[62] "Memo on Visit to U.S. Embassy Rome by German Cultural Counselor Dr. Sattler," File "Ownership – Italian," Records Maintained by the Fine Arts and Monuments Adviser, 1945–61, RG 59.

the Munich Central Collecting Point, who had opposed the 1948 restitution actions.[63] The fine arts officer also took a dim view of Siviero. She claimed that American MFA&A officers believed that Siviero was a communist and that Howard's exclusive reliance on Siviero's advice and recommendations was improper.[64] In an effort to diffuse the situation, Secretary of State John Foster Dulles cabled the American Embassy in Rome in an attempt to discourage the offer of the *Discobolus* copy. Dulles instructed the embassy to inform the Italians quietly that the offer could prove embarrassing to the United States and to request that the offer not be made.[65]

While the diplomatic actions were occurring behind the scenes, old controversies about Siviero and the restitution of looted Italian art at the end of the war broke out in the Italian press. Siviero claimed that he was responsible for the return of three thousand works of art to Italy, which had been illegally sold to Germany before the war. Former military government officials countered that the American Army was responsible for this activity, and, in any event, the number involved was far less than three thousand.[66] The claims and counterclaims rapidly descended into personal attacks, with Siviero stating that the legalism inherent in American Protestantism had infected the MFA&A in Germany, specifically Herbert S. Leonard, and hindered Italian efforts to regain works of art sold to Germany before the end of the Axis alliance.[67] With this bitter, old debate resurfacing, the State Department decided it was not possible to fend off the Italian offer of the *Discobolus* copy. Basically, the State Department believed that settling the public dispute with Italy was more pressing than soothing German irritation, particularly because the latter had kept their position private and out of the press. When President Giovanni Gronchi visited Washington in February 1956, he presented the copy to President Eisenhower in a Rose Garden ceremony.

The Germans fared better in a struggle to prevent the seizure of certain cultural properties in Italy for reparations. The properties in question were four German libraries created in Italy in the previous century and subsequently supported by private foundations and various German government offices. The libraries in question – The Hertziana Library, the Archeological Institute, the German Art Historical Institute of Florence, and the German Historical Institute – were viewed by the Italians as assets of the former

---

[63] Ardelia Hall, "How the Exceptional Return of Eighteen Works of Art by OMGUS to Italy Took Place, 4 June 1954," File "Ownership – Italian," Records Maintained by the Fine Arts and Monuments Adviser, 1945–61, RG 59.

[64] Ibid.

[65] "Proposed Gift of the Discobolus Copy to the United States Government (A-295), 21 October 1953," File "Ownership – Italian," Records Maintained by the Fine Arts and Monuments Adviser, 1945–61, RG 59.

[66] Frederick Hartt to Ardelia Hall, 6 January 1955, Records Concerning Restitution, Library of the National Gallery of Art, Washington, D.C.

[67] Siviero, *Second National Exhibition*, p. 20.

Reich and thus appropriate for seizure as reparations.[68] Ardelia Hall, supported by Ambassador Robert Murphy, argued that these libraries were legitimate institutions and not Nazi propaganda tools. They had contributed to Italian art study and should not be treated as German foreign assets. The State Department accepted the Hall-Murphy position and came to an impasse with the Italian government over the issue. As an interim measure, an international federation administered the libraries.[69] Again, the United States was caught between two of the countries it viewed as indispensable for maintaining an anticommunist front in Europe. As in the dispute over the restitution of allegedly illegally exported works of art, the American government left final resolution of the issue to the Italians and Germans. In an effort to avoid antagonizing either country, no other course was feasible. With quiet support from the Vatican and other Western governments, the Germans eventually succeeded in preventing the seizure of the libraries.[70]

Relations with the other Western Allies were cooperative and friendly. Except with the French, there were no serious difficulties. The Belgian restitution effort went smoothly, for example, though the problem of restitution-in-kind arose toward the end of the occupation. With one thousand items still missing, the Belgians worried that Allied differences would prevent any effective restitution-in-kind.[71] OMGUS assured the Belgians that adequate American machinery existed, and all requests would receive consideration based on the merits of the case.[72] OMGUS noted it had received no claims to date but did urge the preparation of a catalog for distribution containing illustrations of the missing items. The openness of the OMGUS stance, and the fact that they had already received six thousand items, allayed Belgian discontent.[73]

Difficulties with the French, unlike those with the other Western Europeans, were varied and not easily settled. Restitution issues, such as restitution-in-kind, freedom of movement for restitution missions, French

---

[68] "German Institutions in Italy (HICOG Cable 1645), 15 November 1950," File "German Art Libraries: Basic Data," German Cultural Assets in Italy, 1945–54, General Records, 1945–6, Records Concerning the Central Collecting Points, Records of the Marburg Central Collecting Point, RG 260.

[69] Ibid.

[70] Ibid.

[71] Lt. F. S. E. Baudoin to Col. John Allen, 28 May 1948, File "Correspondence – June 1948," Correspondence and Related Records, 1946–9, Records of the Reparations and Restitution Branch, Records of the Restitution Section, RG 260.

[72] Lt. Col. G. H. Garde to Lt. F. S. E. Baudoin, June 1948, File "Correspondence – June 1948," Correspondence and Related Records, 1946–9, Records of the Reparations and Restitution Branch, Records of the Restitution Section, RG 260.

[73] Lester K. Born, "Final Report, Monuments, Fine Arts and Archives Section, 30 December 1948," File "Final Report – Reparations and Restitution," Reports and Related Records Re: Restitution, 1945–52, Records of the Reparations and Restitution Branch, RG 260.

refusal to participate in interzonal exchanges, and the French desire for indefinite restitution, reflected basic antagonism toward the Germans and the expectation of a long occupation. All of these directly contradicted American policies and proclivities. The United States, which was not despoiled by the Nazis, wanted a speedy end to restitution. Therefore, the Americans strove for interzonal exchanges and finally set termination dates for their restitution program. The United States was also concerned that the restitution program not create bitter feelings among the Germans. Therefore, the United States effectively prevented any restitution-in-kind program and likewise restricted the travel of the French restitution mission. Differences with the French prevented a tripartite agreement on internal restitution. The French, for example, had no provision for successor organizations.[74] Only in Berlin was Allied agreement on internal restitution possible, and this occurred in July 1949.

One case in particular epitomizes the complexities and frustrations involved with American-French restitution relations. This involved the Photo-Marburg Company, a commercial organization selling photographs of architectural monuments and art objects. Photo-Marburg was also part of the Art History Department at the University of Marburg.[75] The head of this organization, Dr. Richard Hamann, had worked for twenty years before the war compiling photographic negatives of items in Europe. These included eighteen thousand negatives from France. Between 1940 and 1944, Hamann and his associates had taken 24,000 photographs of French monuments and other works of art.[76] The French informally contacted the MFA&A Section in OMGUS regarding the return of these negatives through restitution procedures. Colonel John Allen, Restitution Branch Chief, at first responded affirmatively. He told the French that the negatives were subject to restitution because the decree of the Vichy government, under which Hamann operated, was not valid.[77] In response to this, the French filed a formal claim.

Theodore Heinrich, MFA&A chief in *Land* Greater Hesse, objected strenuously. In February 1947, he prepared a detailed critique of the case. No doubt, Heinrich was influenced, in part, by the fact that the University of Marburg was in Greater Hesse. Heinrich claimed that Hamann had continued his prewar pattern of practices, which included seeking

---

[74] R. J. Cassoday, Memorandum on restitution in Berlin (87 2/3), File "Berlin Restitution," General Records, 1944–50, Property Division, RG 260.

[75] Memorandum, "Restitution of Photographic Negatives to France (102 1/3), 15 April 1948," File "Photo-Marburg," Reports and Related Records Re: Restitution, 1945–52, Records of the Reparations and Restitution Branch, RG 260.

[76] Ibid.

[77] Col. John Allen, "French Claim on Photo-Marburg, 1 April 1947," File "Photo-Marburg," Reports and Related Records Re: Restitution, 1945–52, Records of the Reparations and Restitution Branch, RG 260.

permission to photograph objects when they were not in the public domain and had paid fees where necessary.[78] In the prewar period, the French had not asked for royalties because they received a file copy of each photograph, and French scholars were accorded publication rights gratis.[79] Heinrich contended that Hamann had used German equipment and material and was not associated with the military. He concluded that 90 percent of the 24,000 negatives related to architectural subjects and were in the public domain.[80] The remaining 10 percent were museum objects in two categories: architectural fragments and old prints or drawings depicting German cities or palaces designed in whole or in part by French architects.[81] Heinrich argued that Hamann had no connection with the Einsatzstab Reichsleiter Rosenberg, nor were his efforts intended to denigrate French achievements.[82]

Former MFA&A officials, L. Bancel La Farge and James J. Rorimer, also entered the fray. La Farge contended that the negatives were not French property and thus were not subject to restitution.[83] In addition, removal of the negatives would do irreparable harm to the integrity of the Photo-Marburg archives. This was a research tool valued by scholars.[84] La Farge urged that the Germans keep at least duplicates, in order to retain their goodwill in cultural matters. He caustically noted that the French were not known for a good cataloguing system or for making their archives available.[85] Rorimer wrote that Hamann had a tremendous following in the United States and that the prewar Marburg Institute had a great reputation for serving cultural institutions.[86] Richard F. Howard, La Farge's successor in MFA&A, thought differently. He believed the French had a strong moral case and that the negatives ought to be returned.[87] In his opinion, pressure from the *Land* government of Greater Hesse, as well as Hamann's connections in the United States and elsewhere, prevented restitution.[88] He thought

[78] Theodore Heinrich, "Photo-Marburg, 10 February 1947," File "Photo-Marburg," Reports and Related Records Re: Restitution, 1945–50, Records of the Reparations and Restitution Branch, RG 260.
[79] Ibid.
[80] Ibid.
[81] Ibid.
[82] Ibid.
[83] L. Bancel La Farge to Col. B. B. McMahon (000.4), 1 April 1948, Executive Office Decimal File, 1948, Records of the Civil Affairs Division, RG 165.
[84] Ibid.
[85] Ibid.
[86] James J. Rorimer to Col. John Allen (000.4), 23 March 1948, Executive Office Decimal File, 1948, Records of the Civil Affairs Division, RG 165.
[87] Richard F. Howard, Memorandum on Photo-Marburg case (102 1/3), 7 December 1948, File "Photo-Marburg," Reports and Related Records Re: Restitution, 1945–50, Records of the Reparations and Restitution Branch, RG 260.
[88] Ibid.

the negatives fell under the category of cultural property removed under exceptional circumstances, similar to the Italian masterpieces exported under Mussolini.[89]

In the face of tremendous conflicting pressures, OMGUS eventually decided in favor of the German position. This was the result of some serious doubts as to whether the photographs were really subject to restitution, the desire not to offend significant sections of the German educational and cultural elite, and the self-interest of American scholars who wanted Photo-Marburg retained intact. Another probable factor was the strained state of French – American relations regarding occupation policy in Germany. As noted before, this was as serious in cultural matters as in political and economic matters. From the American point of view, the French were constantly criticizing restitution efforts and proving uncooperative in any American proposals or projects. In a case open to contending points of view, the psychological state of conflict may have tipped the scales against the French. The French were informed on 25 May 1948 that 90 percent of the objects photographed were in the public domain and, consequently, no loss to the cultural heritage of France.[90] Allen rather curtly told French MFA&A authorities that the claim was dropped, although they could provide further documentation if they wished.[91] Understandably, the French regarded this as another example of American obstruction in their quest to recover all they had lost.

The French protested that the regulations on proving ownership were too tight and that only looted objects of major war criminals were returned. OMGUS officials recognized this unhappiness but attributed it to political differences. They maintained most nations understood that the Americans had returned the vast majority of looted items in their zone. Both Lester K. Born, the archival advisor, and Richard F. Howard, head of MFA&A, did recommend that the United States respond sympathetically if any major works of art were uncovered after the termination of cultural restitution. This controversy obscured the fact that France regained an estimated two-thirds of the items looted by the Germans.[92] In fact, more than 1.6 million items, contained in 4,000 claims, were identified, packed, and shipped to the countries of origin.[93] Although everything certainly was not returned, the volume of restituted objects clearly indicates a major American commitment and achievement.

[89] Ibid.
[90] OMGUS Cablegram (V-35110) to the War Department on the Photo-Marburg case (000.4), 24 August 1948, Executive Office Decimal File, 1948, Records of the Civil Affairs Division, RG 165.
[91] Ibid.
[92] Lester K. Born, "Final Report, Monuments, Fine Arts and Archives Section, 30 December 1948," File "Final Report – Reparations and Restitution," Reports and Related Records Re: Restitution, 1945–50, Records of the Reparations and Restitution Branch, RG 260.
[93] Ibid.

## International Law Evolves

During the Cold War period, international law on restitution and the protection of cultural property began to develop in new directions. In addition to the continued emphasis on protecting cultural property during wartime, efforts to prevent the illegal export and sale of cultural objects, particularly those of indigenous cultures, came to the forefront. This reflected the postcolonial environment, which began in the 1950s, and the demand of newly emerging nations for assistance in protecting their cultural patrimony. Again reflective of the international environment, the United Nations, specifically the UN Educational, Scientific and Cultural Organization (UNESCO), took the lead in negotiating new arrangements.

The Hague Convention of 1954 for the Protection of Cultural Property in the Event of Armed Conflict sought to redress the grievous wrongs committed during World War II. Article 1 of the Hague Convention provided a blanket, if general, protection to all cultural objects. Article 8 provided for a limited number of refuges and centers of great significance to be identified by signatories to the convention and listed in a register to be maintained by UNESCO.[94] These refuges, identified by distinctive markings, must remain immune from all attack, except in cases of "unavoidable military necessity" and if cultural property was used for military purposes.[95] The protocol to the 1954 convention addressed the restitution problem. The protocol prohibits the signatories from exporting cultural property from occupied territory; and if such occurs, mandatory restitution is required at the end of hostilities.[96] Though eighty-eight nations signed the convention and seventy-five announced adherence to the protocol, there were significant abstentions. The Soviet Union, Great Britain, and the United States declined to support the convention. Cold War and nuclear tensions undermined even the façade of international unity on the principles of protecting and restituting cultural property. As the Department of State explained, "[T]he major difficulty is that adherence to the Convention would seriously limit the options of the United States in the event of nuclear war or even in some cases of conventional bombardment."[97]

In 1977, protocols were signed that strengthened the 1949 Geneva Conventions on the conduct of hostilities. The articles once again prohibited any acts of hostility against works of art or places of worship and required signatories to not use cultural objects for military purposes or as objects of reprisals.[98] Signatories to the 1949 conventions, which included almost all

---

[94] Library of Congress, *Report for Congress: Protection of Cultural Property under International Law and the Laws of Selected Foreign Nations* (cc 96.6), April 1996, p. 21.
[95] Ibid.
[96] Ibid., pp. 21–2.
[97] Ibid., p. 21.
[98] Ibid., p. 22.

nations, accepted the new provisions without dissent. But the most path-breaking developments in international law involved a broader perspective than looting and restitution during times of war. The explosion of new nations on the world stage, along with a rising demand and market in the developed nations for artifacts of native cultures, prompted concerns for what came to be defined as the world's cultural heritage. The 1970 UNESCO Convention on the Means of Prohibiting and Preventing the Illicit Import, Export, and Transfer of Ownership of Cultural Property was the first international undertaking seeking to control illicit cultural trade during peacetime. Despite detailed provisions requiring signatories to return items stolen or illegally exported in contravention of the laws of the country of origin, adherence and enforcement has been limited. With the exception of Australia, Canada, and the United States, most art-importing nations have not signed the convention.[99] The convention's limited definition of cultural property, as well as the practical difficulties in determining at the point of importation if laws of other countries have been broken, have for all practical purposes stymied implementation of the convention.[100]

The World Heritage Convention of 1972 moved beyond the somewhat limited definitions of cultural property in its 1970 Convention. The 1972 Convention provides not only for the protection of cultural monuments and sites but also, for the first time, the natural heritage. The 1972 Convention requires that property within its purview "must be of outstanding universal value from the point of view of history, art, science, aesthetics, anthropology, conservation, ethnology, or natural beauty."[101] The United Nation's continued efforts in 1978 to set up mechanisms for the protection and restitution of cultural property, as well as provisions in the 1982 Law of the Sea Convention, attest to continued strong international interest in the protection of cultural heritage.[102] This interest is also expressed in numerous bilateral and regional agreements.

Yet, whether in war or peace, the protection of cultural heritage remains illusive. Countless armed conflicts, such as the Iraqi invasion of Kuwait and ethnic cleansing in Kosovo, demonstrate that cultural heritage and identity remain at risk. The explosion of national claims and countless court cases involving antiquities and works of art attest to the volatile and lucrative nature of cultural protection and restitution even in peacetime. The abrupt end of the Cold War, however, has provided the opportunity for a fresh start, particularly in resolving the bitter legacy of World War II.

[99] Ibid., pp. 25–7.
[100] Ibid.
[101] Ibid., p. 22.
[102] Ibid., pp. 23, 29.

# Restitution at Home

## *The American Scene*

Though American military authorities in Germany sought to control and manage the cultural property in its possession, the effort was always a struggle. Military personnel "liberating" mementos, some quite valuable, and the underground market for art often came together to thwart government policies and objectives. Over time, the problem of looted or displaced works of art entering the United States became a nagging problem for the American government.

### American Policy

Given the vigorous effort of OMGUS to return looted cultural property, a similar stance was required for art that slipped through to America. The Roberts Commission was wrestling with the potential problem of stolen art entering the United States as early as September 1944. As the thefts by Americans came to light, such as the highly publicized case of the Hesse crown jewels, the government had to take action. This case indicated the problems to come. In April 1945, General George Patton's Third Army requisitioned the castle of the former Hesse ruling house for its headquarters. Princess Margaret of Hesse, sister of Kaiser Wilhelm II, mother of the notorious Nazi art procurer Prince Philip, and granddaughter of Queen Victoria, was given four hours to vacate the premises, which she and other family members did with much chagrin. What no one knew at that point was that priceless jewels belonging to the family had been buried under flagstones in the subbasement of Kronberg Castle.[1] After the Third Army moved forward, the castle was used as an officer's club and rest house. At this point, an army sergeant found the jewels and turned them over to the Women's Army Corps (WAC) officer in charge, Katherine Nash. A few months later,

---

[1] Lynn Nicholas, *The Rape of Europa: The Fate of Europe's Treasures in the Third Reich and the Second World War* (New York: Alfred A. Knopf, 1994), pp. 354–5.

the family discovered that the jewels were missing, and the Army's Criminal Investigation Unit began an investigation.[2]

Fairly quickly, suspicion focused on Captain Nash and her lover (later husband) Colonel Durant. Upon return to the United States and interrogation, the couple confessed and the jewels were recovered, along with a great deal of other valuable items, including letters to Queen Victoria, books, medals, and watches. The Army returned the Durants to Germany for trial, and the couple received substantial prison terms.[3] The Army congratulated itself on resolving this high-profile and embarrassing case. But, in fact, other less spectacular items were being shipped back to America by military personnel. MFA&A officers were overwhelmed dealing with the hundreds of repositories and transporting what they found to the central collecting points. They had no time to police the hundreds of military detachments scattered across the country. Nor could the MFA&A men inspect and protect every castle, church, or museum. Clearly higher level policy making and action were needed.

As was often the case, the Roberts Commission stimulated policy making. With the commission's work drawing to a close, Secretary-Treasurer Huntington Cairns wrote Assistant Secretary of State John Hilldring proposing a plan of action. Cairns, on behalf of the commission, proposed to write to individuals already identified as holding objects or collections belonging to other nations, instructing them to turn over the materials to a local military command. According to the Roberts Commission proposal, German or Japanese items would go to the respective military governments. Items from other countries would be sent to the local American embassy for transmittal to national authorities.[4] With the likelihood of other material coming to light, the commission proposed to send a circular to American museums, universities, libraries, and art dealers alerting them to items already known to be in the United States and how to identify and handle other suspicious items that came to light.[5] This reflected an earlier commission initiative, which had requested museums, art and antique dealers, and auction houses to report any items with a doubtful provenance to the commission, which in turn would contact Customs and Treasury Department officials.

The State, War, Navy Coordinating Committee evaluated the Roberts Commission proposals and initiative in determining government policy. The State Department representative presented the Roberts Commission position, and the committee approved a general policy position that stated:

[2] Ibid.
[3] Ibid.
[4] U.S. Department of State, *Bulletin* no. 399 (23 February 1947): 359.
[5] Ibid.

The introduction of looted objects into this country is contrary to the general policy of the United States and to the commitments of the United States under the Hague Convention of 1907 and in the case of objects of a value of $5,000 or more is a contravention of Federal law. It is incumbent on this Government, therefore, to exert every reasonable effort to right such wrongs as may be brought to light.[6]

To put flesh on the policy bone, the committee agreed that the State Department would send out a circular to museums, libraries, university departments of fine arts, art and antique dealers, and auction houses and booksellers announcing government policy and requesting that all relevant information be forwarded to the State Department. The State Department also was authorized to approach all those known to hold possibly looted objects and to seek the return of the items in question. In case of refusal and if the object was worth more than $5,000, the State Department would seek prosecution by the Department of Justice under the terms of the National Stolen Property Act.[7] That former or currently serving military personnel were considered the most likely candidates to hold suspicious objects is clear from the fact that the War and Navy departments were to defray the expenses of the program.[8] The policy and procedures were issued by the State Department in a February 1947 bulletin. Clearly the government admitted there was a problem and then focused attention on recovery and restitution.

## Returns – The First Decade

In addition to the State Department's circular in February 1947, supplemented by a reminder circular in 1950, the efforts of the department's arts and monuments advisor, Ardelia Hall, were critical in making progress on the government's commitments. Actively involved since 1944 in supporting the Roberts Commission and the OMGUS MFA&A program, Hall was simply indefatigable. Ely Maurer, a deputy counsel in the State Department's Legal Advisor's Office and one who also labored for decades on restitution issues, remembered Hall as "a persistent, zealous person, passionate in her attempts to recover stolen cultural property and she succeeded greatly in that effort."[9] Much of Hall's attention was focused on the domestic scene, where she often provided the focus and energy to recover and return looted objects.

---

[6] Ibid., p. 358.

[7] Ibid.

[8] Ibid., pp. 358–9.

[9] Ely Maurer, "The Role of the State Department Regarding National and Private Claims for the Restitution of Stolen Cultural Property," in *The Spoils of War: World War II and Its Aftermath: The Loss, Reappearance, and Recovery of Cultural Property*, edited by Elizabeth Simpson (New York: Harry N. Abram, 1957), p. 143.

Most domestic restitution occurred during the first decade after the war. Through Hall's efforts, a number of institutions reported items with suspect provenance. Most of these were obtained when servicemen or dealers sought to sell the items. When she could not get cooperation from holders of suspected looted property, she turned to federal agencies with law enforcement or investigative powers, such as the Department of Justice, the Customs Service, or the Internal Revenue Service. When members of the military were involved, Ardelia Hall turned to the Department of Defense for aid.[10] Sixty-six cases were brought forward for restitution involving 1,586 objects. All the items returned by the time the major effort was concluded in 1954 belonged to state or municipal collections in Europe. The most valuable of the objects had entered the United States through trade and commercial channels. Items returned included a fourteenth-century work by Petrarch, *De Africa*; a collection of 250 seals, gems, and other items from the State Coin Collection in Munich; the Dutch archives of the Netherlands East Indies; and a tenth-century manuscript with one of the two surviving pages of the Hildebrandslied from the State Library at Kassel.[11]

Hall could proudly report that many European institutions were ecstatic to receive their lost treasures. The mayor of Mainz, for example, was deeply appreciative of American efforts to recover and return the Mainz Psalter in time for the 1950 Johannes Gutenberg celebration. The return of the Petrarch manuscript to the Biblioteca Civica of Trieste prompted the Italian ambassador to the United States to declare "his warmest gratitude and deep appreciation of the assistance offered by the American authorities in the recovery of the masterpiece."[12]

The goodwill engendered by these efforts reinforced the three principles that formed the basis for the State Department's restitution work. The domestic restitution program was viewed, fundamentally, as morally based. After all, stolen property ought to go back to the owner. Just as importantly, the program was considered sound foreign policy and excellent public relations. Both factors were critical in the postwar struggle for Europe. Finally, restitution was in America's self-interest: Art is the heritage of all, and the United States certainly wanted to regain any of its lost or stolen cultural heritage.[13] Despite Ardelia Hall's achievements, it is difficult to believe that she more than scratched the surface. Millions of servicemen mailing home mementos of varying quality and value as well as the active and secretive art market must have meant that many items came into the United States in violation of law and regulations. Only decades later would some of the most valuable items begin to surface.

---

[10] Ibid.
[11] U.S. Department of State, *Bulletin* no. 797 (4 October 1954): 493–8.
[12] Ibid.
[13] Maurer, "The Role of the State Department," p. 142.

## The Courts Decide

Not all the looted art that was located in the United States was voluntarily returned. In the 1960s, as the war faded and art started to come on the market, cases came to the fore and subsequently ended up in fiercely contested litigation. The courts increasingly became the venue for the recovery and return of looted property. The issues involved were always complex, involving entanglements such as statutes of limitation for returning stolen art, disputed ownership, and diplomatic controversy. An excellent example that illustrates the entangling qualities of cultural restitution involved three paintings taken by an American sailor from the Weimar Museum. When the theft was uncovered in the United States, the Office of Alien Property, custodian of former enemy property seized in the United States, vested or took charge of the paintings. In the 1960s, as the Office of Alien Property began to liquidate its holdings, the Federal Republic of Germany requested the return of the three paintings. These valuable items were a Rembrandt, a Terborch, and a Tishbein. The State Department introduced legislation in Congress that permitted the return of the three works of art.

Though Congress approved the bill in late 1966, a further problem ensued. The German Democratic Republic claimed the items because they came from Weimar, located within East Germany. Because the United States did not at that point recognize the GDR, the claim was summarily rejected. After the paintings were returned to the Federal Republic, contention continued. The grand duchess of Saxony-Weimar-Eisenach filed suit claiming the paintings as the property of her family. Eventually, a West German court ordered the Rembrandt awarded to the grand duchess. It is amazing to note that the three paintings involved a larcenous American sailor, an act of Congress, two competing governments, and deposed German royalty.

A similar situation came to light in 1966 and was fought out for years in the U.S. federal courts. Two Dürer paintings, also stolen from the Weimar Museum, surfaced in 1966 in the possession of a Brooklyn lawyer, Edward I. Elicofon.[14] Elicofon asserted that he had purchased the items in good faith in 1946 from an American serviceman who claimed to have bought them for $450. A friend of Elicofon's remembered seeing the paintings in a book on stolen art and publicly exposed the matter.[15] Ely Maurer brought the matter to the attention of Undersecretary of State George C. McGhee, who then invited Elicofon to lunch and sought to persuade him to return the paintings because of a possible violation of the National Stolen Property Act and the need for good foreign relations. When Elicofon rejected the overture, the State Department urged the Federal Republic to institute a lawsuit.[16] At

[14] Ibid., p. 143.
[15] Ibid.
[16] Ibid.

the same time, the GDR claimed the paintings for the Weimar Museum. Because the United States soon granted diplomatic recognition to the GDR, the State Department refrained from any involvement in the litigation.[17] Once again, cultural restitution intersected with American foreign policy.

The issue dragged on in the courts, with arguments mostly focused on the statute of limitations. In New York, the statute of limitations begins when the owner of a stolen object learns of its location and current possessor and demands the return of the item. The original owner has three years from the refusal of the current possessor to file suit.[18] With millions of dollars at stake, Elicofon rejected the claims made by the GDR, the Federal Republic, and the grand duchess of Saxony-Weimar-Eisenach, who entered this case as well. Though the Brooklyn lawyer lost the argument that the "demand and refusal" law did not apply in this case, he claimed that the Weimar Museum had not made a diligent effort to locate the paintings. The court also rejected this argument, and after eight years of litigation the paintings were returned to the Weimar Museum.[19] The "demand and refusal" rule, codified in another Holocaust art restitution case, *Mengel v. List*, was the most significant advance for claimants, at least in the important arena of New York State litigation. As in the Elicofon case, the defendant had to return an artwork (a Chagall) purchased in good faith from a reputable art dealer.

It is important to note the role of the U.S. government in these cases. When efforts at mediation failed, as in the Elicofon case, the State Department urged the aggrieved parties, two foreign governments recognized by the United States, to file a civil lawsuit and pursue the issue using its own resources. Even foreign governments found this an expensive and difficult route to pursue. In the years to come, as individual claimants came forward, referrals to the American court system posed sometimes almost insurmountable obstacles.

The two German states were also embroiled in another case. In April 1945, American forces operating in Thuringia, destined to belong in the Soviet zone of occupation, were ordered to move any uncovered cultural treasures westward. One treasure found in a salt mine was the stamp collection of the German Reich museum. American authorities moved the museum from Berlin to Frankfurt. An inventory in 1949 uncovered the fact that eight stamps worth $500,000 were missing. When the stamps surfaced in Philadelphia in the late 1970s, experts alerted the government. When the owner, a former Army captain, was questioned, he claimed that a German he had befriended gave him the stamps in gratitude. Customs agents convinced the

---

[17] Ibid.

[18] Lawrence Kaye, "Laws in Force at the Dawn of World War II," in *The Spoils of War: World War II and Its Aftermath: The Loss, Reappearance, and Recovery of Cultural Property*, edited by Elizabeth Simpson (New York: Harry N. Abrams, 1997), p. 104.

[19] Ibid.

former Army officer that he possessed looted property, and he turned the stamps over to the government in hopes of an award.[20] Complications arose when both the Federal Republic and the GDR claimed the stamps. The East Germans felt they owned the stamps because the collection was once housed in Berlin, the site of their capital. The West Germans claimed the stamps because they had the bulk of the collection. Quiet diplomatic efforts continued until the collapse of the Berlin Wall and the reunification of the two Germanies. The stamps were returned to Frankfurt, where the segments were once again unified into a single collection.

Another case with foreign policy complications involved a painting by Tintoretto, *The Holy Family with St. Catherine and Honored Donor.* According to Maurer, rumor had it that a Russian general took the painting from Dresden at the end of the war and sold it to a Jewish man, who subsequently emigrated to Israel. This individual commissioned Raumond Vinokur to take the painting to the United States and sell it. Undercover FBI agents arrested Vinokur in December 1979 for attempting to sell stolen property.[21] The GDR claimed the painting because Dresden was in its territory. The Israeli owner of the painting sued in U.S. federal court for the return of the treasure. The vagaries of the litigative process came to the fore in this case when the Israeli owner ultimately triumphed and retained the painting.

The court cases that began to appear in the 1960s indicated the strengths and weaknesses of the American legal system. The concept that a thief could not pass on a good title favored the dispossessed. Yet statute of limitations provisions for filing suits varied among the state jurisdictions, with New York State the most favorable for claimants. But civil litigation was a burdensome, arduous, and expensive process. The U.S. government refrained from taking sides whether claimants were foreign governments or private individuals. After the mid-1950s, the government no longer issued circulars or reminders about looted art and remained aloof to the greatest extent possible from court cases. These cases were regarded as basically serendipitous, not requiring a government program or response. This attitude would remain unchallenged until the dramatic events of the 1990s.

## German War Art

A related but distinct cultural question was the disposition of German war art brought to the United States by the Army. This matter brings to mind to some extent the most bitterly fought battle related to cultural property in the early occupation period: what to do with Class "C" items, German works

---

[20] Ely Maurer, "Memorandum for the Files – Eight Postage Stamps, 4 May 1981," File "Protection of Cultural Property – 8 Postage Stamps – IV," Records of the Legal Advisor: Office of Educational, Cultural and Public Affairs, Subject Files, 1945–97, RG 59.

[21] *The Washington Post*, 14 December 1979.

of art that some American officials wanted to use as reparations. As already noted, the uproar over this was so intense that only 202 masterpieces were brought to the United States for "preservation." German war art, although undoubtedly German in origin, was not in the final analysis treated as if in the same category as other Class "C" property, which remained in Germany. These were works of art commissioned by the *Staffel der bildenden Kunstler* to depict Germans in combat and work situations.[22] In the minds of many American officials at the end of the war, these were paintings that fell under the Yalta Conference communiqué that pledged to eradicate Nazi and militarist influences from German cultural life. Contemporary opinion came to view these paintings as basically nonideological.

If this was the sole motivation for confiscating war art, then the Army would have destroyed these items. However, in June 1945 Secretary of War Stimson created the Historical Properties Section to collect war-related items for display in the Pentagon. An MFA&A specialist, Captain Gordon Gilkey, collected 8,722 items, at the command of the chief of the USFET Historical Division, which were sent to the United States. It seems clear that War Department officials and military historians at that point believed these paintings were legitimate spoils of war. By the end of the occupation period, military historians were becoming skeptical whether all these paintings were Nazi war art. After repeated discussions with the judge advocate general's office, historians convinced the Army that sixteen hundred of the paintings were nonpolitical and nonmilitary and thus had been taken in error. Though at first reluctant to accept a partial restitution, the Germans eventually took these paintings back.

The rest of the collection was scattered across the United States in hospitals, military posts, and various Pentagon corridors, but the war artists and their heirs unsuccessfully petitioned for the return of their works. No progress was made until a Virginia congressman, G. William Whitehurst, introduced a bill in Congress on 6 April 1978, returning ten paintings to the Navy of the Federal Republic. This resulted from Whitehurst's visit to Kiel in January 1978 where two former German naval attachés to the United States sought his assistance. Whitehurst argued that this was military art, not Nazi art, and all but one thousand paintings deserved return. The congressman noted that Japan received its war mementos when the United States returned Okinawa in 1972.[23] The Whitehurst bill met little opposition, and the ten paintings were returned. With this event, momentum grew for a final disposition of the whole matter. State Department specialists urged Secretary of State Alexander Haig to return the rest of the collection as a goodwill gesture during the May 1981 visit of Chancellor Helmut Schmidt.[24] Because the

[22] John Paul Weber, *The German War Artists* (Columbia, S.C.: Cerberus, 1979), pp. 11–129.
[23] *Washington Post*, 27 May 1981.
[24] Ibid.

government had appropriated the paintings, congressional action was required. In May, Congressman Whitehurst, along with several other sponsors, introduced H.R. 4625, which provided for a final return to Germany, pending a review by a commission to weed out any genuinely Nazi-inspired works of art. The bill was swiftly approved by Congress and signed by President Reagan in March 1982.

The Secretary of the Army established the German War Art Committee to identify those items that must remain in the United States. The committee, chaired by Walter A. Baker, assistant general council for the Army, had representatives from the State and Defense departments, the National Gallery of Art, and the Holocaust Memorial Council. The members worked throughout the summer and fall of 1982 to translate congressional intent and international obligations into practical decisions concerning the 6,900 works of art. The committee carefully screened the art to ensure that no items that were to be returned showed Nazi symbols, glorified Nazi leaders or the party, or could otherwise be useful in reviving militarism. The committee also had to keep in mind that congressional intent was to allow the Army and Air Force to retain artwork integral to museum operations or those that were useful for educational or historical purposes. Overriding all else, though, was the committee's desire to implement the spirit of the law, which was to return as much as possible to Germany. In keeping with that feeling, the committee decided that only 226 works of art were to remain in the Army collection and 101 in the Air Force collection. At last, the idea of art as war loot passed. This would have pleased the MFA&A staff in OMGUS who so heartily opposed such a concept as both uncivilized and un-American.

What happened during the Cold War decades of the 1950s through the 1980s was the resolution of cases Ardelia Hall had on hand and the resolution of a few court cases. From all appearances, cultural restitution had run its course. Information about what was in the Soviet Union and Eastern Europe was locked behind the Iron Curtain. Restitution organizations such as Jewish Cultural Reconstruction ceased operation or focused on monetary compensation from Germany. What governments in Europe had done with restituted objects was little understood, and the workings of the art market remained cloaked in secrecy. The provenance of artworks hanging in American museums were sketchy at best. All this was about to change, suddenly and dramatically.

# Renewed Ferment

*Restitution in the Post–Cold War Era*

## A Seismic Shift

The collapse of the Soviet Union and the end of the Cold War dramatically affected restitution efforts, particularly in the cultural arena. From an issue that only occasionally merited newspaper headlines or court decisions came a continuing series of revelations that focused international attention in a manner not seen since the immediate post–World War II period. As communist regimes fell, archives were opened to scholars, journalists, and those seeking lost property for the first time. In Moscow, for example, the *Literaturnaia Gazeta* in October 1990 revealed the existence of ten million German library books seized by the Soviet Trophy Commission at the end of the war. Articles in the journal revealed that the books were scattered throughout Soviet territories, most suffering from severe neglect and deterioration.[1] Revelations about "trophy" art taken by the Soviets and filling the museums of Moscow, Leningrad (soon to be renamed Saint Petersburg), and other cities came to light. As significantly, long-lost foreign archival materials were located in the Soviet Special Archives, renamed in June 1992 as the Center for the Preservation of Historico-Documentary Collections. Extensive materials from France, Belgium, Germany, the Netherlands, and Liechtenstein were uncovered and publicized to the world.[2]

The early 1990s was a period of great hope and expectation as free expression and activity began in Eastern Europe, Russia, and the other states of the former Soviet Union. A harbinger of better times was the 1990 treaty between the Federal Republic of Germany and the Soviet Union on "Good Neighborliness." An article in the treaty provided that "missing" or "unlawfully

---

[1] Patricia Kennedy Grimsted, "Displaced Archives on the Eastern Front: Restitution Problems from World War II and Its Aftermath," *Janus: Archival Review* (February 1996): 51.

[2] Patricia Kennedy Grimsted, "'Trophy' Archives and Non-Restitution: Russia's Cultural 'Cold War' with the European Community," *Problems of Post-Communism* 45 (3) (May/June 1998): 3–6.

transferred" art, located in either Germany or the U.S.S.R., "will be returned to their owners or legal successors."[3] This was followed by a 1992 German-Russian Cultural Agreement providing for restitution in an effort to resolve the numerous issues left from the war. With German reunification, the Federal Republic began a massive transfer of funds to facilitate Russian troop withdrawals from the former East Germany. In this spirit, a somewhat reluctant German government also provided funding for microfilm equipment purchases the Russians said they needed to film captured German records and to return the records.[4]

The collapse of the command-and-control economy left destitute public institutions, including museums, libraries, and archives. Even though archives were being opened for the first time, access was difficult because of poor intellectual control, massive holdings in need of preservation, and facilities that were in a sad state of disrepair and with staff often unpaid. Yet the spirit of openness was contagious. In 1992, the Netherlands negotiated the first archival restitution agreement with Russia and began to assist sorely pressed Russian archivists. Russia also in 1992 negotiated restitution agreements with Belgium, France, and Liechtenstein, promising the return of materials seized almost fifty years before.[5]

The opening up of governments and archives in the East caused a resurgence of interest and hope for claimants and their heirs. Jewish and non-Jewish victims again sought long-delayed justice. The World Jewish Congress (WJC), in particular, was a strong advocate for the rights of Holocaust survivors and their heirs. A staunch advocate of restitution since the days of World War II, the WJC under the leadership of Edgar Bronfman, Israel Singer, and Elan Steinberg pressed in Europe and the United States for an accounting of looted assets.

The march of time also played a role in the resurgence of interest in restitution. Looters were dying. Collections of looted art, obtained wittingly or unwittingly, were coming into the market, and the emergence of the black market in the chaos of the dying Soviet empire brought a veritable deluge of art into the international arena, resulting in numerous legal cases. The 1990s would prove as crucial for restitution as the 1940s had been.

## A Spring Thaw

The German agreements with the Soviets and the Russians in 1990 and 1992 seemed to augur well for resolving long-standing restitution issues. Other agreements also provoked hope. In an agreement with Poland, for

---

[3] Thomas R. Kline, "The Russian Bill to Nationalize Trophy Art: An American Perspective," *The Spoils of War International Newsletter* (August 1997): p. 32.

[4] Grimsted, "Displaced Archives on the Eastern Front," p. 59.

[5] Grimsted, "'Trophy' Archives and Non-Restitution," pp. 7–8.

example, "death books" from the Auschwitz concentration camp captured by Soviet forces were returned to the Poles.[6] Western nations were also eager to reach agreements with the Russians. The Russian-Dutch archival agreement resulted in the return of six hundred books and a shipment of books originally looted by the Nazis from the International Institute of Social History in Amsterdam. Likewise, two Russian-French agreements signed in November 1992 gave promise of resolving long-standing questions about missing records and archival holdings.[7]

But the French, like the Dutch, had to basically barter to get materials returned. The French provided six container trucks to transport their records. Additionally, they paid for microfilming records that were to be restituted. Initially, all went well. Four of the six trucks were filled and returned with military intelligence files from the Deuxieme Bureau, which the Nazis had stored in Czechoslovakia and which the Soviets took in 1945.[8] In return, the Russians received logbooks from Russian and Soviet ships that cruised in the Mediterranean in the 1920s and the personal papers of Russian diplomat Nikolai Ignat'ev.[9] The Belgians also had to make special arrangements to ensure restitution took place. They had to pay the custom duties involved in providing microfilm stock and chemicals so that Belgian records could be microfilmed. After several years of delay, microfilmed copies of 20,154 files were sent to Belgium.[10]

By May 1994, almost three-quarters of the French archival materials were returned to Paris. But the period of the thaw was drawing to a close. There had been some progress on the library and archival fronts, but little progress had taken place in the art arena. Though governments, owners, and heirs had a much better understanding of the art in Russian state collections, little to nothing was returned. National pride, Russian financial need, and an exploding black market all contributed to a new freeze.

## Russian Reaction

Though Russia had only admitted in 1990 that the Soviet Trophy Commission had seized vast quantities of art and other valuable cultural property and begun to make restitution arrangements with Western nations, a nationalist reaction soon asserted itself. This was predictable, given the huge losses in life and property suffered by the Soviet Union and the widespread feeling that the seized art was only just compensation for losses incurred. The involvement of the Russian parliament in the restitution issue began

[6] Grimsted, "Displaced Archives on the Eastern Front," p. 58.
[7] Ibid., p. 59.
[8] Grimsted, "'Trophy' Archives and Non-Restitution," p. 8.
[9] Grimsted, "Displaced Archives on the Eastern Front," p. 59.
[10] Grimsted, "'Trophy' Archives and Non-Restitution," p. 8.

in 1994 when the Duma halted the controversial French restitution effort. Then, in April 1995 parliament placed a blanket embargo on all restitution.[11] The upper chamber of the parliament, the Council of the Federation, used a study prepared by the Russian Academy of Sciences to draft two laws designed to codify restitution policies and procedures. By early June 1995, the lower house, the Duma, had rejected both drafts. The strong communist and nationalist contingents in the Duma rejected the idea that any of the items seized at the end of the war were looted property requiring return to the country of origin. The actions of the Trophy Commission, sanctioned by decrees of Stalin, were considered an adequate legal basis for seizure and retention. Vitriolic speeches in the Duma and inflammatory press accounts led a majority of Russians to support a policy of no return.

The Duma passed a redrafted bill, "On Cultural Valuables Removed to the U.S.S.R. as a Result of World War II and Located in the Territory of the Russian Federation," on 5 July 1996, but the Council of the Federation rejected the bill. After mediation and slight revisions, the bill was passed by both the Duma and the council in early 1997 and sent to the president of the Russian Federation, Boris Yeltsin, for his signature.[12] Yeltsin vetoed the law on 17 March as contrary to international law and as a unilateral decision by the parliament. After his veto was overridden, Yeltsin appealed to the Constitutional Court to sustain his decision. After losing in the court, the president was ordered to sign the law. Though Yeltsin continued to protest about the voting procedures in the upper chamber and that the law violated the Constitution and international agreements signed in 1990 and 1992, restitution was effectively shut down.[13]

The Duma's bill asserted that all "cultural valuables" in the territory of the federation were the property of the state "irrespective of the possessor and the circumstances which led to this actual possession." For the Duma, retention was "a partial compensation for the damage suffered by cultural property of the Russian Federation." Though some exceptions were made for religious organizations, private charities, and those who lost property "because of their active fight against Nazism (Fascism)," processes for claims were complex, difficult, and basically designed to thwart returns.[14] The Duma's actions complicated Yeltsin's already rocky efforts to integrate Russia into the rest of Europe. The Duma's action flouted Russian commitments made when joining the Council of Europe to "settle rapidly all issues related to the return of property claimed by Council of Europe member

---

[11] Ibid., p. 9.
[12] Ibid., pp. 9–11.
[13] "International Discussion of the Russian Law," *Spoils of War International Newsletter* (August 1997): pp. 9–10.
[14] Kline, "The Russian Bill to Nationalize Trophy Art," p. 32.

states." European states with restitution agreements with Russia were disheartened to find their claims summarily rejected and international commitments ignored.[15]

Nationalist belligerence and the lack of an accurate historical perspective were clear factors in the 1997 Duma debate. For example, in justification for refusing to return cultural property, Duma members pointed to the American retention of five hundred files from the Communist Party archive in Smolensk. These files, which the United States retained for intelligence analysis, were only a small portion of the much larger Smolensk collection that the Americans returned in 1945. The Russians did not publicly acknowledge this return until 1991. Further, the Duma members either ignored or did not know that microfilmed copies of the files in American possession were widely available. In addition, the archivist of the United States had offered to return the original records in the 1960s, but the Communist Party's Central Committee had declined the offer because the files documented the impact of the 1930's Soviet collectivization effort.[16] All the difficulties were not solely on the Russian side. In 1992, the U.S. Senate had intervened to stop the return of the Smolensk Archives until an unrelated claim for a library collection looted in 1918 from the Lubavitcher Hasidic community was resolved.[17] Yet, this debate about five hundred files obscured the historical fact that the United States had returned in the immediate postwar period 500,000 cultural items and four freight cars of archival materials.[18] Further, in 1989 the American government returned prerevolutionary Russian consular files stored in the U.S. National Archives, and in 1997 Harvard University had returned files of the post–World War I Georgian government in exile, which the university had preserved. The relatively minor dispute over the Smolensk files was allowed to obscure the historical record.[19]

The collapse of the Iron Curtain and the opening of archival records helped make the 1990s a turbulent decade in restitution. The onslaught of more information not only produced increased hope for returns but also rekindled old animosities. The 1995 symposium in New York City on the "Spoils of War," sponsored by the Bard Graduate Center for the Study of the Decorative Arts, brought both phenomena to the fore. Conference participants heard papers and discussed international law on looting and cultural property, national losses suffered during the war, postwar restitution, and the emerging frontier of new restitution issues. The spirit of this international gathering, the first of its kind, was marred by the still-present passions of World War II. Russians and Germans sparred over losses attributed to one

---

[15] Grimsted, "'Trophy' Archives and Non-Restitution," p. 3.
[16] Grimsted, "Displaced Archives on the Eastern Front," p. 49.
[17] Ibid.
[18] Ibid., p. 46.
[19] Grimsted, "'Trophy' Archives and Non-Restitution," p. 14.

another, and other national representatives expressed concerns over their still-missing heritage.[20]

When Vladimir Putin, Yeltsin's successor as president of the Russian Federation, approved in May 2000 the legislation barring the return of cultural property to Germany and other claimants, a complete reversal had taken place from the spirit of the early 1990s.[21] But restitution and compensation matters in the 1990s and into the new century went beyond cultural treasures and property.

## A Matter of Justice

As a targeted enemy of the Nazis, the Jewish community had experienced particularly grievous losses. The 1990s witnessed a renewed Jewish effort to resolve long-lingering issues related to looted assets. At the forefront of this effort was the World Jewish Congress (WJC).[22] The WJC had been a prominent player in Jewish restitution matters going back to the postwar days of the JRSO and the JCR. The confluence of the end of the Cold War, the availability of newly declassified records, and pressure from Holocaust survivors and their heirs all contributed to a surge of new activity.

The key actor in the American government, who eventually took the lead in the complicated arena of restitution, was Stuart E. Eizenstat. A senior White House advisor to Jimmy Carter, Eizenstat in the mid-1990s was serving as the U.S. Ambassador to the European Union. Eizenstat was asked by Assistant Secretary of State for European Affairs Richard Holbrooke to take on a special "limited" mission. He would serve as the president's special envoy for property restitution in Central and Eastern Europe, focusing primarily on the return of religious property seized by the Nazis and later confiscated by the communists. The long-term goal, as Eizenstat saw it, was to encourage the building of a "civil society" in the former communist states that respected private property, the rule of law, and the rights of minority groups.[23]

In late 1995 and early 1996, action began on a related front. Researchers working for the WJC began reviewing records held at the U.S. National Archives in an effort to trace the disposition of gold looted by the Nazis. In particular, the WJC wanted to ascertain the role of Swiss banks during and after the war in handling so-called "Nazi gold." For decades, Jewish

[20] Elizabeth Simpson, editor, *The Spoils of War: World War II and Its Aftermath: The Loss, Remembrance, and Recovery of Cultural Property* (New York: Harry N. Abrams, 1997).

[21] "Putin Approves Law Barring Return of Art," *Washington Post*, 27 May 2000, p. 20.

[22] William Slany, U.S. Department of State, *U.S. and Allied Efforts to Recover and Restore Gold and Other Assets Stolen or Hidden by Germany During World War II*, Publication 10468 (Washington, D.C.: U.S. Department of State, 1997), p. iv.

[23] Stuart E. Eizenstat, *Imperfect Justice: Looted Assets, Slave Labor, and the Unfinished Business of World War II* (New York: Public Affairs, 2003), p. 23.

restitution organizations had complained about the difficulties that survivors and heirs encountered in gaining access to bank accounts, insurance policies, and other assets. The WJC researchers began to uncover documentation indicating that substantial amounts of "Nazi gold" remained in Swiss banks. Alerted by the WJC, New York Republican Senator Alphonse D'Amato, chair of the U.S. Senate Banking Committee, began a highly publicized effort to draw international attention to the Swiss "Nazi gold" issue.[24]

The explosive legal, political, and diplomatic issues involved in the Swiss case, and by implication other European states, led President Clinton to charge Stuart Eizenstat, by this point undersecretary of commerce, with leading an interagency task force to prepare a report. The president wanted the report "to describe, to the fullest extent possible, U.S. and Allied efforts to recover and restore this gold and other assets stolen by Nazi Germany, and to use other German assets for the reconstruction of postwar Europe."[25] Eizenstat led the eleven-agency effort over an intense seven-month period that studied fifteen million pages of documentation, a million of which were newly declassified and made available for research.[26] The report, issued in May 1997, documented that a substantial amount of gold sent by Nazi Germany to Swiss banks had never been restituted to heirs or turned over to the postwar Tripartite Gold Commission. The records also indicated that there were serious questions about how other neutral states had dealt with looted assets, including art and other cultural property. There was significant adverse political and public reaction in Switzerland. Yet as a direct result of the American report and pressure from the media and Jewish and non-Jewish groups, an international conference was held in London in December 1997 to explore and fully expose Nazi-era confiscation of gold and other monetary assets. The conference was a milestone event toward building an international consensus to resolve long-standing restitution grievances.[27] It was, in fact, the first gathering since the Paris Peace Conference of 1946 to focus on the unfinished legacy of World War II. The operating agenda for Eizenstat and the American delegation was to get international agreement to open archives from the Holocaust and World War II era for purposes of the historical record and for information relevant to resolving claims issues.[28]

---

[24] Slany, *U.S. and Allied Efforts to Recover and Restore Gold*, p. iv.
[25] Ibid., p. iii.
[26] Ibid.
[27] William Slany, U.S. Department of State, *U.S. and Allied Wartime and Postwar Relations and Negotiations with Argentina, Portugal, Spain, Sweden, and Turkey on Looted Gold and German External Assets and U.S. Concerns about the Fate of the Wartime Ustasha Treasury*, Publication 10557 (Washington, D.C.: U.S. Government Printing Office, 1998), p. iii.
[28] Eizenstat, *Imperfect Justice*, p. 113.

By this point, a number of nations, including Switzerland, appointed national commissions to study the record of wartime governments and present an objective, historical account as the basis for resolving claims that the WJC and others were about to press.[29] In fact, the Swiss commission led by Swiss historian Jean-François Bergier, after a five-year investigation, essentially supported the findings of the Eizenstat report on the active cooperation between the Swiss National Bank and Nazi Germany. The London conference brought the question of gold and monetary assets to international attention and contributed to a final resolution of the gold issue. At the closing session of the conference, Eizenstat pushed into territory that was difficult for the British and several other European governments. He brought up the issue of looted art and other categories of assets that were in many ways an even more difficult problem than dealing with "Nazi gold." He asked American journalist Hector Feliciano, author of *The Lost Museum*, to give an introductory statement. In his book, Feliciano accused the French of keeping some two thousand looted artworks in French museums. Though the French were unhappy with Feliciano, Eizenstat believed that in pushing for accountability and rectifying historical wrongs, the international community could not ignore other looted assets, including art. So, at his urging the delegates decided to meet a year later in Washington to explore issues related to art, insurance, and communal property and to develop equitable approaches to resolving restitution claims.[30]

While preparations went forward for the Washington conference, Eizenstat was designated by the president to lead the effort for a second, and more detailed, interagency historical study. This second report, issued in June 1998, focused on U.S. and Allied relations and negotiations with key neutral states concerning the disposition of German assets, particularly those that resulted from looting. The goal was to confront the largely hidden history of Holocaust-related assets, including the role of the U.S. government. The report documented, at best, an incomplete effort for the governments involved and, at worst, active efforts to prevent restitution to survivors and heirs.

Throughout 1998, Eizenstat, by this point the undersecretary of state for economic, business, and agricultural affairs, and his aides focused on two arenas: dormant Swiss bank accounts and laying the groundwork for dealing with art claims. During the year, Eizenstat helped engineer a path-breaking $1.25 billion settlement between Swiss banks and the holders and heirs of dormant accounts from the Holocaust era. While he labored on the Swiss banks issue, he was keenly aware of what was happening on the art front. The American museum community was intensely aware of the great interest in looted art. A drumbeat of scholarly and popular publications throughout the

---

[29] Slany, *U.S. and Allied Wartime and Postwar Relations*, p. iii.
[30] Eizenstat, *Imperfect Justice*, pp. 190–1.

decade had contributed growing public interest. Lynn Nicholas in *The Rape of Europa* (1994) attracted a wide audience with a riveting portrayal of Nazi looting and restitutions immediately after the conflict. Konstantin Akinsha and Sylvia Hochfield in *Beautiful Loot* (1995) provided great detail about Soviet looting during and after the war. In addition to Hector Feliciano's work on looting in France, Jonathan Petropoulos in *Art as Politics in the Third Reich* (1996) brought to the fore the place of art in the Nazi regime. Governments, art galleries, auction houses, and museums all faced increasing scrutiny.[31]

In response to rising concerns and questions, the Association of Art Museum Directors (AAMD) created in January 1998 the Task Force on the Spoliation of Art During the Nazi/World War II Era (1933–45). Chaired by Philippe de Montebello, director of the Metropolitan Museum of Art, the task force developed a set of principles to guide museums through the thicket of determining whether an artwork had been looted and how to deal with the situation. The principles called for them to research their collections for looted art and to publish the information gathered in a "centralized and publicly accessible database."[32] Further, museum directors and staff were encouraged to seek all possible information on the provenance of potential acquisitions and to refuse to acquire any work with a questionable provenance. As a precaution, the principles also called for obtaining warrantees of valid title for new acquisitions, and, most significantly, mediation was urged instead of complex and lengthy litigation to resolve claims.[33]

Montebello presented the principles and guidelines on 4 June 1998, just in time for the organizing meeting preparing for the Washington Conference. Eizenstat was pleased with the AAMD's work. The principles of thorough documentation and public access to information via the Internet were at the core of what he believed needed to be done. He also fully realized the difficulties involved in pursuing the litigation path to resolving conflicts. Aging Holocaust survivors and their heirs had little time and few resources to pursue years-long, expensive litigation. Mediation was surely the best route to pursue. But the organizing meeting was an eye-opener for Eizenstat. The Netherlands, the United Kingdom, France, and Germany resented the attempted imposition of American principles on their museums. There were other problems. The Russians consented to attend the conference but believed there was no legal basis for restitution. Furthermore, they believed an agenda item should be further German compensation for Russian losses. Eizenstat had to assure the Germans this would not be on the agenda. The Germans then agreed to participate.[34]

[31] Ibid., pp. 189–90.
[32] Ibid. p. 193.
[33] Ibid.
[34] Ibid., pp. 194–5.

Eizenstat realized that the AAMD guidelines were not acceptable in their current form, so he and his State Department team developed eleven principles "that looked new and different but kept the AAMD's essential points."[35] The general goal was that the eleven principles would aid in managing the complex issue of looted art, so that claims could be adjudicated and the art markets could proceed without the continued threats of litigation and public criticism. The principles (see Appendix B) envisioned a massive research effort to trace looted art through extensive provenance research (principles 1–3), flexible ways of dealing with gaps in proving ownership (principle 4), publication of the results of research and encouraging equitable and expeditious resolution of issues (principles 5–7), flexible solutions (principle 8), proceeds from heirless art sold to benefit Holocaust victims and communities (principle 9), encouragement to add outside experts to government commissions (principle 10), and development of internal processes in each country to apply the principles (principle 11).[36]

From the beginning, the conference encountered dissent and criticism. The French delegation, for example, was infuriated when Ronald Lauder, chairman of the WJC's Committee on Art Recovery, accused the French government of hiding records that would prove Jewish ownership of artworks hanging in French museums.[37] The eleven principles came in for press scrutiny and criticism. Some viewed them as a balancing act between the claims of the Holocaust victims and the need for the lucrative U.S. art market to have a litigation-free, stable environment. The U.S. delegation, despite the intervention of Britain's Lord Greville Janner, did not favor another international conference on the topic. Rather, the emphasis was to be on getting governments to open their archives and implement the principles of the conference.[38] Resolution, in the U.S. view, would come from consensus rather than from confrontation. Despite the highly charged atmosphere, the delegates accepted the nonbinding art restitution principles. But this happened only after Eizenstat inserted language in the final document that countries with different legal systems "could act within the context of their own laws."[39] With this, the conference adjourned. The next day, the U.S. National Archives sought to underscore the critical importance of access to records in resolving assets issues by hosting a one-day seminar on how researchers could use the archives to find records of wartime thefts.

---

[35] Ibid.

[36] J. D. Bindenagel, editor, U.S. Department of State, *Washington Conference on Holocaust Era Assets, November 30–December 3, 1998: Proceedings* (Washington, D.C.: U.S. Government Printing Office, 1999), pp. 416–19.

[37] Walter V. Robinson, "Jewish Group Says Looted Artworks May Number 1,700," *Boston Globe*, 3 December 1998, p. A01.

[38] Ibid.

[39] Eizenstat, *Imperfect Justice*, p. 198.

Though some observers had doubts about the outcome of the conference, Stuart Eizenstat saw it as a "moral victory."[40] Events since the Washington conference provide some justification for his opinion. In 1999, the International Council on Museums called on its members to follow the principles of the Washington conference. Austria ordered the return of 250 paintings to the Rothschild family and 2,000 additional artworks to other victims the Nazis. In December 1999, the German Ministry of Culture issued a statement on behalf of all German museums pledging to return confiscated art. Though not legally binding, the principles did get international attention and stirred some to act. In 2001, the Association of American Museums (AAM) announced an initiative to create a Nazi-era provenance Internet portal. This would be a central website and serve as a short-cut to other sites listing artworks in American museums with gaps in provenance. This was clearly what Eizenstat and his colleagues had in mind.[41]

The principles and spirit of the Washington conference also played a part in ending the long-running dispute over the Smolensk archives. As Patricia Kennedy Grimsted, an associate at the Ukrainian Research Institute at Harvard, put it: "The Smolensk archives had become a symbol of the problem of displaced archives and the restitution problems that arose after World War II."[42] In December 2002, the collection was returned in a ceremony at the Russian Ministry of Culture. When copies of the Smolensk archives of Ukrainian origin were presented to the Ukrainian ambassador to the United States shortly after the Moscow ceremony, Deputy Assistant Secretary of State for European Affairs Steven Pifer specifically noted the impact of the Washington conference principles on the decision to return the materials.[43] But another result of the conference indicated the limits to international cooperation. At the Vilnius International Forum on Holocaust-Era Looted Cultural Assets, held in October 2000, delegates split over the question of heirless Jewish property. The Israeli delegate stated that Israel was the only legitimate heir to the property. This provoked a bitter, negative reaction from the French, other Europeans, and some local Jewish community leaders.[44] The controversy that the JCR encountered with this issue was alive and well in Vilnius in 2000. All in all, though, the impact of Eizenstat's two reports and the London and Washington conferences was to raise the level of political attention to restitution and compensation issues to the highest point in decades.

[40] Ibid., p. 199.
[41] Ibid., pp. 199–200.
[42] Celestine Bohlen, "A Stray Record of Stalinist Horrors Finds Its Way Home," *New York Times*, 14 December 2002, pp. C1, 3.
[43] Reported to the author in an e-mail from the Department of State, "Smolensk, Ukraine," 20 December 2002.
[44] Eizenstat, *Imperfect Justice*, pp. 203–4.

## Scrutiny at Home

The Holocaust and restitution also received congressional attention during the very active year of 1998. In June, Congress created a Presidential Advisory Commission on Holocaust Assets in the United States (PCHA). In the fall, President Clinton appointed Edgar Bronfman to chair the commission. Bronfman, former chairman of Seagram and president of the WJC and the World Jewish Restitution Organization (WJRO), had a high level of interest and commitment. The commission had government officials, members of Congress, and Holocaust survivors as members. With its report date extended to 31 December 2000, the commission established three research teams to review and analyze documentation in the U.S. National Archives and other repositories to determine what actions the U.S. government had taken concerning Holocaust-era assets in the United States.[45] The major recommendation in the final report was the establishment of a "federally-sponsored public/private foundation to serve as an institutional focal point and coordinator of efforts that will involve the private sector, the States, and individual citizens both in the United States and abroad."[46] Also noted were "ground-breaking" agreements with federal and nonfederal institutions regarding "best practices to be followed in the identification, recognition, and restitution of Holocaust assets to their rightful owners."[47] This meant, in practice, incorporating the AAMD guidelines into the final recommendations and developing an understanding with the Library of Congress (LC) and the National Gallery of Art on handling JCR-donated books (LC) and adding a data field to the National Gallery's database to aid restitution research.

Unlike the domestic reaction to the Eizenstat reports and the international conferences, the response to the PCHA's final report was decidedly mixed. Critics, including scholars working for the commission, thought that the report broke little new ground, did not successfully grapple with how much stolen art passed through American hands, and failed to review critical records. Lynn Nicholas was blunt in her assessment: "[T]hey were so anxious to find smoking guns in the misdeeds of the U.S."[48] Marc Masurowsky, director of the commission's research team on gold and monetary assets, was scathing in his critique. To Masurowsky, the teams "reinvented the wheel," rehashing ground already covered and not examining museum holdings or records. Another staff member, Helen Jung, complained that the report did not explore "the ways art was laundered in the U.S." Commission member Benjamin Gilman, a New York congressman, was equally harsh: "The tents

---

[45] *Report to the President of the Presidential Advisory Commission on Holocaust Assets in the United States* (Washington, D.C.: U.S. Government Printing Office, December 2000), pp. 1–2.

[46] Ibid., p. i.

[47] Ibid.

[48] Ralph Blumenthal, "Panel on Nazi Art Theft Fell Short," *New York Times*, 3 March 2003.

were folded much to the chagrin of many of us. I felt we should have been doing much more than we did."[49]

Commission member Stuart Eizenstat in his observations sought to provide some balance. He cited the lack of time available to the commission and a narrow mandate that was limited to assets flowing through official U.S. control. Private galleries, art houses, and auction houses were not part of the commission's purview, and this, from Eizenstat's perspective, limited the effectiveness of the commission from the beginning. Chairman Bronfman echoed Eizenstat in lamenting the lack of time.[50] All the points of criticism were basically valid. To really have explored the topic would have required access to records in the private sector, and this was probably not a realistic expectation. The research strategy was flawed and two and a half years was too short a time for such a complex topic. This was truly an opportunity missed and one not likely to occur in the near or medium-term future.

A second initiative from Congress was the Nazi War Crimes Disclosure Act of 1998. The act required the government to locate, identify, inventory, recommend for declassification, and make available at the National Archives all classified records relating to Nazi war criminals, war crimes, persecutions, and looted assets. The Interagency Working Group (IWG) set up by the president in January 1999 had a mix of federal agency officials and three public members appointed by the president.[51] The original three-year term set for the IWG was extended by a year, and the terms of reference were clarified to explicitly include Japanese war crimes issues. The mix of federal and non-federal members in an interagency working group format was unusual if not unique. Public members Elizabeth Holtzman, a former member of Congress from New York; Thomas Baer, a film producer; and Richard Ben-Veniste, a Washington lawyer and former Watergate prosecutor, argued for the hiring of professional historians who could put the mass of declassified records into historical context. By the end of 2002, the IWG process had resulted in the declassification of over six million pages of relevant material, with significant releases from the Army's Counter-Intelligence Corps, the Central Intelligence Agency, and the Federal Bureau of Investigation. Though this effort is the federal government's single largest special-purpose declassification effort, a complete evaluation of the IWG awaits the issuance of its final report and historians' analyses.

Not all the efforts at scrutiny were performed by government commissions. Museums across the country began to implement the principles

---

49 Ibid.
50 Ibid.
51 National Archives and Records Administration, *Interim Report to Congress on Implementation of the Nazi War Crimes Disclosure Act* (College Park, Md.: National Archives and Records Administration, 1999), pp. 1–2. Information also provided by the author, who served as IWG chair from 1999 to 2002.

enunciated by the AAMD concerning looted art and provenance research. One case involved the Franz Snyders painting *Still Life with Fruit and Game*, noted earlier in this work as one item among the millions stolen from individuals and private collectors. This one had been stolen from Mme. Edgar Stern, whose collection had been confiscated in 1941 in Paris by the Nazis. Resolving this case was a real detective story and illustrative of the difficulties in determining art provenance. The work had been donated to the National Gallery of Art in 1990 for its fiftieth anniversary celebration. Curator Nancy Yeide, charged with provenance research on items falling within the AAMD guidelines, identified the Snyders work as one among several requiring detailed research.[52]

She had to first study the history of the era to understand the organizations and individuals involved in looting. In tracing the provenance information on the Snyders *Still Life* she had to check the Art Looting Investigation Unit list of those involved in looting to see if there were any "red flags." Though Yeide did not find the painting listed in the Art Loss Register, she did find a reproduction in the Haberstock Gallery catalogue for 1967. Then Yeide contacted the donor and found out that he had acquired the work from a German collector, Baron von Pöllnitz. At this point, the curator had two "red flag names." Through much research and correspondence, Yeide discovered that Herman Göring in a 3 May 1941 visit to the Jeu de Paume had obtained a Snyders *Still Life* and then exchanged it with Haberstock, who in turn gave it to von Pöllnitz.[53] Yet though there was a preponderance of evidence, physical and archival, that the gallery's painting was the work seized from the Sterns, definitive proof was lacking. Based on the evidence, though, the gallery decided in November 2000 to return the painting.

This case is illustrative of the great challenges involved as museums begin to review their holdings. The National Gallery of Art has in place extensive case files on its acquisitions, with automated information available since 1992. The gallery also has the resources available for a professional to work full-time on the research. Many museums have much less complete documentation at hand and lack the staff resources for extensive investigations. The sources available for research are scattered in America and Europe and many, such as the collections at the U.S. National Archives, are voluminous and require sophisticated research techniques. Though Yeide and two professional associates have published a manual on art provenance research, the task is daunting. Public museums may, over time, successfully research their holdings, but there is a question of whether private institutions have the will or resources to do the job. The issues involving private collectors are

---

[52] Nancy H. Yeide, Konstantin Akinsha, and Amy L. Walsh, *The AAM Guide to Provenance Research* (Washington, D.C.: American Association of Museums, 2001), p. 69.
[53] Ibid., p. 70.

even thornier, and it is very unlikely that these collections will become the subject of review and scrutiny.

The intense activity of the public arena during the 1990s was matched or exceeded by events in the private sector and the courts.

## American Dilemmas

The passage of time, the transfer of looted art either to heirs of looters or through sales to others, and the opening of East German archives and cultural sites with the fall of the Berlin Wall in 1989 all contributed to a surge of lawsuits in U.S. courts as long-lost art and cultural treasures began to surface. A veritable flood of lawsuits and law enforcement actions occurred throughout the late 1980s, the 1990s, and into the new century. In essence, the legal claims boiled down to the need to prove ownership, to establish that a theft had taken place, and to deal with the passage of time and the statute of limitations. The cases that came into American courts were not only legally complex but often fraught with diplomatic problems.

One of the most notorious cases was that of the Quedlinburg treasures. In April 1945, an American soldier, Lieutenant Joe Tom Meador, stole valuable treasures of the church of St. Servatius in Quedlinburg, which were stored in the Altenburg cave for protection.[54] As early as December 1945, records at the Munich Central Collecting Point noted that twelve extremely valuable items, including reliquaries and jewel-encrusted manuscripts from the ninth and tenth centuries, were missing.[55] However, the church's location in East Germany and the Cold War events that ensued meant that no effort to locate and recover was possible. Meador indicated his awareness that his actions were illegal by mailing his hoard in several small packages to his parents telling them the items were "very, very valuable" and that they not be shown to anyone.[56] After Meador's death from cancer in 1980, his heirs, brother Jack Meador and sister Jane Meador Cook, attempted to sell the treasures through a middleman, lawyer John Torigian. In October 1988, Torigian approached a London art dealer, who in turn offered one of the two manuscripts, the Samuhel Gospels, to the foundation for Prussian Cultural Heritage in Berlin for $9 million. The Foundation asked its researcher at the U.S. National Archives, Willi Korte, to look into the matter.[57]

---

[54] Constance Lowenthal, "Case Study: The Quedlinburg Church Treasures: Introduction," in *The Spoils of War: World War II and Its Aftermath: The Loss, Reappearance, and Recovery of Cultural Property*, edited by Elizabeth Simpson (New York: Harry N. Abrams, 1997), p. 149.

[55] Willi Korte, "Search for the Treasures," in *The Spoils of War: World War II and Its Aftermath: The Loss, Reappearance, and Recovery of Cultural Property*, edited by Elizabeth Simpson (New York: Harry N. Abrams, 1997), p. 150.

[56] "The Quedlinburg Indictments," *ARTnews* (March 1996): 35.

[57] Korte, "Search for the Treasures," p. 151.

After some research, Korte determined that the manuscripts came from the Quedlinburg church, then in East Germany. By November 1989, the Berlin Wall had fallen and Korte was able to approach the church to get authorization to act on its behalf. By this point, Korte had interested a *New York Times* reporter, William Honan, in the case and had located the heirs and treasures in Texas. At Honan's suggestion, Korte approached Thomas Kline, a lawyer experienced in looting and restitution cases, to handle the legal front. Korte, Honan, and Kline represented the three key factors needed to resolve this and similar cases: effective research, press attention, and legal acumen.[58] While the investigation moved forward, the German foundation feared that it would lose the Samuhel Gospels and approached the German government for assistance. Acting through intermediaries in Switzerland, the Germans offered the Meadors almost $3 million as a "finders fee." The representatives of the Meadors accepted the offer and returned the priceless manuscript. To prevent deals for the other objects still controlled by the Meadors, Korte and Kline tracked them down in Whitewright, Texas.[59]

To stop a pending sale after tentative negotiations broke down, Kline went to federal court in Dallas in early May 1990 and obtained an injunction preventing any further sales and requiring that an inventory of objects be turned over for use in litigation.[60] International attention fueled by William Honan's stories in the *New York Times* and the threat of prolonged litigation led the Meador heirs to accept an out-of-court settlement in 1992. Accepting the already received "finder's fee" for the Samuhel Gospels as the financial basis for settlement, the Meadors relinquished nine precious objects to the original owners, the church in Quedlinburg.[61] Trouble for the Meador heirs, though, was just beginning. Jack Meador, Jane Meador Cook, and John Torigian were indicted under the provisions of the National Stolen Property Act for trafficking in stolen goods.[62]

The Quedlinburg case in many ways was rather straightforward. The church's ownership was well documented over the centuries, the theft was noted in 1945, and, under American law, a thief can never pass on a good title for a stolen object. Yet the federal government, other than the judicial system, played little to no role in resolving the situation. Private initiative and the expensive and time-consuming process of civil litigation were the only tools at hand. Other cases would prove to be more complex, reflective of the decades that had passed since wartime looting.

---

[58] Ibid.

[59] Ibid.

[60] Thomas Kline, "Legal Issues Relating to the Recovery of the Quedlinburg Treasures," in *The Spoils of War: World War II and Its Aftermath: The Loss, Reappearance, and Recovery of Cultural Property*, edited by Elizabeth Simpson (New York: Harry N. Abrams, 1997), p. 156.

[61] Ibid.

[62] Schwerin, "The Quedlinburg Indictments," p. 35.

The international art markets have operated rather informally over time, with little or no extensive provenance research for sales of artworks. This practice led to numerous problems as looted art has surfaced, causing great embarrassment to museums and collectors alike. One case highlights the complex issues involved. Drug company heir Daniel C. Searle purchased for $850,000 in 1987 a Degas pastel, *Landscape with Smokestacks*. Searle, a trustee of the Art Institute of Chicago, planned to donate the artwork to the institute and left it to the museum's experts to authenticate ownership. The experts failed to uncover that at one point Hans Wendland, a well-known German art dealer during the war who had traded Old Masters to Göring in exchange for modern works, had sold the painting to Hans Frankhauser, his brother-in-law and a Swiss textile merchant. Both men appeared in lists prepared by the Art Looting Investigation Unit as collaborators in the Nazi art world.[63] It appears that the museum's experts were not aware of such documentation.

In 1996, the heirs of the original owners, a Dutch Jewish couple, Friedrich and Louise Gutmann, filed suit in the U.S. Federal Court in Chicago, as the lawful owners of the painting. Aided by researcher Willi Korte and lawyer Thomas Kline, the heirs linked the Degas owned by the Gutmanns to Wendland and hence to the sale to Searle. The Gutmanns' daughter, Lili, and her two nephews, Nick and Simon Goodman, sought to reclaim ownership in the name of the only major Western European Jewish art collectors who died at the hands of the Nazis.[64] In August 1998, when the judge in the case ordered a jury trial, Searle's attorneys settled the case. Searle gave half interest in the painting to the Gutmann heirs and the other half to the Art Institute of Chicago. The museum was to acquire the painting by paying the heirs half the appraisal value of the work.[65] Good intentions and inadequate research were not likely to be an adequate defense in the case of a clearly looted work of art. With American law providing no good title, ever, for stolen property and the National Stolen Property Act making it illegal to transport stolen property across national or state boundaries, Searle and his attorneys needed to settle. But there were also pressures on the plaintiffs to settle. It was not certain how the federal judge in Chicago would rule on issues relating to due diligence recovery efforts by the heirs and the statute of limitations. All sides benefited from not prolonging the litigation.

Reflecting the murky nature of art provenance and sales over time to well-intended purchasers, Nick Goodman noted, "This settlement, which allows

---

[63] Walter V. Robinson, "Holocaust Victims' Heirs Given Share of a Degas," *Boston Globe*, 14 August 1998, p. A01; Joe Lauria, "An American Resolution," *ARTnews* (October 1998): 54.

[64] Ibid.

[65] Ibid.

us to preserve the pastel's history in one of the country's finest art museums, represents a fair resolution to this complex issue." Realizing also the tortuous nature of litigation, he also said, "We are very happy with the settlement. Here's a chance to show the rest of the world we can be civilized gentlemen about this, and hopefully other families will take our example." A bit more jaundiced view was expressed by Korte: "This is a great day for the Art Institute. The museum gets a very nice landscape they wanted from the beginning, and they avoid a number of embarrassing questions at the trial."[66]

Other cases, all of which required complex research, press attention, and legal follow-through, highlighted the tangled legal and diplomatic realities in the post–Cold War era. Among the most illustrative were the artworks stolen from the Kunsthalle Bremen, a private German art museum. The first case came to light in 1995 when the Kunstverein Bremen, parent organization of the Kunsthalle Bremen, sought to recover three drawings seized from a Russian refugee, Yuly Saet, in a New York sting operation. Saet claimed he had legally obtained the drawings before emigrating to the United States and that he had the right to offer them to a New York dealer for sale.[67] The dealer, suspicious of Saet's ownership claim, contacted Dr. Constance Lowenthal, then director of the International Foundation for Art Research. She notified authorities, and they seized the items. Though Saet was not criminally prosecuted, the ownership issue had to be settled. Bremen won on a motion for summary judgment, which Saet did not contest. The court agreed that the museum had proven original ownership and loss through theft.[68]

A much more complex case, again involving drawings from the Bremen museum, consumed the entire 1990s. The issue at hand involved twelve drawings worth an estimated $15 million, stolen when Karnzow castle, the repository for the Bremen collection, was looted by Soviet soldiers in 1945. The drawings included Dürer's *Women's Bathhouse* drawn in 1494. Apparently, the Soviet authorities seized the twelve drawings from the soldiers, and the items found their way to a museum in Baku. The drawings were first exhibited in 1993 after Azerbaijan declared its independence. When the Kunstverein Bremen requested their return, the drawings again disappeared, supposedly part of a theft of some 287 artworks.[69] The drawings next surfaced in 1995 in New York City, home to an extensive Russian underworld ring located in Brighton Beach. When the auction house Sotheby's was

[66] Ibid.
[67] Thomas R. Kline, "U.S. Court Orders Return of Drawings Stolen after World War II to *Kunsthalle Bremen*," *Spoils of War International Newsletter* No. 1 (19 December 1995): 40–1.
[68] Ibid.
[69] Thomas R. Kline, "Recent Developments in the Recovery of Old Master Drawings from Bremen," *Spoils of War International Newsletter* No. 5 (5 June 1998): pp. 15–18; Seth Kugel, "Back from Baku," *ARTnews* (September 2001): 56.

approached about a sale, a one-day delay in notifying authorities about the firm's suspicions permitted the artworks to disappear yet again.[70]

At the same time, a Russian-Japanese businessman and former wrestler, Masatsuga Koga, contacted the German Embassy in Tokyo about selling the drawings. When Koga came to New York in September 1993, he was trapped in a sting operation set up by the U.S. Customs Service, the German government, and the Bremen museum. Six of the drawings were seized at that point. Later, the other 6 drawings, as well as 180 works from the Baku museum, were recovered in Brooklyn. Indicted for violating the National Stolen Property Act, Koga pleaded guilty and cooperated in the prosecution of his alleged confederate, Azerbaijani prosecutor Natavan Aleskerova, who was arrested when she came to New York to meet her son. Also indicted, though not apprehended, was Aleskerova's ex-husband, an ex-wrestler and nightclub owner in Baku.[71] In her defense against the criminal charges, Aleskerova asserted that the Allied Control Council and the Soviet military administration had authorized seizures of German cultural property. Thus, the drawings were not stolen but legally acquired, a proposition disputed by the U.S. government and the Kunstverein Bremen.[72] A further complicating factor was that Thomas Hoving, the respected former director of the Metropolitan Museum of Art, cast doubts on the authenticity of the drawings, stating they were "seriously questionable from the standpoint of condition and attribution."[73] Aleskerova buttressed her case by pleading that regardless of the original authority to seize the drawings, they were copies and hence not subject to a criminal prosecution.[74] Aleskerova was convicted of conspiracy and was sentenced to eleven months in prison.

Once criminal actions were completed, the federal district court for the Southern District of New York faced the question of ownership. To resolve the conflicting claims between Baku and Bremen, the "stakeholder" holding the property in the case, the federal government, filed two "interpleader actions" with the court asking for resolution of the matter. Thus, the government was out of the matter with the resolution left to the contending parties and the court.[75] Azerbaijan withdrew its claims and even turned over two drawings it held to the Bremen museum. Finally, in July 2001 the Dürer drawings were returned to Bremen.

Yet another contentious case brought together all the complicated elements affecting cultural restitution. In early January 1998, Manhattan District Attorney Robert Morgenthau issued a subpoena preventing the

[70] Ibid.
[71] Ibid.
[72] Ibid.
[73] Ibid.
[74] Ibid.
[75] Ibid.

return of two Austrian paintings at the conclusion of an exhibition at the Museum of Modern Art.[76] The paintings, by Austrian impressionist artist Egon Schiele, were part of Austrian collector Rudolph Leopold's Schiele collection and on loan to the New York museum for a temporary exhibition. This unprecedented interruption of the international museum world's practice of sharing collections for exhibit purposes created a fierce reaction in Austria and concern elsewhere.[77]

Morgenthau's subpoena was overturned by the New York court of appeals. At that point, the U.S. Customs Service entered the fray at the behest of the U.S. Attorney's Office and seized the two paintings under the terms of the National Stolen Property Act. Eventually, the U.S. federal court determined that one of the paintings, a landscape titled *Dead City III*, was not stolen property, and it was returned to the Leopold Foundation in Vienna. This despite the fact that this work was part of a collection of Schiele paintings seized from cabaret artist Fritz Gruenbaum, who was later killed by the Nazis. The other work, *Wally*, a painting of Schiele's mistress that the Nazis took from Viennese art dealer Leah Bondi Jaray remains the subject of a forfeiture claim.[78] A federal district court judge dismissed the forfeiture claim on the astonishing basis that the painting ceased being stolen when seized by the U.S. Army at the end of the war and returned to Austria. The U.S. Army, despite the judge's confusion, was not a police force, but was acting on military and political requirements. The painting remained a stolen work of art never returned to the original owner or heirs. The Army's temporary stewardship did not resolve legal issues or ownership. To prevent this pernicious ruling from standing, and potentially undermining all such cases, the federal government amended its complaint to clarify the actual role of the U.S. Army in restitution matters. Artworks and other looted property seized by the U.S. Army remained stolen property. Likewise, the items remained stolen property after return to the country of origin until turned over to institutional or private owners. This case alone shook the international museum world and threatened the framework of understanding and settling restitution cases.

Some cases posed diplomatic as well as legal issues. One of these involved the continuing fallout from the Lubomirski case. Poland and Ukraine both pressed claims for the return of the twenty-seven drawings given to Prince George by the U.S. government. MFA&A officials at the time doubted the legality or appropriateness of the decision. The two countries also raised doubts about the American handling of the case. Not surprisingly, Ambassador J. D. Bindenagel, Eizenstat's successor as special envoy for Holocaust

[76] Walter V. Robinson, "New York DA Bars Return of Austrian Art," *Boston Globe*, 9 January 1998, p. A01.

[77] Ibid.

[78] Eizenstat, *Imperfect Justice*, pp. 191–2.

issues, conducted a study that determined that the U.S. government had appropriately returned the items to the prince. With the drawings in six American museums and elsewhere, the two claimants face a daunting legal challenge that may go on indefinitely. Bindenagel's advice was: "Now it's up to the parties [Poland and Ukraine] to get together themselves and discuss the issue of the sale of the Lubomirski Dürers after they were returned."[79] The long-standing diffidence of the U.S. government to get involved in specific cases, aside from those clearly involving criminal acts, remains in place.

Fortunately, not all American restitution cases involved lengthy criminal or civil proceedings. Some were settled amicably. In one case, an article in the newsletter *Spoils of War* on the fate of archives and libraries of German Freemason lodges, looted first by the Nazis and then lost, sparked a resolution. Ely Maurer, colleague of Ardelia Hall and longtime assistant legal advisor at the State Department, reported to the article's author that the Grand Lodge's charter had been located at the Library of Congress. Apparently, a U.S. officer had found the charter at a castle in Thuringia and had taken it to prevent seizure by the Soviets. In turn, the officer had turned over the document to the Library of Congress for safekeeping. In November 1998, the charter was turned over to German Freemasons.[80]

A similar case involved the return of a Martin Luther manuscript from the Concordia Historical Institute in St. Louis, Missouri, to the Kulturhistorisches Museum in Magdeburg, Germany. As was the case with the freemason charter, the Luther manuscript was found by a U.S. officer, a Baptist chaplain, and handed over to a Lutheran chaplain, Theodore P. Bornhoeft.[81] He sent the manuscript to the Missouri Synod's Concordia Historical Institute for safekeeping, requesting that the following notice be put in the book:

Presented to the Concordia Historical Institute for safekeeping, by former Army chaplain Theo. P. Bornhoeft until the opportunity presents itself when he can safely return and present it to the City of Magdeburg, which is now occupied by the U.S.S.R.[82]

After the reunification of Germany, institute director Rev. Daniel Preus sought to fulfill Bornhoeft's pledge. At the ceremony of return held at the institute on 20 February 1996, German Consul General Gabriele von

---

[79] Sylvia Hochfield, "Dürer Claims Continue," *ARTnews* (March 2002): 66.
[80] Petra Kuhn, "Valuable Documents Returned to German Freemasons by the U.S.," *The Spoils of War International Newsletter* no. 6 (February 1999): 55–7.
[81] Klaus Goldmann, "The Return of the Luther Manuscript, 'Wider Hans Worst' (Against Hans Worst), to Germany," *Spoils of War International Newsletter* No. 2 (15 June 1996): 41–2.
[82] Ibid.

Malsen-Tilborch focused in her remarks on the heart of the matter:

There were and still are other people in other countries who consider it a quite legitimate punishment and a rightful compensation for their losses to keep for themselves cultural treasures taken away from a country that started the war. On the other hand, to deprive a country of the better parts of its identity means to deprive it of its chance to improve, to heal, to become a valuable member of the family of man and to make its contribution to it.[83]

The Consul General thus provided a succinct summary of the Russian-German impasse and the urgent need for reconciliation and settlement.

[83] Ibid.

# Looking Ahead

## Two Eras

The tumultuous activity over the past decade in cultural restitution as well as compensation and reparations for other World War II and Holocaust-era losses has hit somewhat of a lull. Whether this is merely a pause or a longer-term phenomenon remains to be seen. The American government is focused almost exclusively on the War on Terror and domestic security. Little attention is paid or emphasis given to restitution matters except in those cases where there are larger issues at stake. The return of the Smolensk archives in 2002 for example, came at a time of great international tension, with the United States desirous of gaining Russian support in the run-up to the Iraq War. In addition, the departure of Stuart Eizenstat from government service removed the single most influential agent pushing for U.S. government attention and leadership in issues relating to Holocaust-era assets. No one of his stature has emerged to rally support within the United States for continued American involvement and to cajole, wheedle, and pressure other governments to push forward what was started in the 1990s. Also, the departures of Rabbi Israel Singer and Elan Steinberg from leadership positions in the World Jewish Congress took from the scene two savvy and experienced negotiators intimately involved in restitution and compensation matters.

It is too early to discern patterns accurately; however, this period in certain ways hearkens back to an earlier time. In the first five years after World War II, there was tremendous restitution activity. The strengths and weaknesses of the American effort have already been discussed, but there is no doubt that much was accomplished. Yet new geopolitical realities and the onset of the Cold War froze the most essential commodity needed for restitution: open access to information. The fate of German and European archives, libraries, and artworks that vanished behind the Iron Curtain were unknown. The fate of cultural treasures was just one more item that got caught up in allegations and propaganda charges. By the late 1940s, a lull in restitution activity and cooperation set in, and for most of the next three decades little happened. Soviet returns of cultural property to satellite states, particularly to the German Democratic Republic, were partial and designed for political ends. In the West, information was not easily accessible. For many years, the records of most governments for the World War II and postwar periods were generally closed to researchers. The disposition of art returned to countries of origin was not well known, particularly items deemed "heirless." Of course, transactions in the art market remained highly confidential. As a result, the record of what was looted and what was returned remained incomplete. So, the lull following intense activity is one element of continuity in the restitution saga.

Another element of continuity is that a handful of individuals in the 1940s and 1990s effectively pushed for government action. Cultural leaders, primarily from east coast institutions, pushed for government involvement in cultural protection. All that flowed from this push – the Roberts Commission, the MFA&A, the central collection points – came from the efforts of a few individuals aligned with perceptive Army officers such as General Clay and General Hilldring. The restitution effort in the 1940s rarely received widespread public or high-level government attention. Yet there was a cadre of individuals at varying levels and ranks dedicated to the mission of restitution, and, within certain parameters, they were highly successful. The 1990s was a different period, but again the roles of key individuals were critical. Without the leadership of the U.S. government, it is impossible to conceive of the Swiss banks settlement, insurance and slave labor settlements, and two international conferences devoted to assets issues, including art. And without Stuart Eizenstat, it is impossible to imagine such U.S. government investment of political capital. Edgar Bronfman, Israel Singer, and Elan Steinberg were critical players in mobilizing Jewish and international opinion on the need to complete the unfinished business of World War II and the Holocaust. Many others in the United States and Europe played important roles, but these few individuals along with several key authors stimulated American political and media interest. It was this interest, allied with similarly disposed individuals in Europe, that pushed the restitution agenda forward.

The roles of Jewish organizations in the late 1940s and the 1990s are fundamentally similar. The major Jewish organizations came together after the war to form the JRSO and the JCR to work with Jewish communities in Europe and America, and particularly with the new state of Israel, to recover and preserve as much of the Jewish cultural heritage as possible. International Jewish organizations facilitated negotiations for Israel with the Federal Republic of Germany for reparations payments for losses incurred by Jews. Certainly, in the 1990s the World Jewish Congress was a central player in all the varied negotiations and debates about restitution and compensation. This interest and commitment can certainly be expected to continue.

Yet another element of continuity between the two periods is in the nature of what was returned. Archival collections that came into Western control were promptly returned. Few if any collections fell into private hands though many were confiscated by the Soviets for intelligence exploitation. Artworks and museum items that were well known and described by the Germans when seized were relatively easy for the Western Allies to return. But many artworks and cultural objects seized were not museum quality and were not described in any detail by the Nazis. Many of these items ended up with the German or Austrian governments when Allied restitution programs ended or with other countries of origin for their own decisions on whether to retain or return to an institution or heir. What was not even dealt with was all the private property that ended up in the hands of neighbors. Books were the most difficult to return. Some library collections were well marked, kept together by the Germans, and easy to return or to turn over to organizations such as the JCR, but many were not identifiable or, as Patricia Grimsted has described, were packed away in the attics of Soviet institutions.

In the 1990s, the same patterns held true. With fits and starts over the course of the decade, the Russians returned the archival collections in its custody. Russian political and economic interests dictated such a course as it sought to forge closer ties with European democracies. As in the 1940s, little progress was made with books and artworks. The million or so books in Russian hands are scattered, and in poor condition, and provenance is difficult to determine. A restitution effort would require a major outlay of precious Russian resources. As to art, the situation is complicated, but for different reasons. Many Russian politicians and citizens regard these items as highly desirable and legitimate spoils of war. There is an acknowledgment that the victims of Nazi persecution should regain their art, but there is little interest in returning art looted from Germany. Art restitution is at a standstill. Although there are significant elements of continuity between the late 1940s and the 1990s, the question is whether the current lull will last for a lengthy period or the dynamics of the present moment are fundamentally different.

## Continuing Imperative

Several factors indicate that the current lull may not be a lengthy interregnum as experienced during the Cold War. The need to complete, to the extent possible, the unfinished works of restitution and compensation to Holocaust victims and their heirs is widely viewed as a moral issue. On all fronts – dormant bank accounts, insurance and slave labor claims, and lost art – there is a belief that what has begun must be completed. The moral imperative continues to stir scholars, Jewish organizations, and institutional and government leaders in America and Europe. A Europe no longer divided along Cold War lines is better able to sustain this moral impetus. This is fueled by a radically different situation from the 1940s: the access to information.

Records in all countries, including Russia, are increasingly open to research. This research will tell the story of what happened to art collections, books, and archives in Russia. It will also tell the story of how the French, the Dutch, and the Austrians, among others, ran their internal restitution programs.

The roles now played by the media and information technology are also radically different from the earlier period. Certainly, there were newspapers, and journal articles during and after the war about looting and restitution. But these were episodic and not sustained. Media interest is now more intense and broad-based, particularly in stories about the holdings of American museums or the action of the U.S. government. The stories today have much more of a "human face" to them. It is not about Hitler or Göring or the treasures they stole. It is about a specific item stolen from an individual or a family or a church. The events recounted are grievous, and the need for accountability is real and present. The increased flow of information about looted art allows those in the media interested in the issue to pursue stories to their conclusion. The tale of the Meadors and their thievery and greed is a moral parable and a riveting story all at once. Governments today in the United States and Europe are held to a higher level of scrutiny and accountability. The various commissions and their reports, aided and abetted by media attention and interest, are often highly critical of the actions taken by their own governments. The Bergier Commission in Switzerland is just one example.

Information technology is another factor that is markedly different from the earlier era. The ability to gather data on looted items, put it all in a database, and then make it electronically available anywhere in the world profoundly transforms research and tracking. By no means does information technology provide a panacea, however. Extensive research, much of it in archives, must occur before databases can be created. But a great deal of such research has occurred, and several databases for art-looting research now exist. A number of victims or heirs have found out about their property from research on the Internet and have taken action. The ability to share information and communicate electronically provides a major impetus for keeping the restitution effort alive and moving forward.

## Moving Forward

Though there is both continuity and divergence between the two periods of intense restitution activity, there is one common factor: the role of leadership – specifically, American leadership. Certainly, the United States conducted the most active and prolonged restitution effort among the Allies. This reflected, in part, attitudes, policies, and plans formulated in the United States over the course of the war, and, in part, the huge volume of materials located in the American Zone. Nonetheless, whether the issue involved heirless Jewish property, claims of refugees from Eastern Europe, or the return

of German-owned property, the U.S. government and military took the lead
in resolving the problem. Clearly, the role played by Stuart Eizenstat and the
U.S. government in the 1990s was the key ingredient in making progress.
U.S. leadership is vitally important in ending the current lull and pushing the
restitution process forward.

During and after World War II, efforts to internationalize the restitution
issue and create a program foundered. Ultimately, what was done took place
for the most part on a bilateral basis. This pattern persisted in the 1990s
with the United States encouraging and assisting negotiations between Jewish organizations and particular industries and governments. The London
and Washington conferences did, however, provide the first international
forums to discuss the whole panoply of restitution and assets issues. The
United States in these various venues basically pursued the roles of advo-
cacy and facilitation. What must happen now is the renewal of high-level
American government interest pursued in an international forum. This forum
needs to include governments, international cultural organizations, and special interest groups such as the WJC. Of all these components, let us begin
first with the United States. Issues related to restitution and the Holocaust are
not partisan. In fact, presidential and congressional advisory panels received
widespread bipartisan support. It is in the United States interest to assist in
resolving disputes that still embroil European governments and cause great
concern among Holocaust victims and heirs in America and elsewhere. From
a diplomatic and political perspective it is in America's national interest to
support the building of "civil societies" in Eastern Europe and Russia. Setting
up mechanisms to address restitution issues is one part of this effort. Such
American involvement would also continue the moral imperative, which was
always a key element in the country's restitution work.

But, as has been demonstrated, leadership has come not in a general sense
but from specific men and women. Who could lead an American government international initiative? The best candidate is Stuart Eizenstat. Though
a senior official in the Carter and Clinton administrations, Eizenstat's work
in the restitution arena was respected and supported. He knows the issues
and the players and believes passionately in the cause. Much preoccupies the
American government at this point in time. Certain members of Congress
have taken a keen interest in issues related to Holocaust victims and heirs.
Several of these members could informally discuss with the Bush administration the necessity and value of continued American government involvement
with restitution. If Eizenstat is not acceptable or declines an offer, then someone of similar public stature and ability must be chosen. A career foreign
service officer, no matter how interested or dedicated, is not likely to have
the stature needed for international negotiations or maintaining high-level
visibility.

There is in place some structure that could support an American initiative.
The State Department has an office of Special Envoy for Holocaust Issues

that could form the infrastructure for an on-going American effort. Moving forward would involve building upon what came out of the Washington Conference and other international gatherings. A forum consisting of the International Council on Archives, the International Council on Museums, and the International Library Council; the WJC; Russia; the United States; and the Council of Europe could provide a stable, on-going institutional framework to address several urgent needs:

1. The need for international specialists to identify literary and archival collections currently in Russian custody and sort out issues of provenance.
2. The need for archives in all countries to be opened and made available for research.
3. The need to create a unified database or series of related databases with information on art, archives, or libraries either still missing or located but not yet restituted.
4. The need to establish a mediation service to assist in resolving claims and disputes.

An international forum could provide the funding, technical support, and expertise needed to resolve to the greatest extent possible cultural restitution issues. This forum would be facilitative and supportive in nature, providing a venue, among other things, for discussion and reaching consensus. This seems to be the only feasible approach. A coercive, overly rigid format would not win needed international support. The forum should have a "sunset" provision, for at some point World War II – era restitution must come to an end. Given the complexity of this international effort, ten years seems to be a suitably lengthy period. Though it will never be possible to return every item stolen or rectify every evil that was perpetrated, good will come from the effort to try. Each item restituted or historical wrong faced is an act of remembrance that will, hopefully, help prevent another Holocaust.

# Appendix A

*Glossary of Terms*

AAM – Association of American Museums.

AAMD – Association of Art Museum Directors.

ACA – Allied Control Authority, the supreme governing authority in postwar Germany.

ACC – Allied Control Council, Germany. The Allies created the Council on 5 June 1945, as the executive arm of the ACA to govern occupied Germany.

Advisory Committee – Advisory Committee on Post-War Foreign Policy Preparation, a U.S. State Department – led entity.

AJDC – American Joint Distribution Committee, an American Jewish relief agency.

ALIU – Art Looting Investigation Unit, created in the Office of Strategic Services in 1945.

Bizonia – Fusion of the American and British Zones of Occupation in Germany for certain functions, primarily economic.

CAD – Civil Affairs Division of the War Department

CCP – central collecting point. Established by the U.S. military to house cultural objects found in the U.S. Zone of Occupation in need of preservation or suspected of having been looted by the Nazis.

CJR – Conference on Jewish Relations. Established in 1936 by American Jewish intellectuals to counter Nazi propaganda.

CORC – Coordinating Committee of the Allied Control Council, Germany.

DPs – Displaced persons. Individuals imprisoned by the Nazis, forced laborers, prisoners of war, and evacuees uprooted from their homes during or after World War II.

DRDR – Directorate for Reparations, Deliveries, and Restitution, Allied Control Authority.

EAC – European Advisory Commission. Created at the Moscow Conference in October 1943 to deal with political questions arising from the anticipated defeat of Germany.

Einsatzgrüppen – Task Forces. SS mobile killing units operating on the eastern front.

Einsatzstab Reichsleiter Rosenberg (ERR) – Rosenberg Task Force. A special task force under Alfred Rosenberg that seized art, libraries, and archives in German-occupied Western and Eastern Europe.

Executive Committee – Executive Committee on Economic Foreign Policy, a U.S. State Department – led entity.

Federal Republic – Federal Republic of Germany, formed in May 1949, from the three western zones of occupation.

*Foreign Relations* – *Foreign Relations of the United States: Diplomatic Papers.* After the initial citation for the various yearly compilations, the footnotes will only list the abbreviated general title of the series, year, volume number, and the title of the volume.

GDR – German Democratic Republic, formed in October 1949 from the former Soviet Zone of Occupation.

Geheime Staatspolizei (Gestapo) – Secret State Police. Organized by Hermann Göring in 1933 and placed under Heinrich Himmler's control in April 1934.

HICOG – U.S. High Commissioner for Germany. Established in the U.S. State Department on 6 June 1949 and in December 1949 replaced OMGUS as the U.S. occupation authority for Germany.

IARA – Inter-Allied Reparations Authority. Established by the Paris Conference on Reparations in 1945.

IWG – Interagency Working Group. Established in 1999 to implement a U.S. law, the Nazi War Crimes Disclosure Act of 1998.

JCR – Jewish Cultural Reconstruction. The JCR was established in April 1947 as a membership corporation of several major Jewish organizations that became the trustee and distributor of heirless Jewish cultural property located in the U.S. Zone of Occupation.

JCS – U.S. Joint Chiefs of Staff. During the war, the JCS served with their British counterparts on the Combined Chiefs of Staff. The JCS became a permanent entity in the National Security Act of 1947.

JRSO – Jewish Restitution Successor Organization. Incorporated in May 1947, the JRSO was designated as the official successor organization in the U.S. Zone of Occupation to obtain title to heirless Jewish assets. The JCR operated as a division within the JRSO.

*Länder* – State governments established by the United States in its zone of occupation.

London Declaration – Issued by the Allies on 5 January 1943, reserving the right to invalidate transactions involving property, rights, and interests in territories directly or indirectly under Nazi control.

Macmillan Committee – British Committee for the Preservation and Restitution of Works of Art, Archives, and Other Material in Enemy Hands.

Established in May 1944 as a counterpart to the Roberts Commission and led by Lord Macmillan.

MFA&A – Monuments, Fine Arts, and Archives Branch/Section. Provided the U.S. Army with specialist officers and guidelines to protect cultural treasures and monuments and to restitute looted objects after the war.

NARA – U.S. National Archives and Records Administration, established in 1934.

NATO – North Atlantic Treaty Organization, created in 1949 to counter Soviet expansionism in Europe.

Nazi Party – The word *Nazi* is derived from the German name for the National-ist Socialist German Workers Party (Nationalsozialistische Deutsche Arbeiterpartei).

NKVD – People's Commissariat for State Security, the Soviet secret police agency.

OMGUS – Office of Military Government for Germany, United States. Estab-lished 1 October 1945 to administer the U.S. Zone of Occupation and the U.S. sector of occupied Berlin. OMGUS succeeded the USGCC (8 May–1 October, 1945) and was abolished 5 December 1949, when its functions were transferred to HICOG.

OSS – U.S. Office of Strategic Services. Established by the U.S. government in June 1942 to conduct intelligence operations against the enemy.

PCHA – Presidential Advisory Commission on Holocaust Assets in the United States. Created by act of Congress in June 1998.

PMGO – U.S. Army Office of the Provost Marshal General, which operated the School for Military Government in Charlottesville, Virginia.

RDR – Reparations, Deliveries and Restitution Division, American Military Government for Germany.

RG – Record Group. After the original citation, footnotes on archival sources will list only the author or type of document, title of the document, file designation, if any, and record group number.

RM – Reichsmark, the currency of Nazi Germany.

Roberts Commission – American Commission for the Protection and Salvage of Artistic and Historic Monuments in War Areas. An advisory commis-sion created on 20 August 1943 under the chairmanship of U.S. Supreme Court Justice Owen J. Roberts. Composed of government and civilian rep-resentatives, the commission was instrumental in creating and supporting the MFA&A.

RSHA (Reichssicherheitshauptamt) – Reich Main Security Office. Estab-lished in 1939 and combined all existing police forces including the Gestapo, the criminal police, and the security service to serve as the main security department of the Nazi regime.

SA (Sturmabteilung) – Storm Detachment. Early Nazi private army.

SANACC – State, Army, Navy, and Air Force Coordinating Committee.

SD (*Sicherheitsdienst*) – Intelligence branch of the SS.

*Sonderkommandos* – Special Detachments. Special units of the SS used for police and political tasks on the eastern front during the war. Some, such as the Sonderkommando Paulsen, focused on looting.

SS (*Schutzstaffel*) – Defense Echelon. Begun as a unit to guard Hitler, by 1936 controlled all police agencies. Declared a criminal organization by the Nuremberg Tribunal because of its persecution of Jews.

SHAEF – Supreme Headquarters, Allied Expeditionary Forces. Created in January 1944 as a joint U.S.-British command for military operations in Europe.

SWNCC – State, Army, Navy, and Air Force Coordinating Committee.

USFET – U.S. Forces European Theater. Established as an independent command in July 1945 with command of all U.S. forces in Europe.

USGCC (Germany) – U.S. Group, Control Council for Germany. Established in August 1944 as a planning group to prepare for the military government of Germany. Redesignated on 1 October 1945 as OMGUS.

UNESCO – United Nations Educational and Social Organization.

Vaucher Commission – Inter-Allied Commission for the protection and restitution of cultural materials, led by Professor Paul Vaucher.

WJRO – World Jewish Restitution Organization.

WJC – World Jewish Congress. Established in 1932 to defend Jewish interests against the Nazis.

# Appendix B

## Washington Conference Principles on Nazi-Confiscated Art

Released in connection with the Washington Conference on Holocaust Era Assets, Washington, D.C., 3 December, 1998.[*]

In developing a consensus on nonbinding principles to assist in resolving issues relating to Nazi-confiscated art, the Conference recognizes that among participating nations there are differing legal systems and that countries act within the context of their own laws.

    I. Art that had been confiscated by the Nazis and not subsequently restituted should be identified.

    II. Relevant records and archives should be opened and accessible to researchers, in accordance with the guidelines of the International Council on Archives.

    III. Resources and personnel should be made available to facilitate the identification of all art that had been confiscated by the Nazis and not subsequently restituted.

    IV. In establishing that a work of art had been confiscated by the Nazis and not subsequently restituted, consideration should be given to unavoidable gaps or ambiguities in the provenance in light of the passage of time and the circumstances of the Holocaust era.

    V. Every effort should be made to publicize art that is found to have been confiscated by the Nazis and not subsequently restituted in order to locate its pre-War owners or their heirs.

    VI. Efforts should be made to establish a central registry of such information.

    VII. Pre-War owners and their heirs should be encouraged to come forward and make known their claims to art that was confiscated by the Nazis and not subsequently restituted.

---

[*] J. D. Bindenagel, editor, U.S. Department of State, *Washington Conference on Holocaust Era Assets, November 30–December 3, 1998: Proceedings*, February 1999.

VIII. If the pre-War owners of art that is found to have been confiscated by the Nazis and not subsequently restituted, or their heirs, can be identified, steps should be taken expeditiously to achieve a just and fair solution, recognizing this may vary according to the facts and circumstances surrounding a specific case.

  IX. If the pre-War owners of art that is found to have been confiscated by the Nazis, or their heirs, cannot be identified, steps should be taken expeditiously to achieve a just and fair solution.

   X. Commissions or other bodies established to identify art that was confiscated by the Nazis and to assist in addressing ownership issues should have a balanced membership.

  XI. Nations are encouraged to develop national processes to implement these principles, particularly as they relate to alternative dispute resolution mechanisms for resolving ownership issues.

# Bibliography

Primary Sources

*Unpublished*

College Park, Maryland, National Archives at College Park. Civilian Records Life Cycle Control Unit (LICON); Modern Military Records Life Cycle Control Unit (LICON).

Civilian Records LICON. Record Group 43. Records of the Allied Control Council, Germany, 1941–1950. Allied Control Council Documents, 1945–1949.

Civilian Records LICON. Record Group 43. Records of the European Advisory Commission, Part 1: Records of Philip E. Mosely, U.S. Political Advisor. Decimal Files, 1943–1945.

Civilian Records LICON. Record Group 59. General Records of the Department of State. Decimal Files, 1940–1944, 1945–1949.

Civilian Records LICON. Record Group 59. Records maintained by the Fine Arts and Monuments Advisor, 1945–1961. "Ardelia Hall Collection."

Civilian Records LICON. Record Group 59. Records of the Legal Advisor, Office of Educational, Cultural, and Public Affairs, Subject Files, 1945–1997.

Record Group 64. Records of the National Archives. Extra-Federal Archival Affairs Cases.

Civilian Records LICON. Record Group 84. Records of the Foreign Service Posts of the Department of State. Records of the Office of the U.S. Political Advisor for Germany, Berlin.

Modern Military Records LICON. Record Group 165. Records of the Civil Affairs Division. Executive Office Decimal Files, 11 June 1946–1947; 1948.

Civilian Records LICON. Record Group 169. Records of the Foreign Economic Administration. "Safehaven." Records of the Office of the Director, Bureau of Areas, European Branch.

Modern Military Records LICON. Record Group 200. Abraham G. Druker/Irving Dwork Papers. Office of Strategic Services, Research and Analysis Branch, Jewish Desk, World War II.

Modern Military Records LICON. Record Group 200. National Archives Gift Collection. Personal Papers of Gen. Lucius Clay, April 1945–May 1949.

Civilian Records LICON. Record Group 239. Records of the American Commission for the Protection and Salvage of Artistic and Historic Monuments in War Areas. Restitution Background Material. London Files, 1943–1945.

Modern Military Records LICON. Record Group 260. Claims Section. General Records, 1947–1949.

Modern Military Records LICON. Record Group 260. Records of the United States Occupation Headquarters, World War II.

Modern Military Records LICON. Record Group 260. Records Concerning the Central Collecting Points. General Records, 1938–1948.

Modern Military Records LICON. Record Group 260. Records of the Economic Division. General Correspondence, 1944–1948.

Modern Military Records LICON. Record Group 260. Records of the Munich Central Collecting Point. Jewish Claims, 1938–1951. Restitution Claims Records, 1945–1947.

Modern Military Records LICON. Record Group 260. Records of the Offenbach Archival Depot. Administrative Records, 1946–1949. Policy and Procedures, 1946–1948.

Modern Military Records LICON. Record Group 260. Records of the Property Control and External Assets Branch. Financial Records.

Modern Military Records LICON. Record Group 260. Records of the Property Control and External Assets Branch. Records of the Section Chief, 1945–1948.

Modern Military Records LICON. Record Group 260. Records of the Property Division. Records of the Office of the Director. Records of the Secretarial Section. General Records, 1944–1950.

Modern Military Records LICON. Record Group 260. Records of the Property Division. Records of the Reparations and Restitution Branch. General Records. Cables Relating to Reparations and Restitution, 1945–1948.

Modern Military Records LICON. Record Group 260. Records of the Property Division. Records of the Reparations and Restitution Branch. Monthly Restitution Reports, June 1946–October 1948.

Modern Military Records LICON. Record Group 260. Records of the Property Division. Records of the Reparations and Restitution Branch. Records of the Museum, Fine Arts, and Archives Section. General Records, 1944–1949.

Modern Military Records LICON. Record Group 260. Records of the Property Division. Records of the Reparations and Restitution Branch. Records of the Restitution Section. Correspondence and Related Records, 1946–1949.'

Modern Military Records LICON. Record Group 260. Records of the Property Division. Records of the Reparations and Restitution Branch. Reports and Related Records Re: Restitution, 1945–1950.

Modern Military Records LICON. Record Group 260. Records of the Property Division. Records of the Reparations and Restitution Branch. Records of the Restitution Liaison Office. Meritorious Restitution Claims. 1948–1949.

Modern Military Records LICON. Record Group 260. Records of Unidentified Allied Control Authority Units. Records of the U.S. Element of the Allied Control Authority. Records of the Reparations, Deliveries, and Restitution Directorate. Masterfile, 1945–1948.

Modern Military Records LICON. Record Group 260. Records of Unidentified Allied Control Authority Units. Records of the U.S. Elements of Inter-Allied Organizations. Records of the U.S. Element of the Allied Control Authority. Enactments and Approved Papers of the Central Council and Coordinating Committee, 1945–1948.

Modern Military Records LICON. Record Group 260. Records of Unidentified Allied Control Authority Units. Records of the U.S. Elements of Inter-Allied Organizations. Records of the U.S. Elements, Allied Control Authority. Records of the Reparations, Deliveries, and Restitution Division. General Records, 1945–1948.

Modern Military Records LICON. Record Group 260. Records of the Wiesbaden Central Collecting Point. Administrative Records, 1944–1951.

Modern Military Records LICON. Record Group 260. Records of the Wiesbaden Central Collecting Point. General Reports, Special Reports, and Investigative Files, 1945–1951. General Records, 1945–1952.

Modern Military Records LICON. Record Group 260. Records of the Wiesbaden Central Collecting Point. Restitution, Research, and Reference Records, 1900–1954. Prominent German Personalities, 1939–1948.

Jerusalem, Israel. Central Archives for the History of the Jewish People. Records of the Jewish Restitution Successor Organization.

Los Angeles, California. Skirball Cultural Center. Records relating to the Jewish Cultural Reconstruction, Inc.

New York, New York. American Jewish Committee. Records concerning restitution.

Palo Alto, California. Stanford University, Department of Special Collections. Papers of Salo W. Baron (M580).

Washington, D.C., National Gallery of Art. Gallery Archives.

Record Group 17. Roberts Commission. Reports and Correspondence.

Record Group 28. Collection of Donated Papers: Monuments, Fine Arts, and Archives Officers. Edith A. Standen Papers.

## Published

Bindenagel, J. D., editor, U.S. Department of State. *Washington Conference on Holocaust Era Assets, November 30–December 3, 1998: Proceedings.* February 1999.

Clay, Lucius D. *Decision in Germany.* Garden City, N.Y.: Doubleday, 1950.

Great Britain, Parliament. *Parliamentary Debates* (Lords), 5th series, vol. 130 (1943–4).

Historical Society of Israel. *The Jewish Historical General Archives.* Jerusalem: The Historical Society of Israel, 1961.

Library of Congress. *Report for Congress: Protection of Cultural Property Under International Law and the Laws of Selected Foreign Nations* (cc 96.6). April 1996.

Murphy, Robert. *Diplomat Among Warriors.* Garden City, N.Y.: Doubleday, 1964.

National Archives and Records Administration. *Interim Report to Congress on Implementation of the Nazi War Crimes Disclosure Act.* College Park, Md.: National Archives and Records Administration, October 1999.

*Report of the American Commission for the Protection and Salvage of Artistic and Historic Monuments in War Areas.* Washington, D.C.: U.S. Government Printing Office, 1946.

*Report to the President of the Presidential Advisory Commission on Holocaust Assets in the United States.* Washington, D.C.: U.S. Government Printing Office, December 2000.

Slany, William S., U.S. Department of State. *U.S. and Allied Efforts to Recover and Restore Gold and Other Assets Stolen or Hidden by Germany During World War II.* Publication 10468. May 1997.

U.S. and Allied Wartime and Postwar Relations and Negotiations with Argentina, Portugal, Spain, Sweden, and Turkey on Looted Gold and German External Assets and U.S. Concerns about the Fate of the Wartime Ustasha Treasury. Publication 10557. June 1998.

Supreme Headquarters Allied Expeditionary Forces. *Handbook for Military Government in Germany Prior to Defeat or Surrender.* London, December 1944.

U.S. Chief of Counsel for Prosecution of Axis Criminality. *Nazi Conspiracy and Aggression,* vol. 1. Washington, D.C.: U.S. Government Printing Office, 1946.

U.S. Department of State. *Bulletin.* No. 399. 23 February 1947.

U.S. Department of State. *Bulletin.* No. 797. 4 October 1954.

U.S. Department of State. *Foreign Relations of the United States: Diplomatic Papers,* 1942, vol. 1, *General.* Washington, D.C.: U.S. Government Printing Office, 1960.

*Foreign Relations, 1943,* vol. 1, *General.* 1963.

*Foreign Relations, 1944,* vol. 1, *General.* 1966.

*Foreign Relations, 1944,* vol. 2, *General: Economic and Social Matters.* 1967.

*Foreign Relations, 1945,* vol. 1, *The Conference of Berlin.* 1960.

*Foreign Relations, 1945,* vol. 2, *The Conference of Berlin.* 1960.

*Foreign Relations, 1945,* vol. 2, *General: Political and Economic Matters.* 1967.

*Foreign Relations, 1945,* vol. 3, *European Advisory Commission; Austria; Germany.* 1968.

*Foreign Relations, 1946,* vol. 2, *Council of Foreign Ministers.* 1970.

*Foreign Relations, 1946,* vol. 3, *Paris Peace Conference: Proceedings.* 1970.

*Foreign Relations, 1947,* vol. 2, *Council of Foreign Ministers; Germany and Austria.* 1972.

*Foreign Relations, 1948,* vol. 2, *Germany and Austria.* 1973.

*Foreign Relations, 1949,* vol. 3, *Council of Foreign Ministers; Germany and Austria.* 1974.

U.S. Department of State. *International Protection of Works of Art and Historic Monuments.* International and Cultural Series 8, Publication 3590 (1949).

U.S. Department of State. *Post-War Foreign Policy Preparation, 1939–45.* General Foreign Policy Series 15, Publication 3580 (1949).

World Jewish Congress. *Bulletin of the World Jewish Congress.* New York. September 1950.

*Interviews and Correspondence*

Baron, Salo W. Columbia University, New York. Correspondence interview, 8 June 1981.

Crosby, Sumner McKnight. Yale University, New Haven, Connecticut. Telephone interview, 16 April 1981.

Faison, S. Lane, Jr. Williams College, Williamstown, Massachusetts. Correspondence interview, 22 November 1982.

Gruenewald, Max. Leo Baeck Institute. Correspondence interview, 12 September 1983.

Hammond, Mason. Widener Library. Correspondence interview, 23 November 1982.

Howard, Richard F. Museum director, Birmingham, Alabama. Telephone interview, 21 April 1981. Correspondence interview, April 1981.

Jaffe, H. L. C. Restitution Officer, Royal Netherland Army. Correspondence interview, 28 February 1983.

Maurer, Ely. U.S. Department of State. Interview, 15 May 1981. Telephone interview, May 1985.

Parkhurst, Charles. National Gallery of Art. Oral history interview by Alfred C. Viebranz. 10 November and 6 December 1988.

Pomrenze, Seymour J. Records Management, Department of the Army. Correspondence interview, 10 May 1981.

Rifkind, Simon A. Former Special Advisor on Jewish Affairs to the Commanding General SHAEF, USFET. Correspondence interview, 24 November 1982.

Smyth, Craig. Director, Center for Renaissance Studies, I Tatti. Telephone interview, 27 April 1983.

Standen, Edith. Former MFA&A Officer. Correspondence interview, 30 September 1982.

Walker, John. National Gallery of Art. Oral history interview by Annie G. Ritchie. 23 October 1990.

## Secondary Sources

*Articles*

Adams, Edward E. "Looted Art Treasures Go Back to France." *Quartermaster Review* (September–October 1946): 19.

Akinsha, Konstantin and Hochfield, Sylvia. "Who Owns the Lubomirsky Dürers?" *ARTnews* (October 2001): 158–63.

Breitenbach, Edgar. "Historical Survey of the Intelligence Department, MFAA Section, in OMGB, 1946–1949." *College Art Journal* 2 (Winter 1949–50): 192–8.

Collins, Donald E. and Rothfeder, Herbert P. "The *Einsatzstab Reichsleiter Rosenberg* and the Looting of Jewish and Masonic Libraries During World War II." *Journal of Library History* 18 (Winter 1983): 21–36.

Gattini, Andrea. "Restitution by Russia of Works of Art Removed from German Territory at the End of the Second World War." *European Journal of International Law* 7 (1996): 1–6.

Goldman, Klaus. "The Return of the Luther Manuscript, 'Wider Hans Worst' (Against Hans Worst), to Germany." *Spoils of War International Newsletter* No. 2 (15 June 1996): 41–2.

Grimsted, Patricia Kennedy. "Displaced Archives on the Eastern Front: Restitution Problems from World War II and Its Aftermath." *Janus* 2 (1996): 49–51.

"'Trophy' Archives and Non-Restitution: Russia's Cultural 'Cold War' with the European Community." *Problems of Post-Communism* 45 (May/June 1998): 3–14.

"Twice Plundered or Twice Saved? Identifying Russia's 'Trophy' Archives and the Loot of the *Reichssicherheitshauptamt.*" *Holocaust and Genocide Studies* 15 (Fall 2001): 191–244.

Hamlin, Gladys E. "European Art Collections and the War." *College Art Journal* 5 (March 1946): 219–28.

Heller, Bernard. "Operation Salvage." *Jewish Horizon* 6 (February 1950): 12–15.

Hochfield, Sylvia. "Dürer Claims Continue." *ARTnews* (March 2002): 66.

Holmes, Oliver W. "The National Archives and the Protection of Records in War Areas." *American Archivist* 9 (April 1946): 110–17.

"International Discussion of the Russian Law." *Spoils of War International Newsletter* No. 4 (August 1997): 9–10.

Jones, Stacy V. "Art for Hitler's Sake." *Liberty* (April 1946): 19–48.

Kline, Thomas R. "Recent Developments in the Recovery of Old Master Drawings from Bremen." *Spoils of War International Newsletter* No. 5 (5 June 1998): 15–18.

"The Russian Bill to Nationalize Trophy Art: An American Perspective." *Spoils of War International Newsletter* No. 4 (August 1997): 32.

"U.S. Court Orders Return of Drawings Stolen after World War II to *Kunsthalle Bremen.*" *Spoils of War International Newsletter* No. 1 (19 December 1995): 40–1.

Kowalski, Wojciech. "Introduction to International Law of Restitution of Works of Art During Armed Conflicts, Part II." *Spoils of War International Newsletter* No. 3 (December 1996): 10.

"Introduction to International Law of Restitution of Works of Art During Armed Conflicts, Part III." *Spoils of War International Newsletter* No. 4 (August 1997): 39–41.

Kugel, Seth. "Back from Baku." *ARTnews* (September 2001): 56.

Kuhn, Charles L. "German Paintings in the National Gallery: A Protest." *College Art Journal* 5 (January 1946): 78–81.

Kuhn, Petra. "Comments on the Soviet Returns of Cultural Treasures Moved Because of the War to the GDR." *Spoils of War International Newsletter* No. 4 (August 1997): 45–6.

Lauria, Joe. "An Amicable Resolution." *ARTnews* (October 1998): 54.

Milton, Sybil H. "Lost, Stolen, and Strayed: The Archival Heritage of Modern German-Jewish History." In *The Jewish Response to German Culture: From the Enlightenment to the Second World War*, edited by Jehuda Reinhauz and Walter Schatzberg. Hanover, N.H. and London: University Press of New England, 1985: 320–31.

Petropoulos, Jonathan. "The Importance of the Second Rank: The Case of Art Plunderer Kajetan Mühlmann." In *Austro-Corporatism: Past, Present and Future*, vol. 4. *Contemporary Austrian Studies*, edited by Gunter Bischof and Anton Pelinka. New Brunswick, N.J. and London: Transaction Publishers, 1996: 177–205.

Plaut, James S. "Hitler's Capital: Loot for the Master Race." *Atlantic Monthly* 178 (October 1946): 73–8.

"Loot for the Master Race." *Atlantic Monthly* (September 1946): 57–63.

Pomrenze, Seymour J. "Offenbach Reminiscences." *Spoils of War International Newsletter* No. 2 (15 July 1996): 18–20.

Posner, Ernst. "Public Records under Military Occupation." *American Historical Review* 49 (January 1944): 213–27.

Poste, Leslie I. "Books Go Home from the Wars." *Library Journal* 73 (1 December 1948): 1699–1704.

"Protective Custody." *Magazine of Art* 2 (February 1946): 42, 73–5.

Robinson, Nehemiah. "Restitution of Jewish Property." *Congress Weekly* 10 (12 March 1948): 11–12.

Roth, Cecil. "The Restoration of Jewish Libraries, Archives and Museums." *Contemporary Jewish Record* 8 (June 1944): 253–7.

Rupnow, Dirk. "The Jewish Central Museum in Prague and Historical Memory in the Third Reich." *Holocaust and Genocide Studies* 16 (Spring 2002): 23–53.

Schwerin, Kurt. "German Compensation for Victims of Nazi Persecution." *Northwestern University Law Review* 67 (September–October 1972): 485–94.

"The Quedlinburg Indictments." *ARTnews* (March 1996): 35.

"Tentative List of Jewish Cultural Treasures in Axis-Occupied Countries." *Supplement to Jewish Social Studies* 8 (1946): 6.

Waite, Robert G. "Returning Jewish Cultural Property: The Handling of Books Looted by the Nazis in the American Zone of Occupation, 1945 to 1952." *Libraries and Culture* 37 (Summer 2002): 213–28.

Walker, John. "Europe's Looted Art." *National Geographic* (January 1946): 41–9.

*Books*

Akinsha, Konstantin and Kozlov, Grigorii. *Beautiful Loot: The Soviet Plunder of Europe's Art Treasures*. New York: Random House, 1995.

Baron, Salo. "The Journal and the Conference of Jewish Social Studies." In *Emancipation and Counter-Emancipation*, edited by Abraham G. Duker and Meir Ben Horin, pp. 1–9. New York: KTAV Publishing House, 1974.

Davis, Franklin M. *Come as a Conqueror: The United States Army's Occupation of Germany, 1945–1949*. New York: Macmillan, 1967.

Derwent, Mary. "Hannah Arendt." in *Lives of Modern Women*, edited by Emma Tennant. Hammondsworth, England: Penguin Books, 1986.

Eizenstat, Stuart E. *Imperfect Justice: Looted Assets, Slave Labor, and the Unfinished Business of World War II*. New York: Public Affairs, 2003.

Estreicher, Charles, ed. *Cultural Losses of Poland: Index of Polish Cultural Losses during the German Occupation*. London, 1944.

Feliciano, Hector. *The Lost Museum: The Nazi Conspiracy to Steal the World's Greatest Works of Art*. New York: HarperCollins, 1997.

Flanner, Janet. *Men and Monuments*. New York: Harper and Brothers, 1947.

Gaddis, John Lewis. *We Now Know: Rethinking Cold War History*. Oxford: Clarendon Press, 1997.

Giles, Robert S. *Archival and Library Restitution in the United States Zone of Germany: A Preliminary Study*. Washington, D.C.: American School of Social Sciences and Public Affairs, 1947.

Gimbel, John. *The American Occupation of Germany: Politics and the Military,*
   *1945–49.* Stanford, Calif.: Stanford University Press, 1968.

Hilberg, Raoul. *The Destruction of the European Jews.* Chicago: Quadrangle Books,
   1967.

Howe, Thomas Carr, Jr. *Salt Mines and Castles: The Discovery and Restitu-*
   *tion of Looted European Art.* Indianapolis and New York: Bobbs-Merrill,
   1946.

Kurtz, Michael J. *Nazi Contraband: American Policy on the Return of European*
   *Cultural Treasures, 1945–1955.* New York and London: Garland, 1985.

Liberles, Robert. *Salo Wittmayer Baron: Architect of Jewish History.* New York and
   London: New York University Press, 1995.

Murphy, Robert. *Diplomat Among Warriors.* New York: Doubleday, 1964.

Nicholas, Lynn. *The Rape of Europa: The Fate of Europe's Treasures in the Third*
   *Reich and the Second World War.* New York: Knopf, 1994.

Peterson, Edward N. *The American Occupation of Germany: Retreat to Victory.*
   Detroit: Wayne State University Press, 1978.

Petropoulos, Jonathan. *Art as Politics in the Third Reich.* Chapel Hill: University of
   North Carolina Press, 1996.

   *The Faustian Bargain: The Art World in Nazi Germany.* New York and Oxford:
   Oxford University Press, 2000.

Reynolds, David. *One World Divided: Global History Since 1945.* New York and
   London: W. W. Norton, 2000.

Robinson, Nehemiah. *Ten Years of German Indemnification.* New York: Conference
   on Jewish Material Claims Against Germany, 1964.

Rorimer, James J. *Survival: The Salvage and Protection of Art in War.* New York:
   Abelard Press, 1950.

Roxan, David and Wanstall, Ken. *The Rape of Art: The Story of Hitler's Plun-*
   *der of the Great Masterpieces of Europe.* New York: Coward-McCann,
   1965.

Simpson, Elizabeth, ed. *The Spoils of War: World War II and Its Aftermath: The*
   *Loss, Reappearance, and Recovery of Cultural Property.* New York: Harry
   N. Abrams, 1997.

Siviero, Rodolfo. *Second National Exhibition of the Works of Art Recovered in*
   *Germany.* Florence, Italy: Sansoni, 1950.

Smyth, Craig Hugh. *Repatriation of Art from the Collecting Point in Munich after*
   *World War II.* The Hague: Maarssen, 1988.

Trachtenberg, Marc E. *A Constructed Peace: The Making of the European Settlement.*
   Princeton, N.J.: Princeton University Press, 1999.

Weber, John Paul. *The German War Artists.* Columbia, S.C.: Cerberus Book
   Co., 1979.

   *A World at Arms: A Global History of World War II.* New York: Cambridge
   University Press, 1994.

Weinberg, Gerhard L. *World in the Balance: Behind the Scenes of World War II.*
   Hanover, N.H. and London: University Press of New England, 1981.

Williams, Sharon A. *The International and National Protection of Movable Cul-*
   *tural Property: A Comparative Study.* Dobbs Ferry, N.Y.: Oceana Publications,
   1978.

Wistrich, Robert S. *Who's Who in Nazi Germany*. London and New York: Routledge, 1995.
Woolley, Sir Charles Leonard. *A Record of the Work Done by the Military Authorities for the Protection of the Treasures of Art and History in War Areas*. London: His Majesty's Stationery Office, 1947.
Yahil, Leni. *The Holocaust: The Fate of European Jewry*. New York and Oxford: Oxford University Press, 1990.
Yeide, Nancy H., Akinsha, Konstantin and Walsh, Amy L. *AAM Guide to Provenance Research*. Washington, D.C.: American Association of Museums, 2001.
Young-Buehl, Elizabeth. *Hannah Arendt: For Love of the World*. New Haven, Conn.: Yale University Press, 1982.
Ziemke, Earl F. *The U.S. Army in the Occupation of Germany, 1944–1946*. Washington, D.C.: Center of Military History, United States Army, 1975.


### Dissertations and Theses

Pease, Louis E. "After the Holocaust: West Germany and Material Reparations to the Jews – From the Allied Occupation to the Luxembourg Agreements." Ph.D. dissertation, Florida State University, 1976.
Poste, Leslie. "The Development of U.S. Protection of Libraries and Archives in Europe During World War II," 2 vols. Ph.D. dissertation, University of Chicago, 1958.
Rothfeld, Anne. "Project ORION: An Administrative History of the Art Looting Investigation Unit (ALIU): An Overlooked Page in Intelligence Gathering." M.A. thesis, University of Maryland, 2000.


### Encyclopedias

*Encyclopedia Judaica*, 1971 ed., s.v. "Jewish Cultural Reconstruction."
*Encyclopedia Judaica*, 1971 ed., s.v. "Jewish Restitution Successor Organization."
*Encyclopedia Judaica*, 1971 ed., s.v. "Salo Baron."


### Newspapers

*Boston Globe*
  9 January 1998
  14 August 1998
  3 December 1998
*New York Times*
  6 January 1948
  30 January 1948
  26 November 1955
  6 March 1963
  6 January 1978
  27 May 2000

14 December 2002
3 March 2003
*The Washington Post*
11 October 1979
14 December 1979
27 May 1981
14 December 2002


*Websites*

Belgium Travel Network (www.trabel.com). "Ghent: *The Adoration of the Mystic Lamb* (1432)." September 2002.
Gombich, E. H. "The Story of Art." The Artchive (www.artchive.com). September 2002.

# Index